Old Homes—New Families:
Shared Living for the Elderly

COLUMBIA STUDIES OF
SOCIAL GERONTOLOGY AND AGING

Columbia Studies of Social Gerontology and Aging
   Abraham Monk, GENERAL EDITOR

The Political Economy of Aging: The State, Private Power, and Social Welfare,
Laura Katz Olson, 1982

Resolving Grievances in the Nursing Home: A Study of the Ombudsman Program,
Abraham Monk, Lenard W. Kaye, and Howard Litwin, 1983

Ages in Conflict: A Cross-Cultural Perspective on Inequality Between Old and Young,
Nancy Foner, 1984

Old Homes—New Families: Shared Living for the Elderly

GORDON F. STREIB
W. EDWARD FOLTS
MARY ANNE HILKER

Columbia University Press
NEW YORK   1984

Photographs of Florida Share-a-Homes in chapter 3 reprinted courtesy of The Center for Gerontological Studies, University of Florida.

Photograph of the Wellsboro Shared Home in chapter 6 reprinted courtesy of Wellsboro Shared Homes.

Photograph of Robineau in chapter 6 reprinted courtesy of the Council for Jewish Elderly, Jewish Federation of Metropolitan Chicago.

Photograph of the Shared Living Project Boston in chapter 6 reprinted courtesy of Linda Kravitz and the Housing Assistance Council.

Photographs of the Abbeyfield House in chapter 8, reprinted courtesy of the Abbeyfield Society.

Library of Congress Cataloging in Publication Data

Streib, Gordon Franklin, 1918–
Old homes—new families.

(Columbia studies of social gerontology and aging)
Bibliography: p. 1
Includes index.
1. Old age homes—United States—Case studies.
2. Group homes—United States—Case studies. 3. Aged—
United States—Dwellings—Case studies. 4. Communal
living—United States—Case studies. I. Folts,
W. Edward (William Edward) II. Hilker, Mary Anne.
III. Title. IV. Series.
HV1461.S87 1984 362.6'1'0973 84-1772
ISBN 0-231-05652-4 (alk. paper)

Columbia University Press
New York Guildford, Surrey
Copyright © 1984 Columbia University Press
All rights reserved

Printed in the United States of America

Clothbound editions of Columbia University Press Books are
Smyth-sewn and printed on permanent and durable acid-free paper

To the memory of Wanda Gillies, pioneer in providing shared housing for older Americans

Contents

Acknowledgments   xiii

Introduction   1

CHAPTER 1. *The Need for Shared Housing*   7

MODERN SOCIETIES AND AN AGING POPULATION   7

MODERNIZATION AND THE DEMOGRAPHY OF THE
ELDERLY   11

BUREAUCRACY, MODERNIZATION, AND SHARED HOUSING   14

CHANGING FAMILY RELATIONS: AUTONOMY AND
INDEPENDENCE   16

THE MASS MEDIA AND IMAGES OF THE OLD   18

SUMMARY   20

CHAPTER 2. *The Continuum of Living Arrangements:
Where and How Older People Live*   23

THE CONTINUUM OF LIVING ARRANGEMENTS   25

AGE-CONCENTRATED VERSUS AGE-INTEGRATED
ENVIRONMENTS   32

ORIENTATIONS TO HOUSING THE FRAIL ELDERLY   33

CHAPTER 3. *Share-A-Home in Florida: A Case Study
of Shared Living*   37

HISTORY OF SHARE-A-HOME   37

THE FAMILY MODEL OF SHARED LIVING   42

THE RESIDENTS   48

THE HOUSEHOLD STAFF   51

COMMUNITY TIES   53

CHAPTER 4. *Everyday Life in Florida Share-A-Homes*   55

BECOMING A RESIDENT: SOCIALIZATION TO SHARED
    LIVING   58

CONTACTS WITH FAMILY AND FRIENDS OUTSIDE THE
    HOMES   63

RESIDENT RELATIONSHIPS   65

VARIATION AMONG THE HOMES   69

RESIDENT-STAFF RELATIONSHIPS   71

OVERVIEW AND DISCUSSION   73

CHAPTER 5. *Diffusion of the Share-A-Home Model*   76

THE ROLE OF MASS MEDIA IN DISSEMINATING INFORMATION
    ABOUT SHARED HOUSING   81

DIFFUSION OF THE MODEL TO OTHER STATES   83

DIFFUSION OF THE IDEA: THE DECISION-MAKING PROCESS   87

ELEMENTS IN THE ESTABLISHMENT OF SHARE-A-HOME-TYPE
    PROJECTS   88

TVA'S DESIGN FOR AN ENERGY-SAVING SHARED LIVING
    FACILITY   92

A SURVEY OF SHARED LIVING FACILITIES   94

CONCLUSIONS   100

CHAPTER 6. *Diversity in Sponsorship, Structure, and Cost:
Fifteen Case Studies of Shared Living*   101

CLASSIFICATION OF SHARED LIVING HOMES 102

CLASSIFICATION OF SHARED LIVING HOMES BY HOUSING STOCK 130

CONCLUSIONS 140

CHAPTER 7. *Alternative Housing Using Existing Households* 146

HOUSE SHARING 146

FOSTER FAMILY CARE 149

GRANNY FLATS 150

CONCLUSIONS 154

CHAPTER 8. *Abbeyfield—Success Story in Great Britain* 156

HISTORY AND ORGANIZATION 157

THE NATIONAL ORGANIZATION 160

LOCAL SOCIETIES 162

RESIDENTS 163

HOUSEKEEPER 164

THE HOUSES 165

FOUR EXAMPLES OF ABBEYFIELD HOUSES 166

PURPOSE-BUILT HOUSES 171

EXTRA CARE HOUSES 173

THE ABBEYFIELD SOCIETY EVALUATES ITSELF 175

CROSS-NATIONAL COMPARISONS IN SHARED LIVING 180

CONCLUSIONS: ABBEYFIELD LOOKS TO THE FUTURE 183

CHAPTER 9. *Problems and Dilemmas in Establishing Shared Living Facilities* 186

INTERNAL FACTORS 187

EXTERNAL FACTORS 200

CONCLUSIONS   208

CHAPTER 10. *Sociological Interpretations*   210

THE CONCEPT OF FAMILY   210

ARE SHARED LIVING ARRANGEMENTS REAL FAMILIES?   211

SOCIAL ROLES AND SHARED FAMILY LIFE   215

THE AMALGAM OF FAMILY AND BUREAUCRACY   218

THE TARGET POPULATION'S PERCEPTION OF SHARED
HOUSING   220

IMPLICATIONS OF DIFFUSION: WILL SHARED LIVING
SPREAD?   223

THREE AVENUES OF DIFFUSION   224

CHAPTER 11. *Shared Housing and Its Policy Implications*   228

SHARED HOUSING AS INCREMENTAL CHANGE   228

CONSEQUENCES OF INCREASED BUREAUCRACY   230

POLICY IMPLICATIONS OF FINANCING SHARED HOUSING   236

ZONING AS AN IMPEDIMENT TO SHARED HOUSING   239

THE ENERGY ISSUE AND SHARED HOUSING   243

LONG LIFE, ADAPTABILITY, AND SHARED HOUSING   245

MODERNIZATION AND SHARED HOUSING: A SUMMING UP   246

APPENDIX 1. *Methods of Research*   249

APPENDIX 2. *Instruments*   253

APPENDIX 3. *Architectural Plans for TVA's Solar Group Home*   274

APPENDIX 4. *Shared Housing Projects in the United States*   276

APPENDIX 5. *Other Source Materials on Shared Housing*   291

References   293

Name Index   303

Subject Index   307

Acknowledgments

There are many individuals and organizations who have given information, support, and encouragement toward the completion of this book. First and foremost is Ruth B. Streib, who has been involved in all the phases of the book: the early exploration of the subject, the field work, the analysis, and the writing. She has shared in many aspects of the project and has had an interest in all phases, particularly its completion.

Many persons in the provision of shared housing for older Americans have been informative and supportive. James Gillies and the late Wanda Gillies, the founders of Share-A-Home, were of primary help at the start of the project. The Gillies opened the doors to Share-A-Home in ways that are uniquely cooperative, and over the years we have maintained close contact, so that the research has an on-going, longitudinal quality that is quite unusual in the social sciences.

Over the years many persons who are or were part of the Share-A-Home organization and its households have been of enormous help to us. They include the office staff, especially May Wheeler, Ruth Michelman, Rosalee Garnsey, and Jim Bonano, the household staffs, and, most importantly, the residents of the homes who permitted us such close participation in their lives for many months.

Desmond Charles, general secretary of the Abbeyfield Society of Great Britain, has been a stalwart supporter and was of great help during our visit to the British Isles. It was through the Abbeyfield Society's good offices that Gordon and Ruth Streib were able to meet many Abbeyfield staff, committee members, and residents, who were generous in sharing their experiences and information. Their cooperation enabled us to add a cross-national dimension to the research.

In the course of the research, the authors visited many facilities in various parts of the United States. The list of these persons is very long, and it would take many pages to list all of the people whose generosity with time and information allowed us to assemble all of the facts reported here. We do wish to acknowledge the splendid cooperation we have received from many older Americans who live in shared living households and who provided information, insights, and interest in our work.

A number of graduate students at the University of Florida in sociology and gerontology gave research assistance to us: William Haas III, Jeffrey Abolafia, Martha Baker, Monday Ekpo, Patricia A. Richeson, and an undergraduate research assistant, Connie Konstant, were most helpful.

Our research has received generous financial support from a number of organizations. The Andrus Foundation of the American Association of Retired Persons was the first organization that supported the research. Fred J. Ferris, administrator of the foundation, and Leo Baldwin, housing coordinator for AARP, were particularly helpful. The Administration on Aging provided support for two years, and two persons on its staff deserve special mention: Marvin Taves of the Washington office and Steven Vilvens of the Atlanta regional office.

The World Health Organization awarded Gordon Streib a Travel Fellowship to visit Great Britain and Sweden to observe housing projects in 1979. Arnold Ross and Associates made a generous gift to the University of Florida Foundation, which assisted Gordon Streib's research on retirement communities.

Many other persons have been interested and helpful. Dan Karney, who was affiliated with the National Ministries of the Baptist Churches, was supportive of our work.

At the University of Florida, we have been fortunate in having colleagues who have maintained an interest in our work and have provided the necessary administrative support. They include the three chairmen of the Department of Sociology during whose terms the research and writing was carried out—Gerald Leslie, Ben Gorman, and Ronald Akers—and the past and current directors of the Center for Gerontological Studies—Carter Osterbind and Leonard Hayflick.

The many drafts of this book and the proposals, reports, papers, and speeches have been typed and retyped by many helping hands. Mary Robinson, Ivy Upshaw, and especially Marylee Vandiver have played crucial roles in keeping our work on course. Their diligence, forbearance, and accuracy are greatly appreciated by the authors.

Charles Webel, formerly of Columbia University Press, and an anonymous professional referee for Columbia University Press, provided useful critiques during the final revisions of the manuscript. Sincere thanks to Anita O'Brien, our copy editor at Columbia University Press.

The senior author particularly appreciates the support for research and writing provided by the University of Florida in his position as graduate research professor. The absence of formal assigned duties provides freedom to conduct research and a kind of intellectual environment that is unique in academia.

Old Homes—New Families:
Shared Living for the Elderly

GORDON F. STREIB

Introduction

The research presented in this book focuses on shared living households for older people. These may be viewed as social experiments in creating "families"—primary group environments that provide services and companionship in a noninstitutional setting. At the same time, these households have organizational linkages to formal organizations—churches, nonprofit corporations, welfare agencies, governmental bodies. The examples described here demonstrate the creative efforts of people concerned about the housing of the elderly as they attempt to devise "solutions" to the demographic trends set in motion by modernization. It is a heartening aspect of American and British societies that so many people are devoting their time and energy to developing small group environments for the elderly. Despite all the publicity in the mass media about the United States as an "uncaring society," these experiments have demonstrated how much effort people devote to making life more pleasant and comfortable for the elderly.

People develop these various schemes in their own communities, so each household has an individual style and pattern. Some have developed shared living projects independently, while others have learned from the experiences of similar groups in other areas and have adapted ideas from projects already established. These experiments are attempts to cope on a small scale with some of the dilemmas and contradictions of modernization. That is why we feel these grass-roots endeavors, although they are limited in number and touch the lives of relatively few people, are important beacons in pointing the way to the future.

The people who start shared living arrangements are optimistic, pragmatic citizens who attempt to use their available resources to cope with local problems that they see in their immediate community. Often they have a religious or humanitarian motivation to use their talents and energies to make the world a better place.

Our research started as a case study of a shared living arrangement in central Florida. Our goal was to record, as contemporary social historians, how this social experiment was initiated and how it operated in its community. As sociologists, we were instructed by the theories of family sociology in the first focus of our study: whether a family could be created by bringing together a small number of unrelated adults who would live as a primary group. It became apparent that the living arrangements were more like households and represented an amalgam group, combining the characteristics of a primary group household and a formal organization, the sponsors. Thus, the second phase of our research effort was guided by the sociology of organizations. We studied the web of connections among the household, the sponsoring organization, and the institutional structure of our society.

The third area of the research falls within the sociological studies of diffusion of an innovation. We learned that these so-called communal living arrangements were receiving attention in the mass media and that the founder of Share-A-Home was also engaged in an educational campaign to tell interested groups and individuals about these arrangements. He was informing other potential sponsors how to form and operate shared living arrangements based upon his model and experience. This presented us with a unique opportunity to study the diffusion of a social idea. We examined the theory of the spread of technological innovations to find how they become diffused in a society, but we found little information on the spread of nonpatentable ideas.

The fourth focus of the research was a comparative study, which resulted from our efforts to observe and analyze the multiplicity of shared living arrangements that had developed independently of Share-A-Home, Inc., the first case study. Fifteen of these case studies are described briefly in chapter 6, and some tentative generalizations are offered.

As the research continued and the knowledge of the phenomenon increased, we learned that there was a group in Great Britain, the Abbeyfield Society, that was operating hundreds of shared living homes for the elderly. American gerontologists were unaware of this development. We felt it would increase our understanding of the care of older persons if we were able to make a study of the same phenomenon in another highly industrialized society. Thus our study of Abbeyfield in chapter 8 provides cross-national comparisons.

Finally, the studies of the Florida organization and the variety of shared living arrangements that we located in other states helped us to understand these new developments we were studying as an important aspect of contemporary American culture. Their formation is an indication of the values, norms, and behavior of Americans. We observed how individuals and groups responded to a social need. This grass-roots "movement" of trying to tackle and solve a local problem represents the kind of pragmatic approach to social needs that is very compatible with American values.

In Sweden, which has been described as a model welfare state, one will not find these varieties of grass-roots endeavors to solve a social problem.[1] The Swedish approach is perhaps more effectively coordinated than these multiple community endeavors, which rely to a considerable extent on the use of nonprofessionals and volunteers. Such voluntary efforts are discouraged in Sweden, for it is felt that if a social situation requires intervention by the community, it should be planned and implemented in a rational, universal way so that the service meets standardized criteria and is equally available to all qualified needy citizens. The comparison of the Swedish situation with that of the United States indicates the trade-off that must be acknowledged when comparing the two societies. For example, the absence of grass-roots initiative and community participation by volunteers is a loss for Sweden. On the other hand, our system loses the advantages of centralized planning in housing and social services.

The works of contemporary sociologists can be considered in relation to three different kinds of goals: explanatory, applied, and ideological.[2] Sociologists may give more attention and emphasis to one goal over another, depending on their training, interests, professional objectives, and political commitments. Sociologists who stress explanations assert that they are "pure" researchers who desire to move the discipline ahead as a basic science. They eschew any interest in practical outcomes.

1. This is the senior author's judgment. For the basis for this assertion see, for example, Castles (1978), Heclo (1974), Wilensky (1975), and Schulz et al. (1974).
2. Collins has a fourth orientation to sociology, the "aesthetic" or "dramatic" approach, which "is merely to produce an intellectual work, the experience of which is a value in itself" (1975:24).

Other sociologists are very interested in practical outcomes and the applied implications of their work. These interests influence the areas of sociological research they choose, the kinds of problems they select, and the way in which they present their results. And finally, the ideological commitments of sociologists may lead them to do research with the goal of social reform or radical social change. Most sociologists, whether they state it or not, have an ideological component in their work. For some it is a stated set of explicit assumptions, and for others it is merely a tacit understanding concerning domain assumptions.[3]

Our work has been influenced by all three types of goals. The initial impetus for this book was sociological understanding and explanation. We found shared living for the elderly to be a unique social grouping, and these small environments provided strategic sites for empirical social research. As the work progressed, it became obvious that outside financial support was necessary if we were going to move beyond a case study to comparative studies of the varieties of these households. We were successful in obtaining financial support from the NRTA–AARP Andrus Foundation, the Administration on Aging (Department of Health, Education, and Welfare), and from a gift of Arnold Ross and Associates to the University of Florida Foundation. Because of the demand for practical information resulting from the presentation of our findings to various groups, we have provided data to a variety of groups and organizations who wished to learn more about the "experiments" and implement them in their localities.

Our commitment to improving the quality of life for older people also provided the impetus to undertake this particular research. We analyzed the problems of older people in modern societies and became aware that this kind of living arrangement was efficacious in dealing with the problems of a growing frail population and that it would be to the advantage of elderly people and their communities if these kinds of households were established. We believe that these shared living arrangements are one important option for housing older people that should be included in the continuum of housing alternatives.

In organizing the research, in carrying it out, and in writing up the results, we have attempted to maintain the objectivity that is ordinarily

3. The phrase "domain assumptions" is analyzed in depth and in relation to several aspects of sociology by Gouldner (1970).

expected in scholarly description and explanation. While the social scientist's primary task is to try to understand and explain social behavior and social organization, the pressing issues involving the frail elderly in our society warrant research that is useful and understandable.

For the sociologist who has as a primary goal description and explanation, it is important to be clearly aware of the importance of the methods of investigation that are appropriate to the subject matter, feasible in the realm of observation, and fruitful in producing results that add to our understanding. We chose the methods and the role of the "field sociologist"—which are similar to those of the field biologist.

While a great deal of biological research is performed in the laboratory, field biology (or natural history, as it was formerly called) is a recognized scientific tradition practiced by biologists who carry out their scientific pursuits in field situations.

The research methods described in appendix 1 provide a view of how we operated as field sociologists, attempting to observe, measure, and classify the "species"—shared living arrangements—that it was our good fortune to come across in the sociological forests. Just as field biologists describe in precise detail the whole animals they discover, the variations of those organisms, and the habitats in which they live, we tried to describe our social species accurately and place it in its broad habitat— the modern world. As field sociologists interested in the conceptual and theoretical aspects of the species, we considered these households in relation to the larger society. In this instance, we indicated how shared living arrangements are one kind of modern microhabitat for older persons, as is shown in the discussion of the continuum of housing in chapter 2.

Most field biologists do not need to justify their observations in terms of immediate practical outcomes. When a sociologist studies a species of social group, however, the question arises as to the utility or value of carrying out such a series of investigations. The sociologist must often justify his or her pursuit of scientific curiosity, particularly when supported by organizations that are concerned with practical outcomes. Thus, the field sociologist must be aware of competing demands—the requirement that he be a detached observer, trying to describe and explain the species in its habitat, and the expectation that he will supply information needed by persons who may want to learn if the research will be of immediate utility to society. In this research, we attempted to meet both demands—those of the detached scientific observer, and those of a resource person responding to requests for practical information that might be used by organizers and practitioners in the housing and service fields.

Since the start of this research, changes in the political economy have increased interest in our results, for there is greater awareness of the need for alternative housing for the frail elderly. This is due to a combination of factors: the increased number of the elderly and the cost of institutionalization; the importance of saving energy for heating, cooling, and transportation; the reduction in government funding for purpose-built housing for the elderly; and the greater awareness of the need for local initiative and support for health, housing, and service programs.

It is our hope that this book may offer insights to those citizens who work at the grass-roots level and are seeking to respond to the social needs in their communities in new and innovative ways, and also to social scientists in the fields of family sociology, social gerontology, and social change who are interested in understanding these amalgam groups.

CHAPTER ONE

The Need for Shared Housing

In recent years there have been a number of attempts to devise new living arrangements for the elderly as a means of solving many of their problems of economic insecurity, declining health, dependency, household management, and loneliness. These new arrangements are predicated on the notion that unrelated adults can live together as a kind of "family." In this book we shall describe and analyze these family-like living arrangements. Our first task is to describe the social context in which they emerged, for they are a contemporary development and are related to fundamental social processes that can be placed under the broad umbrella concept of modernization.

MODERN SOCIETIES AND AN AGING POPULATION

Modernization is one of the major contemporary themes that has occupied the attention of writers, intellectuals, government officials, businessmen, and the average concerned citizens. Modernization touches the lives of all. One of the hallmarks of modernization is change—not necessarily "progress" but change, for modernity means the rejection or modification of old methods, customs, and material objects, and the substitution of new ones. Adaptation to change is one of the hallmarks of a vital society.

Charles Frankel, the philosopher, has captured the essence of modernization:

Technology, plainly, is the fundamental dynamic element in modern society. It affects everything from the size, shape, look, and smell of our cities and suburbs to the mobility of populations, the character of social classes, the stability of the family, the standards of workmanship that prevail, and the direction and level of moral and aesthetic sensibilities. (1959:198)

When most persons see or hear the word "modernization," they do not think of older persons and their living arrangements. They think instead of jet planes, nuclear reactors, computers, and word processors, and not of a lonely widow in frail health, living alone in housing that she cannot afford. What is the connection between these two images? In this book we will explore some ramifications of how modernization affects the living environments and housing possibilities for older persons. We will describe how older persons and younger persons, groups and organizations respond to one facet of modernization—the growing number of older persons over seventy-five years of age, sometimes called the frail elderly or the old-old. We will describe the social context that creates the need for new kinds of households and living arrangements and show how modernization brings about social situations to which persons and groups respond by creating new kinds of household arrangements.

Modernization is a mixture of positive and negative features. To some it has been a bane and to others a blessing. Most persons, however, if given a choice, would vote for modernization and its results, rather than the kind of social and physical conditions that existed a hundred and two hundred years ago.

Modernization theory has been widely used in studies of aging. Williamson et al. (1982) have provided a cogent summary and critique of the ways in which modernization theory has been utilized by different writers, particularly Cowgill and Holmes (1972) and Cowgill (1974). (See endnote, pp. 21–22.)

Our discussion of modernization differs in several respects from Cowgill's, namely, we do not consider modernization to be a theory in a precise sense, for we refer to it as a framework, or orientation, which provides a way of organizing complex materials related to modern societies. Furthermore, we are not concerned with the status and power debate that plagues those who try to determine the effects of modernization. Cowgill's revision (1974) indicates the intricate way in which institutional structures and social processes are woven together, resulting in lowered status of the elderly. Instead, we deal with the *consequences* of modernization: an increasing number of frail older persons over seventy-five who have no kin, or do not wish to live with kin, and who need a supportive environment.

Cowgill offers a useful framework relating modernization to aging and specifies four salient aspects of modernization: health technology, economic technology, urbanization, and education. For the purposes of this book, we view Cowgill's orientation as explaining the antecedent factors that are integral to modernization and its impact on the family life of the elderly.

Health Technology. The basic scientific discoveries in health technology are very important for understanding the general context that sets the stage for our research on alternative housing because health and medical developments, which in recent years have resulted in greater longevity, are closely related to demographic patterns. In health technology, we include sanitation, antibiotics, and the large array of sophisticated drugs, modern diagnostic techniques, and such technological advances as kidney dialysis, cardiac bypass surgery, implantation of pacemakers, and the like. Their use has resulted in an increase in life expectancy for many persons and a greater proportion of older people. This is the "gerontological miracle" of modern times. Modernization has also resulted, however, in a greater amount of chronic disease and the slow deterioration of many who survive. Stub has pointed out, "There is little evidence that the projected increases in expected length of life, at the older ages, will allow the very old to escape a period of preterminal deterioration, although the length of this period might be relatively short" (1982:372). The alternative living arrangements discussed here are one type of social arrangement that has been organized to cope with this period of preterminal deterioration.

Economic Technology. This involves the use of inanimate power with automated machines, resulting in greatly increased productivity. The industrial method of production requires new occupations which tend to be filled by younger people, and in the process, the elderly are displaced. The increased productivity resulting from efficiencies of a modern industrial system means that the society can support a large percentage of people who are not in the labor force. This is the fundamental basis for a welfare state that provides the sustenance and economic support for people who do not work. This factor is very important to the elderly, for it means that they can receive pensions—Social Security—and, in addition, private pensions if they have worked for companies with pension plans. The result of this important facet of modernization with regard to the elderly is that they have much more autonomy than older people experienced in any previous time in history. They can live independently—they are not "beholden" to anyone and are not subject to the dictates of family pressures. All of this is a satisfactory arrangement for both the older people and their families, until the time comes when the elderly person, often a widow, can no longer live alone. Then suddenly the whole way of life for the widow *and* the families must be reconsidered.

Urbanization. Closely related to modern economic technology is the increasing concentration of population in urban areas—or urbanization. The significance of this to our theme of housing for the elderly is that younger persons, attrracted to the new jobs resulting from advanced technology, must have the mobility to leave their childhood homes and seek jobs in cities. This often leaves the elderly in rural areas or small towns. Furthermore, the demands of the job may require the younger persons to move several times in their careers, often to areas far away. This is a completely accepted facet of modern American life. People expect that their children, if successful, will probably live in another area. It is considered selfish for a parent to attempt to keep children nearby, rather than encouraging them to realize their potential and take advantage of career opportunities or promotions that require moving.

Education. Finally, the fourth salient dimension of Cowgill's theory of modernization is the process by which the young receive technical training on a mass scale to obtain the skills necessary to become part of the technically trained labor force in both the health and industrial fields. The highly trained people in the younger generation, both men and women, are not available to stay home and take care of the frail elderly. They are looking for jobs in industrial and professional employment—opportunities which often draw them away from the location where they formerly lived. Such work is more interesting and more remunerative than staying home to take care of an older relative. Hence, as our older population grows in number, there is a need to develop some kind of living arrangements to fill the void left by the departure of the younger generation. Even when members of the younger generation do not relocate away from older kin because of job opportunities, they are employed outside the home and feel they do not have the time or energy to devote to caring for old family members. They would often prefer to contribute monetarily to some other living arrangement in the same town.

MODERNIZATION AND THE DEMOGRAPHY OF THE ELDERLY

The consequences of modernization, we have pointed out, are manifested in the life expectancy, numbers, and distribution of the aged, in sex ratios, and in marital status of the elderly. To give a background for our discussion on the need for new forms of housing arrangements, it is necessary to relate a few demographic facts prepared for the Select Committee on Aging of the House of Representatives in 1982.

During the eighty years between 1900 and 1980, the total population of the United States grew almost threefold, while the older population (age sixty-five and over) grew almost eightfold. In 1981, there were 25.5 million older Americans, comprising 11 percent of the population (Select Committee on Aging, House of Representatives 1982). Thirty-eight percent of these were over 75, and almost 10 percent were over 85. At age 65, the life expectancy for women was 18.4 years, and for men, 14 years. The report states that life expectancy at the upper ages has also increased since the 1950s, and current decreases in death rates from cardiovascular conditions will extend life even further.

Most older persons are women, for the death rates are higher for males than females at every age. In 1981, there were 148 women per 100 men for the total population of persons age 65 and over. This breaks down as follows: in the 65 to 74 category, the ratio is 131 women to 100 men. It rises to 180 women to 100 men for those 75 years and over, and 229 women to 100 men for the eighty-five and over category.

In 1980, most older men (78 percent) were married, but most older women (51 percent) were widows. There were 5.3 times as many widows as widowers. Among women 75 and older, almost 70 percent were widows.

The disparity in living arrangements of older men and women was highlighted in the committee report: "Three quarters of the older men (75.5 percent) lived in families that included a wife, but only slightly more than a third of the older women (38 percent) lived in families that included the husband. Four of every ten older women lived alone" (Select Committee on Aging 1982:27). Almost four times as many older women lived alone or with nonrelatives than did older men.

Seventy-two percent of the elderly owned their homes as compared to 64 percent of younger persons, according to the 1980 annual housing survey. The elderly tended to live in older structures. Therefore, an older widow is very apt to be "overhoused" in a structure with inadequacies: problems with plumbing, electrical wiring, roofing, etc. Because of a declining income, she may find it difficult to meet the cost of needed repairs.

In regard to health status, over two-thirds of the noninstitutionalized elderly reported that they were in good health. Twenty-two percent reported themselves in fair health and almost 9 percent in poor health. It is those in the last two categories—in fair or poor health—who are candidates for shared housing, for they may need help in shopping, food preparation, and transportation. A 1977 national survey cited in the committee report showed that of the 22 million older persons not in institutions, 2.1 percent were confined to bed, 2.6 percent needed help to get about the house, 6 percent needed help to get about the neighborhood, and 8.4 percent needed help outside the neighborhood.

A few facts on income are pertinent. Older persons have about one-half the income of younger persons, for retirement from gainful employment usually brings a reduction of around 50 percent in income. In 1980, the median income was $12,881 per year for older families and $22,548 for younger families. This means that half of the families headed by an older person had incomes of less than $248 a week, compared with $434 a week for half of the families headed by persons under 65 years of age.

These demographic facts point to the emergence of a large new category of older persons, primarily women, who live alone in owner-occupied dwellings that are too large for their needs and, in many instances, too expensive to maintain as private dwellings. Moreover, a third are in lowered health condition so that they need a supportive environment in order to maintain themselves and carry out the activities of daily living. Finally, since so many men and women are widows or widowers, many wish to avoid the loneliness and isolation that often mark the last years of life. The combination of these factors points to the need for the development of alternative living arrangements.

The Federal Council on Aging (1978) has given particular attention

them. Despite romantic views of intergenerational living, most people acknowledge that it often results in grave problems and family tensions. Younger generations have different life styles, and it is often difficult to incorporate an older person. If there are grandchildren in the home, this widens the gap in life style and attitudes.

One might ask what has brought about the increased independence on the part of the older generations. Certainly the improved economic situation of many elderly is of prime importance. Most of the elderly in modern societies like the United States have a steady source of income in social security, plus pensions, savings, and home ownership. There has been considerable discussion about the adequacy of the elderly's income in the United States in works by Kutza (1981), Olson (1982), Schulz (1980), and Schulz et al. (1974). Although the income is inadequate in many cases, when judged by experts and the older persons themselves, the fact is that the *regularity* of the source creates a foundation for economic independence that did not exist for millions of older persons before a national system of old-age economic supports was established. Thus, modernization and the resulting social security system enable the elderly to maintain an independence unknown throughout most of history.

We believe this kind of economic independence is basic for understanding the structure of relations of older families and their adult children and grandchildren. We tend to agree with Baum and Baum when they state that "diachronic solidarity" is one of the basic clues to understanding older people and their social relations in modern society. By this term, Baum and Baum describe a a kind of "self-perpetuating form of intergenerational solidarity." In more precise language, diachronic solidarity is "a social identity shared with successive generations that always connects the younger with the older in a perpetual chain of community lasting through time indefinitely" (1980:8).

The fact that the generations do not choose to live together does not mean that a sense of responsibility is lessened and emotional ties are diminished. In fact people emphasize that close affectional ties can be preserved only if they maintain separate residences from their children. Thus, modernization has shaped a new form of intergenerational solidarity in which family relationships and help patterns are fundamentally different than they were in earlier periods of American history. They also differ tremendously from societies that do not have an economic system productive enough to support elderly people independently from family and kin.

In countries like Russia and China, older people often live with relatives in an intergenerational household. The elderly woman often has a function of child care, or standing in lines to do the daily shopping, while the daughter works. Because of the extreme housing shortage in these two countries, grandparents have no choice but to live with relatives (Butterfield 1982; Hollander 1973). In the United States, however, older women have generally eschewed the child-care role. Many will readily express the attitude that they have done their share of child rearing—let the younger people handle this responsibility. Therefore, working mothers usually rely on nursery schools or day care centers for child care rather than enlist the aid of grandmothers. Furthermore, if the elderly woman is frail, she is in need of care herself, rather than being able to assume the responsibility for the upbringing of an active child.

THE MASS MEDIA AND IMAGES OF THE OLD

The mass media of communication are one of the hallmarks of modern society, for the highly integrated communications networks influence and shape the lives of everyone. This highly sophisticated system not only reports news and current happenings, but also has an important role in "image building"—presenting information that forms people's ideas of norms and customs and shapes their expectations of the world we live in.

In their treatment of the elderly, the mass media often present a distorted picture, focusing on pathetic "human interest" stories. There is a great deal of material presented in newspapers and magazines and on television deploring "society's treatment of the old." Usually, the reporter finds a pathetic story of some lonely, elderly person and relates in detail the unfortunate conditions, the loneliness, the health problems, the poverty, the uncaring family, and then concludes with a condemnation of our modern society for "throwing the elderly on the scrap heap." This sad picture is placed against a backdrop of a romantic portrayal of society in historical times, which supposedly provided a warm and caring primary group environment for the occasional rare individual who reached advanced age. However, Williamson et al. (1982) observe that the "good old days" for the elderly in preindustrial America existed only for the wealthy and powerful and that the elderly poor often suffered considerably.

The respect accorded the elderly in nineteenth-century America, according to the historian Achenbaum (1978), was partially due to their nearness to death and hence to "the eternal life." Old age was described as the transitional stage of development that moderated between life and death, and "the elderly's proximity to the supernatural enhanced their special value" (Achenbaum 1978:35). (This kind of respect would be considered a dubious goal in modern secular America.) Writers in the middle nineteenth century, says Achenbaum, believed that understanding the meaning of suffering remained the foremost comfort of age, and that the elderly's meekness of spirit, delight in prayer and the Bible, piety, and resignation to God's will established them as moral exemplars. We would note that this is hardly what contemporary writers have in mind when they speak of the respect accorded to the elderly in the "good old days."

Fischer, another contemporary historian, questions that there was ever a "golden age" for the elderly. Writing about Colonial America, he states: "More than today, old age was filled with pain, both physical and psychological. Young people were not very kind to their elders. The irony was striking: old people received respect without affection, honor without devotion, veneration without love" (1978:224).

Peter Laslett (1976, 1979), the English demographer, also emphasized that the advantages of the mythic past for the elderly have been largely overstated and that the multigenerational household was not the usual method for taking care of the aged. In preindustrial England, the elderly did not move to live in the households of their married children, nor did the married children come to live with them.

Corinne Nydegger, writing about the myths of family life in other societies, also observes: "It is necessary to emphasize that most of our cherished beliefs about the treatment of the aged at other times and in other places are proving to be illusions" (1983:26). She adds that there is little question that the elderly and their children in our historic past valued the independence of separate residence as much as do contemporary families, and many elderly persons were not cared for by their families if other alternatives, such as institutions or hired help, were available.

Thus, we must be aware that many of the glib generalizations about modern society's "abandonment of the elderly" that one hears in the mass media should be questioned. Almost everyone wants the advantages resulting from modernization: a longer life, social security, modern health care, and residential independence. Modernization has other consequences, however, some of which are undesirable for older persons, such as residential mobility of their children. Furthermore, the advantages of modernization are not shared equally by all members of society. Thus, there are indeed a certain number of isolated, lonely, frail people who need help. Gerontologists must not generalize from these as representing the modal pattern. It should be added, however, that sometimes these cases are highlighted in order to mobilize public support for legislative or for assistance programs.

It is the expectation and hope that a caring society can use its facilities and resources more efficaciously to reduce the number of underprivileged elderly in need of services. Indeed, this is the motivation of people who organize shared family living for the elderly.

SUMMARY

The preceding discussion has described the consequences of modernization for a growing older population. One consequence for the elderly is that some older people find themselves in need of help for aspects of daily living: housing, food preparation, transportation for necessary services and occasional recreation, companionship, etc. The approach to these needs in a highly organized technological society is often formal and bureaucratic; the proliferation of nursing homes has been the major response to these needs. However, the skills and expense of trained health care personnel and the ancillary professional staff that are an integral and required part of a modern health care facility are not always needed by the frail elderly. Therefore, one needs to consider an alternative model that meets the needs of daily living and avoids the expense and impersonality of bureaucratic structures.

Endnote

Modernization is the broad social process which was defined by the social historian David Landes as:

Such developments as urbanization (a concentration of the population in cities that serves as modes of industrial production, administration, and intellectual and artistic activity); a sharp reduction in both death rates and birth rates from traditional levels (the so-called demographic transition); the establishment of an effective, fairly centralised bureaucratic government; the creation of an educational system capable of training and socialising the children of a society to a level compatible with their capacities and best contemporary knowledge; and of course the acquisition of the ability and means to use an up-to-date technology. (1969:6)

Other writers have described modernization from other perspectives. C. E. Black (1966) analyzed modernization in comparative historical terms, emphasizing political integration, while Daniel Lerner (1958), a political scientist, pioneered in the empirical use of survey techniques to study modernization in five countries in the Middle East. These works do not focus on aging as did Cottrell (1960) in his synoptic work, "The Technological and Societal Basis of Aging."

American sociologists and gerontologists have also looked at other societies for clues about the causes and effects of modernization. Japan has received particular attention because it is considered a modern society that has been able to provide high status for the old. Palmore's (1975) book, *The Honorable Elders,* presents a picture of Japan as an exception to the idea that the status of the aged declines with modernization. His contention has been challenged in reviews by Chadwick (1976) and by Kiefer (1976). David Plath, an anthropologist specializing in Japanese culture, wrote a very skeptical account of the high status of the elderly in modern Japan and questioned whether Japan offered the possibility of making aging "a peak experience." He concluded his analysis in these words: "I continue to doubt that the Japanese culture offers a much better—or much worse—model for that social order than the American one" (1972:149).

Two important studies of the impact of modernization on Japan are reported by two anthropologists who returned to the villages they studied at two points in time. Smith (1978) studied an agricultural village in 1951 and again in 1975, and Norbeck (1978) did his first ethnographic study of a Japanese fishing village in 1950–51 and then returned in 1974. One quotation from Norbeck captures the many changes relating to the elderly that modernization has brought: "The second category of troubled people, the most elderly in the community, is more numerous and their circumstances affect a larger number of other people. As a class, they constitute a great and growing social problem in the entire nation" (1978:331).

Quadagno (1982) has also provided a useful framework as to how industrialization (modernization) has affected older persons. She states that there are at least three approaches: 1) the analytic, mainly derived from the sociological perspective called structural functionalism (Cowgill 1974; Cowgill and Holmes 1972; Bengtson et al. 1975); 2) the historical, in which periods or epochs are set off by their unique characteristics (Achenbaum 1978; Fischer 1978); and 3) a policy approach, in which modernization is viewed as a set of plans developed and implemented by the leaders or elites of developing countries (Cherry and Magnuson-Martinson 1981).

The Continuum of Living Arrangements:
Where and How Older People Live

If a sample of people were asked, "Where do the elderly in the United States live?" the following would be among the answers given.

They live in declining neighborhoods in the decaying core of central cities.
They live in low-income public housing projects.
They live in deteriorated single-room occupancy hotels.
They move to retirement communities or mobile home parks.
They are shunted off to nursing homes.

Actually, all of these answers are correct, for a small percentage of the elderly live in one of these or in one of a number of specialized types of housing. According to Carp, however, "Most older people reside in ordinary housing in their communities" (1976:249). She adds that very little is known about their housing and how it accommodates them or their needs in regard to the living environment.

When a disability occurs among the elderly, housing changes are considered in about half of the cases, according to a nationwide survey reported by Newman (1976). The two major alternatives are moving into the household of relatives or entering a nursing home. Changes are very likely to be considered when the person is over 75 or is female. Newman states:

The move to an institution, such as a nursing home, was shown to be more probable when the disabled person's spouse was alive at the onset of the disability and when the child with the greatest responsibility for the decision making in relation to the disabled person had a relatively high family income. (1976:317)

In earlier and more traditional times, among the options to be considered were for the elderly person to move in with children, or for children to move in with parents. These solutions are increasingly rejected in urban America, by both the adult children and the elderly themselves. As we pointed out in chapter 1, both generations prize their freedom and independence; the older generation does not want to endanger the affectional ties with their children by living with them.

Furthermore, because of the mobility of the younger generation, moving in with children often means that the older persons would have to move away from their friends, activities, church, and familiar environment to another city or state. Another factor that reduces the feasibility of traditional family solutions is the increasing number of persons living to their eighties and nineties. This means that the "children" may have retired themselves, and they are anticipating a period of freedom and travel after their work years are over. They are not oriented to spending their remaining years of health in providing nursing care for a frail parent, but they are receptive to seeking other possibilities. Furthermore, some sixty-year-olds have their own health problems and cannot be counted on to provide nursing care to an 80- or 90-year-old parent.

One recent solution for the moderately dependent elderly person is the initiation of home care services in order to maintain the person in her residence as long as possible. Her needs are met by supplying Meals-on-Wheels, housekeeping services, visiting nurses, therapists, and transportation services. When there is a multiplicity of services, the coordination of activities becomes complicated and the costs escalate. If the person lives in a rural area, or far from the location where the services originate, the transportation costs become excessive. Provision of home care services may not alleviate the loneliness and fears concerning personal safety. This includes fear of crime and the fear of a fall or heart attack in which the person could not reach a telephone to summon help. To meet this contingency, programs have been initiated using electronic summoning devices to signal for help. However, such technological solutions have limitations. Sometimes they do not function adequately, for the batteries wear out. Some elderly people find it cumbersome to wear the devices all of the time. In addition, the service is expensive, usually costing from $15 to $25 a month.

All of these factors have stimulated interest in developing new housing alternatives for the frail elderly. There is a realization that nursing care and the hospital-like environment of nursing homes are not necessary for many older people who simply need meals prepared, a safe environment, and someone to "keep an eye on them." There is also a realization that "family" type environments are more satisfying emotionally and psychologically than institutional environments.

THE CONTINUUM OF LIVING ARRANGEMENTS

Alternative family and living arrangements can be understood in relation to the continuum of housing in which older persons live, ranging from living independently and autonomously in a private house or apartment to a full-care institution where twenty-four-hour-a-day skilled nursing care is provided. Understanding the continuum enables one to see where the various alternatives lie. In figure 2.1, a graphic presentation shows the kinds of housing, ranging from the least supportive to the most supportive. A conventional house is regarded as the least supportive and the life care facility or nursing home as the most supportive. Mangum states: "Supportiveness refers to the degree to which the

FIGURE *2.1. Continuum of Living Arrangements: From Private Home to the Nursing Home*

Least Supportive ⟶	Most Supportive
Conventional Housing (Comprises about 80% to 90% of elderly housing)	Retirement Housing (Comprises 10% to 20% of elderly housing)*
Apartments Condominiums Houses	Nursing Homes Life Care Facilities Board and Care Homes Shared Living Homes Retirement Hotels Retirement Apartments (high-rise) Retirement Villages Mobile Home Parks (retirement)

SOURCE: Adapted from Mangum 1979), fig. 1.

*The estimates are based upon figures in Struyk (1977). Other statistics are found in Struyk and Soldo (1980) and in Berghorn et al. (1978). See also Lawton (1980).

housing environment provides for the routine and special needs of the resident, as well as the extent to which the resident is freed of responsibility for maintaining the housing environment"(1979:90–91).

Conventional housing is considered to be the single family house in which the owner takes care of meals and other traditional services and also has the responsibility for maintenance and repair of the property, including yard upkeep. The owner has multiple responsibilities: paying taxes and insurance premiums; maintaining the house to the standards of the local housing code; repairing plumbing, heating systems, and roof; keeping the house painted and the yard maintained, with grass cut and weeds controlled; preventing insect or rodent infestation; and, in cold climates, keeping walkways free of ice and snow. All of these tasks are an integral and accepted part of home ownership. However, older people in declining health sometimes have extreme difficulty in coping with these tasks personally or finding and paying someone to perform them satisfactorily.

There has been little research on how the elderly fare when they remain in owner-occupied dwellings. Struyk and Soldo (1980) point out that older people often must spend more than the recommended 25 percent of their income for housing. Their income declines upon retirement, but they usually remain in the same house. This may result in a housing situation in which they have more space than they need, and the cost of maintenance may constitute a financial burden. In short, many widowed elderly persons in private homes are "overhoused."

One suggestion to ease the problem of the financial burden of home ownership for the older person living alone is discussed by Scholen and Chen (1980). They propose that housing annuities be established, by which a person receives yearly "loans" in the form of monthly annuity checks to supplement his current income. These loans would be repaid at a later date from the equity in their houses. Thus, the elderly themselves would have the use of the equity they have built up, rather than having it pass on to their heirs upon their death.

Apartments and condominiums offer certain advantages over single family houses in regard to supportive services. There is usually a manager who takes care of many of the necessary tasks: maintenance of the yard, landscaping and upkeep, and repair of the basic physical structure.

Planned retirement communities offer more supportive services than are usually available in more conventional housing. The residents usually choose this kind of housing arrangement after carefully studying all other possibilities. The persons who choose this environment are apt to be those who take active control of their lives, and they tend to be above average in educational attainment and income levels when compared to the average retiree. Retirement communities are relatively recent on the American scene and are unique to this culture, for they are not found in other developed, industrialized societies (Streib, La Greca, and Folts 1984).

The dwelling units in retirement communities may vary in style, design, quality, and cost. They can be single family homes, duplexes, triplexes, or manufactured homes (formerly called mobile homes). There is usually an arrangement for management to take care of the common facilities and property. In the case of many manufactured home parks, the management owns the lots and pays the taxes. Personal security or crime is less of a worry, for there is sometimes an entry gate with a security guard. The communities may be located in isolated areas because the land is less expensive and there is no need to be near employment opportunities. The distance from urbanized areas is also a security factor, for it reduces the possibility of criminal activity. Transportation may be provided for shopping and for religious and medical services, so the residents may not need to drive a private automobile. Many activities are organized by residents and use community facilities, so some residents spend most of their time in the community. Altogether, the environment offers many supports and provides some definite advantages to people in declining health who still wish to remain active.

Retirement communities have been the focus of research for a generation, dating back to the early work by Hoyt (1954) and Webber (1954), when they were called "trailer parks." The more recent work by Johnson (1971), Jacobs (1974), and Bultena and Wood (1969) focused upon the high degree of resident satisfaction. In a study of an affluent retirement community in central Florida in which a random sample of participants were interviewed, it was found that 78 percent were "very satisfied" and only 3 percent were dissatisfied with living in the community (Barr 1977). They particularly valued safety and security, easy home maintenance, community facilities, and social atmosphere. Osgood (1982) found that residents developed new and meaningful roles, and a sense of "communityness" emerged.

Critics of retirement communities have asserted that they are geriatric ghettoes, cut off from the mainstream of social life and community participation. The two major detailed studies that focus on the relation of retirement communities to their surrounding environment are the work of Heintz (1976) and Haas (1980). They found that the residents of the two communities they studied participate widely in the civic life, voluntary organizations, religious activities, and political sphere of the adjacent communities.

The next step in the continuum is high-rise retirement apartments. These are similar to retirement communities in the kinds of facilities and services they offer. The main difference is that dwelling units are clustered together in one or more structures, comprising what might be called a vertical rather than a horizontal retirement community. Some may have dining facilities within the complex.

Retirement hotels are another type of living arrangement preferred by some elderly usually single individuals. Albrecht (1969), who studied retirement hotels in Florida, found that active, young, and independent retirees often choose this type of housing. Health is an important consideration; in fact, some retirement hotels or clubs require a statement from a physician indicating that the individual is ambulatory and self-sufficient.

Albrecht reported:

Concern for residents is not unusual. One hotel has a breakfast roll call, others make various checks on them and sometimes neighbors, friends or buddies take care of this and report illness to the management. . . . The retirement hotels visited keep records of next of kin or others to be notified in case this is necessary. (1969:79)

Thus, these hotels provide services beyond those of the usual commercial hotel. They allow residents to be independent and come and go as they please, without reporting to anyone or accounting for their activities. In addition, the food was usually good in the places studied, and the residents enjoyed the companionship and recreational facilities. Albrecht concluded, however, that there are potential problems if the person's physical or mental health condition deteriorates.

A slightly different picture was painted in a careful study by Stephens (1976) of elderly tenants in a slum hotel in a large midwestern city. She found that this type of housing seemed to be preferred by male loners who wished to avoid social involvement. Indeed, the work of Stephens emphasized that many of the older residents cling fiercely to their autonomy and privacy in the slum hotel and regard it as preferable to living in any kind of an institutional setting, which might offer more services.

Two other recent studies of elderly hotel residents in Seattle and San Diego reported similar findings, particularly that the residents were highly independent and self-reliant. The Seattle team reported:

They are reticent to enter dependent relationships with 'helpers' which they perceive could compromise their self concepts. They either lack contact with or under-utilize existing social services which they distrust because they believe representatives of these agencies have the power to deny them the life style of their choosing. (Lally et al. 1979:72)

In San Diego, the investigators found that the most effective services and social supports were those provided by the hotel staff and neighborhood shopkeepers (Erickson and Eckert 1977). Similar results have been reported by Ehrlich and Ehrlich (1982) in a study in St. Louis.

The next kind of housing on the continuum is shared living homes, which are the focus of this book and will be discussed in detail in later chapters.

Boarding homes, foster care homes, or Board and Care Homes comprise the next step in the continuum. These were probably utilized more frequently in the past than in the contemporary scene, but there is renewed interest in them. In a study done in Missouri, the investigators classified homes into three groups: small—one or two or three persons, generally not licensed; medium—seven or eight persons; and large—up to thirty persons, the legal limit in the state (Habenstein, Kiefer, and Wang 1976). All groups are operated for profit, although in the marginal or smaller ones, profit is often minimal; they may just break even. These homes are operated by local people in small towns, and there is often community involvement in the homes. Most families consider them a much more desirable living arrangement than nursing homes when a frail or impaired person is unable to take care of herself, or when the relatives cannot take her in. The average age of the residents was 82, and half of the older people were unable to pay the charges with their own funds.

The physician was the person who initiated the move to the boarding home in a third of all moves. While the decision to enter is primarily a family matter, the doctor facilitated the decision by his recommendation. Since such a decision was nearly always an unwelcome
one, the physician's role was to ratify the unpleasant step that the family must take.

The Missouri boarding home situation has an interesting feature in
that all residents in licensed homes need a sponsor—a responsible person concerned with the welfare of the resident. It may be more than
one person, but in 60 percent of the cases, the sponsor was a son or
daughter.

The Missouri investigators reported that although the smaller boarding homes are financially marginal operations in modest family homes,
the quality of care and the amount of concern and personal attention
was often higher than that observed in larger, well-appointed homes.
In 1973, when a new law on licensure was placed on the books, many
small and medium-sized homes were closed. The pressure to comply
with the rigid regulations caused considerable soul-searching on the part
of the small operators, and many felt that "the game was not worth the
candle," in their words. The larger homes, with larger fees, were clear-
cut profit ventures with an extra fee for anything beyond the standard
necessities. Bigger boarding homes bring about economies, a technical
division of labor, and a more rigid scheduling of activities, including
meals, bedtime, visiting hours, and the like.

At the most supportive end of the continuum are life care facilities,
which are often multi-level housing arrangements. They can include
small cottages, apartments, single rooms, and shared rooms. Meals are
usually served in a central dining facility and other supportive services
such as recreational facilities, a beauty shop, religious services, and
transportation may be provided. Many life care facilities also provide a
health care facility or nursing home. These are similar to free-standing
nursing homes.

The life care facilities provide a continuum of living arrangements
in one location with the possibility of acute or chronic nursing care.
These facilities represent the most comprehensive form of living environment for the elderly provided in our society, giving the most complete range of housing options and services in one location. However,
they are able to take care of only a small proportion of America's older

population, and they are quite expensive. Usually there is an initial entrance fee ranging from $30,000 to as much as $100,000 depending on the luxury of the accommodations chosen, and there is a monthly service charge from $600 to $2,000 per person.

Nursing homes are the final point on the continuum. Often the elderly—and their kin—will make many compromises and consider any alternative to avoid institutionalization because of the negative perceptions held about nursing homes by both young and old. The orientation in the literature ranges widely. Some reports aare written from the advocacy point of view, in order to expose the conditions, such as works by Butler (1975), Mendelson (1974), and Townsend (1971). There are other investigations written from a scholarly and dispassionate stance, such as Tobin and Lieberman (1976), Gubrium (1975), and Glasscote et al. (1976). These writers attempt to analyze how long-term care settings operate and how they affect the older people who reside in them.

Tobin and Lieberman (1976) offer a detailed analysis of the institutional effects of living in a nursing home. They studied the period before admission, at the time of admission and during the first year of residence. They were interested in analyzing the process of institutionalization and how it relates to vulnerability and survivorship. They point out that homes for the aged are in reality becoming chronic disease hospitals, and the population now and in the future is apt to be older and sicker.

Gubrium's (1975) work is based upon participant observation of one rather large nursing home focusing upon the nature of the physical setting and how it shapes and forms the life in the home. He also analyzes the social structure—the strata of the staff and how these relate to the everyday activities, "bed and body work." The realities of the social relations among the clients are insulated from the top staff. It is the floor staff who carry the routine work of the home, coping with the "annoyance of superiors and the residents."

A comparative approach is illustrated by the work of Glasscote and associates (1976), who studied sixty nursing homes and thirty-one bed and board homes. The importance of this study is the compilation of observations on ninety-one facilities. They can offer valid generalizations about the nursing home industry, which is not possible in the rather select sample studied more intensively by Tobin and Lieberman and by Gubrium. This team of thirteen investigators began its study with a skeptical orientation about the quality of care in nursing homes, but concluded, "The majority of the 91 facilities . . . we visited were, in many important respects, better than the innumerable attacks on nursing homes had led us to expect" (1976:147).

AGE-CONCENTRATED VERSUS AGE-INTEGRATED ENVIRONMENTS

Among the several crucial theoretical and policy issues in the field of social gerontology, one of the most significant is that of age segregation or age integration. The issue of age segregation may be a misnomer, for it would perhaps be more precise to write of "age concentration" (Berghorn et al. 1978), for the terms refer to the age composition found in a community or living arrangement. Rosow (1967) uses the terms residential density and residential concentration, and he designates neighborhoods as being "normal," "concentrated," or "dense" according to the percentage of households with an older member.

Retirement communities and other age-dense residential settings have been viewed with disfavor by some gerontologists and sociologists (Rose 1962; Jacobs 1974). Advocates for the old, such as Maggie Kuhn, have spoken widely and vigorously against retirement communities, and she has called them "geratric playpens." There are complex reasons for the opposition to age-dense environments Segregated environments evoke images of racial or religious segregation. Some hold (without evidence) that the "healthiest" environment for the elderly is a mixture of all age groups, interacting together and offering mutual help. There is also an implication that persons who prefer their own age group are somehow warped or deviant, for it is "normal" to prefer living with a mixture of ages.

A variety of studies in different geographical locations and covering a range of settings offer some convincing evidence showing the positive outcomes associated with a high degree of age density. Rosow's (1967) classic study of age density in Cleveland, Ohio, neighborhoods demonstrated the social benefits of a residential environment that has a high proportion of age peers. Hochschild's (1973) detailed case study of one small apartment building offered confirmatory qualitative data on how age-concentrated housing may have positive outcomes for older persons. Congruent findings were reported in Johnson's (1971) study of a mobile home community in the San Francisco Bay area.

Carp's (1966) landmark study of a low-income, high-rise public housing project showed how age-dense housing (a new environment for the residents) enhanced the morale of the residents as shown by increased activity, more informal social contacts, and a decrease in disengagement.

While housing environments were not the focus of the study by Berghorn et al. they did examine the relationships between neighborhoods that were age homogeneous and life satisfaction. They found that "elderly people residing in neighborhoods with high concentration of older residents have higher levels of life satisfaction" (1978:106).

Gubrium (1973), reporting on a study in Detroit of three types of environments differing in the degree of age concentration, found that age concentration has a positive impact on the morale of persons.

In retirement communities, the research findings are very convincing that age concentration is a preferred environment and has positive consequences from the perspective of the residents (Bultena and Wood 1969; Jacobs 1974; Barr 1977; Osgood 1982).

Lawton has raised several questions about age segregation or age integration, and he argues that "this issue remains unsettled" (1980:93). One implication of these studies from many regions of the United States is that there is no one desirable form of retirement environment that is endorsed by all older persons or can be recommended for all elderly people. The professionals may not agree about the research findings on the optimum retirement environment, and the elderly hold varying opinions of what is the most desirable place to live. The options shown in the continuum of living arrangements provide a realistic set of alternatives in the context of a complex society when viewed by professionals and by the residents.

ORIENTATIONS TO HOUSING THE FRAIL ELDERLY

The previous discussion has indicated the variety of housing structures and living arrangements for the elderly. Now let us consider more specifically the ways of meeting the housing needs of the frail elderly— those persons who are no longer physically capable of maintaining single family residences but do not require institutionalization. Three major approaches are: 1) by providing specialized physical structures, 2) by supplying economic assistance, and 3) by altering social arrangements. The first, physical structures, involves the conventional method of building new housing for older persons that takes account of their physical conditions and the need for a smaller space. Often there are safety features built into the apartments, such as grab bars in the bathrooms, wider doorways, or communication systems. This housing can be provided either in segregated units designed only for older persons, or in integrated units or neighborhoods that are age heterogeneous.

Under Section 202 of the 1959 Housing Act and Section 236, of the 1974 Housing Act new housing has been constructed with the specific needs of older persons in mind. The earliest buildings were concerned merely with shelter and did not take account of social services, food services, and health or medical services. The federal housing law required that persons who live in these buildings should be able to take care of themselves. A basic problem is that people may be able to take care of themselves when they move in, but their condition could change quickly, due to a broken hip, a stroke, or arthritis. Therefore, services have been added to older structures in some instances (Ehrlich and Ehrlich 1982).

The first approach involves providing clean, safe housing in which the older person lives by herself and is able to summon help if needed by using call buttons or telephone systems. This is very important in emergencies, but it is less helpful in day-to-day problems that occur with chronic disability. It provides privacy and the continuation of a person's independent life style that he or she has always known. Research on this kind of housing (Carp 1975) shows that the long-term residents of a high-rise public housing project are very satisfied with their housing, and the longitudinal study of one project shows that the residents have a more favorable mortality rate than those who were on the waiting list but were not provided with an apartment.

There are several problems with an approach that seeks only physical structure improvements as the solution for the housing needs of the elderly—namely, the high initial cost, which must be paid from tax funds, the long period of time necessary to plan and build such a project, and the small number of dwelling units available in contrast to the large demand. For a full discussion of public housing, particularly in relation to the elderly, see Struyk and Soldo (1980).

The second major approach to meeting housing needs is by providing economic supplements, such as rent subsidy programs. These programs allow persons of low income to receive a subsidy so they can
continue to live in their present housing or move to housing that they
could not otherwise afford. The individuals must pay a quarter of their
income toward their housing cost, and the subsidy meets the additional
cost above this amount. The philosophy is that the program is designed
to provide financial assistance for those whose housing cost is a financial burden.

Although Section 8,[1] the most common of the government supplement programs, is undoubtedly an important feature of some shared
living facilities, private loans and grants are by far the most common
means of providing rent supplements to needy residents in the small
group homes we studied. It is necessary that housing units receiving
Section 8 subsidies be licensed and monitored by an appropriate state
agency.

The third approach to meeting the housing needs of the frail elderly
is the manipulation of social characteristics. This is the orientation that
will receive major attention in the following chapters. This approach is
classified as social because the major emphasis is directed to organizing
and managing the housing by taking account of social factors rather
than physical environment or economic considerations. This approach
does not imply that one overlooks the nature of the building, its location, the neighborhood, and other physical features, nor does one ignore
cost and economic issues. The major orientation, however, is that an
individual or group of persons consider the *social environment* of the
elderly as being of paramount importance in their welfare. Persons who
favor this approach emphasize that an environment providing sociability, concern, companionship, and attention in a noninstitutionalized setting is paramount in meeting the needs of the frail elderly.

Because of the desire of the elderly to remain in family-type environments rather than move to institutions, a great deal of interest has been
stimulated in developing new housing alternatives for the frail and de-

1. Section 8 refers to a federal program that assists eligible households in paying their rents through
a direct cash payment to landlords. The idea behind Section 8 is to induce developers, builders,
and financial institutions to provide decent housing to low-income people. This program was created by the Housing Assistance Payments Program of the Housing and Community Development
Act of 1974 (Title II, Section 8; 43 USC 1437f).

pendent segment of this population. There is a realization that nursing care and the hospital-like atmosphere are not necessary for many older people, for they simply need meals prepared, a safe environment, and "someone to keep an eye on them."[2] There is a realization that small group environments will meet these needs.

In this book, we are focusing on shared living homes, which are smaller in size than most other types of supportive housing and represent a more family type of arrangement. They provide a level of support that is much less expensive for the resident. In the chapters that follow, we shall describe and analyze a variety of shared living facilities, both in the United States and in Great Britain.

2. There are other alternatives to institutionalization than the shared housing experiments described here. For example, Highland Heights is a carefully planned, medically oriented residential facility for the chronically impaired. A detailed account of this unusual kind of social experiment is found in Sherwood et al. (1981).

CHAPTER THREE

Share-A-Home in Florida:
A Case Study of Shared Living

One important and interesting experiment in shared living is taking place in the Orlando, Florida, area. Here, groups of older people and paid domestic staffs reside in ten large houses known as Share-A-Homes, which are located in residential neighborhoods in and around the city. While the Share-A-Home model is only one of a number of experiments in shared living for older people in the United States, it is of particular interest for two reasons. First, it has survived and grown in Florida for over a decade, and, second, the Share-A-Home model has been adopted by a variety of sponsoring groups in other states.

HISTORY OF SHARE-A-HOME

The history of the development of Share-A-Homes in Florida provides a case study in determination and commitment to ideals. The first home was founded by James Gillies, who had been employed as an institutional food consultant and had worked with nursing homes in Orlando for a number of years. Disturbed by what he observed in some of these homes, he became convinced that some alternative to institutional care could and should be found for many older people.

In 1969, Gillies and his wife leased a large, old estate in Winter Park, Florida, near Orlando. His goal was to establish a "family" of unrelated older people who could no longer live independently but who neither wanted nor needed institutional care. Very soon twelve older men and women resided in the home, each paying a monthly contribution. This money was used to operate the house and to pay a modest salary to

Gillies and his wife to take care of all the cooking, housekeeping, and transportation for the "family."

In 1972, Gillies founded Share-A-Home of America, Incorporated. This nonprofit, tax exempt corporation has a board of directors composed of interested people from the community. The corporation works to establish new Share-A-Homes by developing community interest and support. The board of directors meets at least quarterly and assumes responsibility for all business affairs of the corporation. Board members promote the Share-A-Home concept in the community and have sought donations of services, goods, and money from local individuals and groups. The board functions primarily to set policies regarding fiscal and other business matters and to promote public relations. It has little contact with the residents or staffs of the homes themselves, and it leaves the day-to-day operating of the homes to Gillies and his small administrative staff. Gillies is employed by the corporation as the general manager, or coordinator, for the homes.

Over the years, new Share-A-Homes opened in the Orlando–Winter Park area, all modeled after the original "family" established in 1969. Gillies and his small staff perform numerous administrative tasks for all of the homes, including screening potential residents and recruiting and training house managers and other staff. In 1980, there were ten separate Share-A-Homes, each employing its own resident house manager and household staff. The administrative office is located in the original Share-A-Home in Winter Park.

Many types of structures have been successfully utilized by the Share-A-Home organization in Florida. The ten homes in operation during the field study varied in size, in type of neighborhood, and in architectural design. Five of the homes were attractive, one-story dwellings built as single-family residences. Each of these homes could accommodate eight residents and one or two live-in staff. These were located in predominantly residential areas. While a few renovations and additions were made in most cases, these homes did not appear any different from any of the "ordinary" houses in the neighborhood.

The five larger homes could house up to twenty residents and two or more live-in staff. Two of these were huge, multiple-story mansions located on beautiful, spacious grounds; one of these had been used as a nursing home. Two others were large, older homes located on the property of a small private college. The remaining home was a two-

The first Share-A-Home started in this home in Winter Park, Florida, in 1969. This luxurious Spanish-style home has extensive grounds, with a lawn at the back sloping to a beautiful lake. Residents enjoy walking to the lake, where they can sit and read, watch the sunset, or feed the ducks.

The wide range of structures adaptable to shared living is shown in these two photos of Share-A-Homes in Florida. The large mansion at the top accommodates fourteen residents.

The house in the lower photo was a normal single-family residence in a suburban neighborhood before being converted to a Share-A-Home.

Flexibility of the shared living concept in adapting existing housing is shown in these two buildings in Winter Park, Florida. The Share-A-Home in the top photo was housed in a vacant convent, rented from the Catholic Church.

The Share-A-Home in the bottom photo shows how a duplex with two three-bedroom units was joined to form a single-family home by breaking through the walls between the two units.

story building formerly used as a Catholic convent and located only a few blocks from the downtown area.

Share-A-Homes and other variations of the shared housing idea that are developing throughout the country present important sociological and social policy issues. The sociological task is an investigation of the nature of these emerging social groups, while policy makers must decide how to respond to them. Are they quasi-families? Are they voluntary adult communities? Are they old-age institutions requiring close regulation and monitoring by outside agencies?

The description of the Florida Share-A-Homes contained in this and the following chapter is based on a year-long study conducted in the homes during 1979 and 1980. This field study included six months of participant observation during which one of the coauthors resided in three of the homes on a twenty-four-hour-a-day basis (Hilker 1983). During this time, she was able to participate in the on-going lives of the groups as well as conduct both formal and informal interviews with residents, staff, and the Share-A-Home administration.

THE FAMILY MODEL OF SHARED LIVING

The founder and general manager of Share-A-Home is a religiously motivated man who believes that older people can create a "family" together and can live the kind of communal life that is described in the Bible. He has spent the last decade starting new homes in his own community and helping other nonprofit groups to start them in other parts of the United States. Although the corporation has no formal connection with any church or denomination, the establishing and maintaining of homes is viewed as a "Christian mission."

The formally stated goal of the Share-A-Home organization is the creation of residences for older people that maximize independence while providing "family-like" support. Considerable attention is given in the organization's public relations literature to the noninstitutional features of these homes. According to a brochure describing the homes, living in a Share-A-Home means "a way of life that allows older people to retain their dignity and self-respect in an atmosphere of compassion and love . . . where there are no institutional constraints." The brochure describes each home as "a legally recognized family of nonrelated individuals" rather than "a nursing home . . . or a retirement home . . . or a commercial establishment."

Staff training sessions conducted by the administration reveal a strong commitment to the "family" ideal. The founder and general manager in particular emphasizes this:

> I still take big exception when one of my staff members says anything about the patients down the hall, or this patient or that patient, because we have no patients in Share-A-Home and I still have trouble getting across the concept that we are a family. . . . I don't rent rooms. These are not boarding houses or motels. We provide a home for a family. We're not an institution in any way, shape, or form. We are a family.

The claim by the administration that these homes are legally recognized "families" is based on the outcome of a lawsuit filed against the original home in 1971.[1] The suit, brought by neighbors of the home, charged that a boarding home was being operated in a neighborhood zoned exclusively for single family dwellings. However, the circuit court judge who heard the case found that the home did meet the definition of "family" as set forth by the local zoning board—"one or more persons occupying a dwelling and living as a single housekeeping unit." Following the court's decision, the organization began gradually to establish other "families" throughout the county.

The general manager professes a strong commitment to the autonomy of the "families," which he believes would be compromised by governmental interference. He is very resistant to the idea that the "families" should be fitted into one of the several categories of group living facilities established by the agency in Florida charged with licensing and monitoring such facilities. Thus far the organization has established and operated the homes without a formal confrontation with this state agency over the issues of licensure and regulation.

The Share-A-Home Corporation is committed to providing safe and pleasant homes for older people who cannot live completely independently for one reason or another. Beliefs about what these older people need and want are clearly articulated by the administration: older people do not wish to be burdens on anyone, and they very much want to feel loved, secure, and protected, and part of a family. The general manager tries to communicate this in training sessions with new staff:

---

1. *Orange County* vs. *Share-A-Home Association of Winter Park, Florida, et al.*, Ninth Circuit Court, Orange County, Florida, 71-3319, October 19, 1971.

This is one question that always comes up—how can you create a family from diverse people? The answer is—the need for love and security. The children, friends, and associates of these people are all gone. They are alone. . . . Being alone is the worst disease in the world.

There is a strong belief that these older people desire a sense of continuity with the past and that they resist sudden change. For change causes anxiety, and this must be avoided according to the general manager:

Staff must dispel anxiety in old people. . . . Living without anxiety is necessary. . . . Anxiety is a major problem of old people. It causes physical and mental problems. . . . Our job is to protect old people.

Protecting the residents involves providing a place to live in which they are not alone and in which they may move about in safety and security. It also involves making sure that the residents have nutritious meals and that they seek medical attention if and when they need it. Staff are instructed constantly to be aware of even the most subtle changes in a resident's appearance or habits, which might suggest some problem or illness. Although the residents are generally healthy, and staff often have no medical training or experience, this need for constant awareness of residents' physical and mental states is emphasized repeatedly to staff.

In addition to protecting residents by providing needed services and by paying close attention to their well-being, the Share-A-Home administration and staff often consciously assume the role of buffer between the resident and the natural family. It is believed that older people and their adult children do not want to live together, and when they do, serious problems may often arise. Shared living is thought to provide a way for the frail elderly person to live independently of his or her children without the stigma of living in a nursing home and without the resentment and tensions that may emerge when parents live with adult children.

Provision of Services. In return for the monthly contribution made by each resident (the administration declines to call this "rent"), a number of services are offered in addition to the actual shelter. The homes provide no nursing care, nor do they have any formal ties with any phy-

Primary sources of income for the residents were Social Security, other pensions, savings, and other assets; only two residents received Supplemental Security Income (SSI). About one-half of the ninety-seven residents paid their monthly contributions entirely from their personal incomes; about 40 percent, thirty-eight residents, received supplements toward the contribution from their families, usually adult children. Other sources of support for the monthly contribution came from private organizations such as churches; only a few of the residents received financial assistance from these sources.

Most of the residents resided in the state of Florida, often in the same county as the Share-A-Homes, before moving into one of the homes. They were typically living alone or with a spouse or other family member before the move; only a few came from nursing homes or other institutional settings. Most of the residents moved into the homes because living alone had become impossible to manage, or because their spouse or other family member had died or become incapacitated. Their personal physicians often suggested that they seek some type of group residential setting, and adult children often made the initial contact with the Share-A-Home office on behalf of their parent.

Among the ninety-seven residents, the length of stay in the homes ranged from one month to six years with a median length of twenty-one months. In the oldest of the homes, which had been open since 1969, the average length of residence for the seventeen individuals living there at the start of the fieldwork was two years and three months.

Applicants to the homes are not admitted if they have medical problems that might be more appropriately treated in a residential setting having a medical component. Therefore, the residents appeared generally healthy, although chronic conditions such as arthritis, high blood pressure, and heart disease were not uncommon. Since there are no medical records kept, the only sources of information about the health status of the residents were their self-reports and the researcher's observations and interviews with staff. Of those fifty-one who took part in the comprehensive interview, three-quarters rated their health as good or excellent, and nearly everyone felt that his or her health was as good or better than others of the same age. Only a few felt that their health problems limited their activities in any significant ways.

Two instruments commonly used to assess the functional capacities of older people were utilized. The Physical Self Maintenance Scale (PSMS) developed by Lowenthal (1964) was used to obtain a description of how adequately all Share-A-Home clients were able to manage their self-care needs.

Most of the residents of Share-A-Homes were able to care for all their personal needs, such as bathing, dressing, toileting, and so forth; this is a definite requirement for admission to the homes. Staff reports and researcher's observations suggest, however, that a small percentage, at least 10 to 15 percent of the total population, did receive some regular assistance in personal care, usually in fastening clothing, getting in and out of the bathtub, or cutting up food. These were usually residents who had lived in the homes for some time and were beginning to falter in their capacity for self-care or else were residents who were recovering from some illness or surgery. The assistance may have come from staff, but just as often it came from other residents, particularly from roommates.

The Instrumental Activities of Daily Living (IADL) scale (Lawton and Brody 1969) was included in the formal interview with the sample of fifty-one residents. The scale contains questions concerning the ability to accomplish household tasks.

Although the residents were not required to perform any housework, those fifty-one residents who were interviewed were asked to judge their present capacity to manage the daily tasks of independent living. Table 3.1 shows the results. While relatively few residents felt they could manage all the housework, shopping, meal preparation, and laundry without help, a considerable percentage felt they could accomplish these things given some help. Doing the laundry would apparently present serious problems for one-third of the residents interviewed. Forty-three of these fifty-one residents did make their own beds every day without

TABLE 3.1. *Perceived Capacity for Independent Living Tasks*

	Housework		Shopping		Meal Preparation		Laundry	
	%	N	%	N	%	N	%	N
Completely unable to do	21.0	11	24.0	12	27.0	14	33.0	17
Could do with some help	61.0	31	45.0	23	47.0	24	45.0	23
Could do with no help	18.0	9	31.0	16	26.0	13	22.0	11
Total	100.0	51	100.0	51	100.0	51	100.0	51

assistance, although the housekeeper would have done this for them if they had preferred.

As another indicator of self-care ability, the residents were asked if they managed all their financial affairs independently. Thirty-one of these fifty-one residents did so, while thirteen managed with some help from a family member and fourteen had turned over the management of all or most money matters to a family member. In the latter cases no formal guardianships had been established, only informal arrangements between the resident and, in most cases, an adult child.

It should be noted again that those fifty-one residents who participated in the interview tended to be the most cooperative and, in addition, the healthiest and most alert. Therefore, the description of the capacities of this particular group to accomplish everyday tasks of living should not be taken as representative of the entire population since the more seriously impaired residents were not included.

THE HOUSEHOLD STAFF

Every one of the ten homes in central Florida employed a manager or managing couple who resided full time in the home and was responsible for seeing that domestic tasks were accomplished. In the smaller homes, the manager often did all the housekeeping, shopping, cooking, and laundry without help, while in the larger homes, other staff were employed to serve as cooks or housekeepers. Live-in staff were paid a small salary in addition to receiving room and board; "room" in this case meant exactly that—a bedroom usually directly adjacent to residents' bedrooms. Rarely did live-in staff have private bathrooms; these were usually shared either with other staff members or with one or more residents.

Most of the managers had high school educations, but none was a college graduate. None of the managers had any professional training in the field of aging, although about one-half had work experiences that were related to their current positions, such as nurse's aide in a nursing home or manager of a mobile home park consisting largely of older residents. At the beginning of the fieldwork, half of the homes were managed by married couples and the other half by women alone. The couples were middle-aged or older; two of these couples were themselves past retirement age. The women managers were divorcees or widows and one had a young child living with her.

Motivations for working in a Share-A-Home ranged from just needing a job to strong commitments to the organizational ideals. All of the managers felt they could get better paying, less demanding jobs, but they chose to work at Share-A-Home out of a desire to be of service to the elderly. A number mentioned strong religious commitments as the motivating factor in their remaining in a difficult and exhausting job. However, even those who expressed the strongest commitment to their work also stated quite candidly that they did not anticipate staying in their jobs for a long period of time. The pressures, they felt, would eventually prove to be too much; the turnover rate clearly reflects this.

Two of the managers were long-time employees of Share-A-Home and had worked continuously for several years in the same homes. The other managers had been employed in the homes for one year or less. Turnover is high, and seven out of the ten homes had different managers by the time the field study was completed. Finding and keeping dedicated managers is seen as a major problem by the Share-A-Home administration.

The other domestic staff, the cooks and the housekeepers in the larger homes, were all women and ranged in age from the early twenties to the sixties. In the largest homes, one or more of these staff resided there on a full-time basis just as the manager did, receiving room and board and a small salary. Most of these women had previous work experiences as either cooks or housekeepers, and a few had worked in the homes for several years. Turnover among these staff was constant, however, and some of the houses had a rapid succession of cooks and housekeepers during the period of the fieldwork. Of the twelve cooks and housekeepers employed at the start of the study, only three were still working at its conclusion one year later.

In informal interviews with those working in the homes, the reasons for high turnover were discussed. For the live-in staff, the major complaints involved inadequate living quarters, the lack of privacy, and the pressures of being constantly at the call of the residents. Some mentioned the awkwardness of having guests over, as they felt they had no place to entertain them except in their bedrooms. Some of the live-in workers felt that they never really got away from their work. They were encouraged by the administration to spend their days off away from the home, and two of the managing couples even maintained small apartments to use on their days off; however, this was not financially possible for most of those who lived in the homes. The managers in the smaller homes felt particularly tied down, as quite often they were the only domestic help there. Consequently, they could never leave the house except on their official days off, as Share-A-Home requires that a domestic helper be present at all times, day or night.

COMMUNITY TIES

Most of the men and women who lived in these shared homes during the field study had been residents of the state of Florida prior to moving into the homes. In fact, over half of them had lived within a few miles of their Share-A-Home. This made it possible for many residents to retain the same physicians, dentists, and other services they had used for years. They were able to go to the same hairdressers or barbers, and they could attend the same churches. They could shop in the same stores and visit the same libraries and other establishments in which they felt familiar and comfortable.

Involvement with the community on at least the minimal level of utilizing commercial establishments and professional services is necessary given the "family" model employed by the administration. While rich in domestic services, there are no other on-site services—no health clinic, no social services department, no canteen or store, no chapel, and no visiting hairdressers or barbers. Residents must, therefore, leave the home to satisfy many of their needs. While some of the residents, especially the very frail ones, depend on their children to bring them personal care items and clothing, even they must go out of the home to secure medical or other professional services.

In some of the largest Share-A-Homes, a variety of community organizations were involved in conducting regular programs and classes or providing special entertainments and events. For example, the local adult education department sent instructors into the homes each week to teach music, art, and other classes. Churches conducted weekly prayer meetings and Bible study classes. Groups of children from local schools and churches periodically visited the residents to provide music and other entertainment. Some of this contact between the homes and community groups, particularly the on-going, informal church programs, allowed the residents to keep involved in local happenings. In one home, the weekly prayer meeting and sing conducted by several members of a nearby church was a time for residents to sing, pray, and hear some local gossip. At the same time, members of the community were permitted an inside look at the home and its residents.

The publicity surrounding the court battle over zoning in the early 1970s has served to keep the local press interested in the Share-A-Homes. The opening or closing of a home always receives attention, and human interest stories about the residents appear quite often. Therefore, although there is no advertising in newspapers or in other media, the Share-A-Homes are well known enough in the area to keep a steady flow of applicants contacting the office.

Members of the board and especially the general manager also endeavor to keep local churches and physicians aware of the existence of the homes. They also appear before civic groups to explain how the homes operate. Letters and a brochure on the homes are sent to ministers, physicians, and others who might come into contact with older people in need of this kind of living arrangement. Through referral from professionals and by word of mouth, the number of homes has slowly grown in the past decade, attesting to Share-A-Home's acceptance by the community.

CHAPTER FOUR

Everyday Life in Florida Share-A-Homes

Daily life in these shared homes is clearly influenced by the Share-A-Home "family" ideology. One way in which this is evident centers around the methods used by staff to accomplish household tasks. For in the attempt to maintain a noninstitutional atmosphere the administration insists that a great many "just-like-home" procedures be followed by every household staff member. Some of these procedures with regard to meal preparation and service have already been mentioned. Staff are expected to pay strict attention to numerous small details in running the homes to insure and enhance that "family" feeling.

The administration believes that household staff should follow a uniform pattern in running the homes so as to help foster and maintain feelings of security in the residents: the residents know what to expect, where, and when. A new resident enters an already well-functioning household, and it is her task to learn how things are done. Although there is little opportunity for her to suggest alternative methods, such as those that she followed in the many years during which she was the mistress of her own household, the staff's goal is to maintain a family-like informality in the homes, to make them so unlike institutions that adaptation to the new routines is relatively easy.

Outside of mealtimes, little staff scheduling of residents' time was observed by the researcher. There were no specified wake-up times, bedtimes, bathing times, or visiting hours; these were seen as unnecessary and not in keeping with the "family" model. Therefore, residents simply did as they wished in their "own" home, creating their own timetables and routines as they chose. There were no areas, not even the kitchen, that were off limits or that were designated as exclusively staff's, except their bedrooms, of course. In fact, the kitchen table was one of the favorite gathering spots for socializing, and there always seemed to be people—residents, guests, and staff—sitting in the kitchens talking and drinking coffee. This kind of informality and lack of clear spatial boundaries between staff and residents is one feature that distinguishes most of these shared homes from other, more institutional types of group living.

There were no check-out systems, and residents came and went from the homes at their discretion. Often it was not necessary for a resident to mention she was going out because everybody knew that, for example, on Wednesday mornings she always took the bus downtown to the library, and on Friday evenings her son always took her out to dinner. Still, most of the residents did tell the manager if they were going out for the day, or if they would be returning late in the evening. In the latter case, the resident would be given a key to the home; residents were not given keys when they moved in, nor were there locks on their bedroom doors.

The individuals within any particular home varied considerably in how they spent their days. It was completely the choice of the resident whether she spent her time away from the home or in the living areas, kitchen, or yard of the home or, for that matter, in her own room. Unlike many other group residential settings where many residents tend to stay inside their private domains, be it apartment or room, very little of this was observed in any of the Share-A-Homes. With the exception of a few of the frailest residents, everyone seemed to spend their time during the day in the common areas of the homes. While many residents had small televisions in their rooms, most preferred to watch the afternoon soap operas and the evening news on the one in the living room of the home. Most of the homes had either front or back porches, patios, or sun rooms, and these common areas received heavy use. Although residents had the option of withdrawing from the company of others, few appeared to do so.

One of the major differences between the large and the small homes was the availability of scheduled group activities: some of the smallest homes had few, if any, such activities. There appeared to be two primary reasons for this. First, organizations such as the local adult education department were unable to offer classes unless a minimum number of twelve could be enrolled; this completely left out small houses of six or eight residents. The same kind of pattern was observed for church groups, who would naturally prefer to conduct their services or study groups for more than a handful of people.

Second, nearly all the residents of these small homes seemed to like the slow pace and lack of scheduled activities and, in fact, had chosen to live in a smaller rather than a larger home for this very reason. With the exception of one woman who had already made application to a nearby high-rise retirement complex because she was bored with the lack of activities, nobody else expressed an interest in having more of such activities.

In five of the larger homes the number of planned activities ranged from one, a bimonthly visit from a pianist, to almost daily events in another of the homes, including prayer meetings, Bible study groups, films, classes conducted by the adult education department, parties and entertainments, and bingo games. The levels of participation in these regularly scheduled events were similar to those documented by researchers in other group living situations for the elderly. There appeared to exist a small core of residents who took part in nearly all the activities, from Bible study to macramé classes. The majority attended only specific events (musical entertainments were always popular), and some residents attended none of them. Only in one of the largest homes did this pattern vary; there the majority attended all the many activities and events that regularly took place.

While the atmosphere often seemed busier in the larger homes, the pace of life in any Share-A-Home was usually slow and relaxed. Without the overlay of regulations, schedules, and medical or other professional care-giving staff, these homes really felt like homes. There were no charts or files, no nurses' stations, no wheelchairs, and no sickroom smells or sounds to create an impossible-to-cover-up institutional atmosphere. Through the conscious efforts of staff, the typical Share-A-Home looked, sounded, and even smelled like somebody's home.

What was unusual, of course, as compared to "normal" households, was that there were lots of very old people sitting together, often in a companionable silence, in those common areas of the home, where if anything happened they would be sure to see it or hear it. In institutional settings, residents have often been discouraged from sitting in groups near foyers and passageways because it gives the appearance of having nothing to do, of not being active and engaged, and because it creates traffic problems. In these shared homes, where there is no pressure to "look busy" in case outsiders come by, and where no areas of the house, except others' bedrooms, are inaccessible to residents, they seem to gravitate toward the living areas, the porches, and the company of others.

BECOMING A RESIDENT: SOCIALIZATION TO SHARED LIVING

An attempt was made to discover why the men and women who lived in these shared homes chose this particular kind of group living. Were they drawn to the home because they shared the founder's religious beliefs about the appropriateness of "communal" living? Were they unhappy in their previous living arrangements which frequently involved living alone?

The majority came because their failing health, increasing frailty, or sensory losses made living alone impossible, or because someone they had been living with died or became too disabled to care for them. They did not come because they shared the "family" ideology of the organizers, although some later began to share this ideology, or because they had any interest in forging new possibilities in human relationships. They came because they had to, and most would have preferred to be able to live completely on their own again.

The fifty-one residents who were interviewed were asked about possible alternatives to Share-A-Home; that is, where else did they believe they could live? Table 4.1 shows that nearly one-third either felt they had no alternative or were not aware of any alternative. About one-quarter replied that their only alternative was a nursing home or some other institution for the elderly. About one-fifth believed they could live in an apartment, but only if they had some domestic help, while another one-fifth felt their only other alternative was to move in with an adult child or other family member. The latter response, however, was almost always accompanied by comments to the effect that this was an undesirable choice as shown by these examples:

I could live with my son in Virginia, but I have no desire to. I want to be around people my own age who I have something in common with, who I can have an exchange with. I don't want to be taken care of. (an eighty-seven-year-old female)

TABLE *4.1. Perceived Alternatives to Share-A-Home*

	%	N
Child or other kin	21.0	11
Institution for aged (includes boarding homes, nursing homes)	24.0	12
Own apartment (with help)	20.0	10
Miscellaneous alternative	4.0	2
No alternative	29.0	15
No response	2.0	1
Total	100.0	51

My daughter says I could live with her, but I'd go to a nursing home before I'd impose on their lives. (an eighty-year-old female)

We could live at our daughter's, but it would disrupt both families. They wouldn't really want us and we wouldn't really want to go there. (a married couple in their eighties)

In these settings, there was no talk of returning to a more independent style of life, no expectation of rehabilitation, and no regarding of these homes as temporary respites from the chores of housekeeping and cooking. The home was seen by most of the residents as the last place they would live before institutionalization or death. The home was viewed as infinitely better than a nursing home, and most residents had a strong desire to maintain their current levels of health and abilities for self-care so they could remain in the home.

Whatever else the Share-A-Home might have been to a resident, it was first and foremost housing—a place to live, and a good place at that. Yet it was not traditional housing, for in these settings an individual moved into an on-going household of older people who were living in very close physical proximity, sharing every meal, sharing the phone, the refrigerator, the bath, and probably even sharing a bedroom with one other person. Living in a shared environment with unrelated people was an unfamiliar experience for most of the residents. A few had resided for short periods in nursing or boarding homes, but most had lived all their lives with family or alone in their own homes and apartments. Even though every effort is made by the staff to model these residences on the idea of "family," it is this aspect of moving into a household of strangers that creates not only opportunities for companionship and security, but also some highly stressful situations.

Applying to become a resident in a Share-A-Home is a simple procedure. A family member of the older person often makes the first telephone contact with the administrative office. A member of the family usually accompanies the applicant to the office to be interviewed by the general manager or some other member of the administrative staff. During the interview, the applicant is asked about his or her self-care abilities and about any medical problems. Also, a subjective assessment of the applicant's mental functioning is made. There are no tests given, and no previous medical or other records are requested. If the applicant seems suitable, he or she is invited to visit one or more of the homes, depending on room availability and personal preferences in terms of size and location. If, after the visit, the applicant wishes to join the Share-A-Home, he or she pays the first month's fee and moves in; there are no leases or contracts, no last month's fee, and no deposits.

The particular home or homes an applicant is encouraged to visit are determined in part also by the administration's feelings about whether the applicant would "fit" into the group already established. This is done purely by intuition and what little background information may come out during the interview. Such background information is not gathered in any systematic way, and, in fact, the administration believes that this type of inquiry is inappropriate. The following is a quote from the general manager:

I don't ever press into the background information, unless someone volunteers information to me. Nowhere on my application does it ask what did you do in your lifetime. I could care less. I'm not interested what their occupation was. They could have spent time in Sing Sing prison . . . because what difference does it make what you were twenty years ago . . . it is from today on that we worry about.

There are two reasons for this resistance to inquiring about the applicant's personal life. One has to do with the idea that the house staff must "love" all of the residents equally. Another quote from the general manager illustrates this:

You treat everybody as an equal and you love everybody with the same compassion and understanding. But you're a human being and if I told you that that man was married five times and beat his wife, you wouldn't want him in the house . . . but if you don't know this and into your hands comes a man who needs help, you're going to help him with the same love and understanding as you have anyone else.

A second reason is that the administration realizes that the other residents might find out something about the applicant's background and reject her from the start. Again, from the general manager:

Once we took a lady seventy-six years old that used to be [a nightclub dancer] and she let it out and two of those women wouldn't talk to her. . . . Now this is where things cause problems within a household. Now it isn't going to make any difference if you are an organ teacher or you were a tap dancer. But if you'd ever been a movie star or something like that, you might not be accepted too well.

There is, therefore, explicit recognition by the administration that the other residents wish to live with others who are socially similar or, at least, socially acceptable to them. However, the Share-A-Home philosophy that old people can create "families" because they *are* old and in need of love and security may cause the administration to ignore variations in backgrounds when it comes to accepting new residents.

New residents are encouraged to bring their own furniture and other personal possessions to furnish their bedrooms. They are asked to arrive in time to sit down to a meal with the other residents so that the manager may properly introduce them; arriving after supper has been served is discouraged. The new resident should have already met the manager and at least her roommate if she is to share a room. Current residents usually know that a new resident is scheduled to move into the home, but they may not know exactly when she is to arrive, and they probably have never met her.

There are no formally established welcoming committees to greet new residents, although in a few of the homes one or more individuals are informally recognized in this capacity. Usually the manager helps the new resident get settled in her room and answers any questions she or her family might have. The new resident receives neither formal orientation nor written guidelines. The routines of the homes, as well as acceptable behaviors, are to be learned by observing and asking questions of staff and fellow residents. A quote from an interview with the general manager shows this:

There is no orientation to family life . . . no lists of dos and don'ts. . . . New members learn from old members what is expected . . . just like a child is socialized . . . if she has a question she can ask the manager . . . and if a new resident gets out of line, the old residents will tell her.

While formal orientation to "family life" is deemed unnecessary and contradictory, the lack of it may present some uncomfortable situations for the new resident. This excerpt from the researcher's field notes describes one resident's first day in shared living in one of the larger homes:

Margo [the new resident] came in for breakfast at 8:00, after all the rest of us had finished . . . later she came to the wing where some of us sat, stopping at each person and introducing herself. . . . Zenoma [another resident] walked with her outside and introduced her to several more residents. . . . Margo had spent the morning making a pest of herself. She "talks your head off" according to Maggie [a resident]. She inadvertently sat in Ellie's [a resident] chair in the living room. Ellie came in, saw her, and stomped out even though poor Margo offered to give her her chair. Both Mona and Nora [residents] told Margo that Ellie "always sits there."

Margo also had an unfortunate proclivity for popping her head into some of the other residents' rooms without knocking (required even when the door is ajar). This lasted only a day or two, until subtle hints from the other residents made it apparent to her that her visits were not appreciated.

New residents are encouraged to stay in the home at least one month before making the final decision either to remain or move out. The staff feel that it takes a while to become accustomed to any new surroundings, and the first few days or weeks are the most difficult to get through, for this is the time when the resident misses his or her old home the most. This month is known as the "thirty-day trial period" by the staff and the residents.

This trial period is also supposed to give the "family" a chance to see if the new resident is acceptable to them. Ordinarily, this trial period passes without comment from other residents, and its ending is not formally acknowledged. Occasionally, however, dissatisfaction on the part of some members of the group will result in the general manager's calling for a secret vote on a new resident. This occurred only once during the researcher's residence in the homes, and it involved a loud and disruptive man. The majority vote was negative, and the man was moved to another home where he apparently tempered his behavior and remained for some time.

One of the stated goals of Share-A-Home is to provide a sense of continuity for the older person. When a new resident enters, she is not expected by staff or the others in the home to assume any new roles. She is expected, instead, to carry on her life just as she did before, only in greater comfort and security. There are no pressures to take up any pursuits that she was not already accustomed to; staff do not vigorously encourage participation in any planned activities and rarely take an active part in getting the residents involved in hobbies or the like. House staff are constantly busy cooking and cleaning, shopping and transporting, and they perceive these as their most important duties.

Just as there is no pressure to be active, there are no jobs to perform that involve either real work or the kind of make-work that has been observed in other residential settings of older people. There are no rehabilitative tasks to perform, and the role of sick person or patient is out of place in these settings. Residents in these shared homes are required to do nothing except to carry on as much as possible in their usual ways in a kind of "holding pattern." The emphasis is on retaining independence and health so that one may remain at one's present stage rather than face the dreaded prospect of entering a nursing home or becoming a burden on one's family.

Yet new role opportunities for many residents do arise, and these are usually unexpected and sometimes not welcomed by them. For as the residents age, some of them become very frail, some become significantly impaired in vision, hearing, and mobility, and still others begin to exhibit signs of mental impairment. For the healthier and more able residents, there are opportunities for helping these others. The content of these helping roles, how and why they arise, and how residents respond to the opportunities to assume such roles are described later in this chapter.

CONTACTS WITH FAMILY AND FRIENDS OUTSIDE THE HOMES

Another focus of our research concerned the degree to which residents kept up contacts with family and friends after they moved into Share-A-Homes. Of the ninety-seven residents residing in the homes at the beginning of the field study, only two individuals had no living immediate family. Fifty-seven of the residents had at least one living child, the majority of whom lived in the state of Florida. The rest had living siblings, grandchildren, nieces, or nephews.

The frequency of contact with the natural family varied from daily visits or phone calls to a single visit per year. The reports of those fifty-one residents who participated in the comprehensive interview is believed to be representative of the entire Share-A-Home population.

Twenty-seven, just over one-half of those interviewed, indicated that they received a personal visit from a family member at least once a week. Eight residents received several visits each month, while twelve received several visits each year. Two residents, both of whom had lived in the homes at least one year, stated that they had never been visited by family members, one because she had no living family, and the other because her only surviving sibling lived out of the state.

Visiting in the homes of family members was less commonly reported than receiving visits. Eleven residents made weekly visits to the homes of family, while another seven made monthly visits and fourteen made yearly visits. Nineteen persons, over one-third of the respondents, never visited in their families' homes.

It is important to note that the presence of the natural families of the residents is not a pervasive aspect of life in any of the ten shared homes. The researcher met a number of family members and noted that their visits were usually brief and occurred in the evenings or on weekends. Residents usually entertained their families in their bedrooms rather than in the common areas of the home. There are no planned "family nights" to which relatives are invited to participate in any Share-A-Home events; however, a relative was observed occasionally eating a meal with a resident in her Share-A-Home.

Contact with friends and associates outside the home was minimal for most of the residents. Only ten of the sample of fifty-one indicated that they ever visited friends outside the home, while eighteen received either a letter or a phone call from a friend on at least a monthly basis. About one-third stated that since their move to the home they saw less of their friends in the community. It was difficult to go back to the old neighborhood and see one's friends because of lack of transportation. Also, some old friends had themselves moved while others had become ill or had died.

Establishing friendships or even acquaintanceships in the neighborhood of the shared home appears to be uncommon. Thirty-seven of the fifty-one residents said that they knew nothing about the surrounding neighbors because they had no contact with them. A few residents were on a first-name speaking basis with their neighbors, but there was little exchange of visitation. None of the ten homes seem to be any different in this respect; the residents of these shared homes keep to themselves, not unlike many suburban households.

RESIDENT RELATIONSHIPS

A major goal of the six-month participant observation study of the homes was to gain some understanding of the kinds of relationships that existed inside the homes. The relationships between residents and between the residents and staff in other residential settings for older people have long interested researchers in the field of aging. How do Share-A-Homes compare with other types of group living for frail older people? Do the conscious efforts of the Share-A-Home organization to avoid an institutional atmosphere result in more positive social relationships than those that have been documented in other settings? Do the "families" vary in the quality of the relationships within them and, if so, what causes the difference?

Among the indicators of the quality of resident relationships was the extent to which residents identified each other as confidants, or persons they would go to with a problem or other personal matter (see Lowenthal and Haven 1968). The residents' responses to situations inside the homes that might involve conflict were explored, as was the involvement of residents in helping relationships. Both observational and interview data were used to assess these indicators of the quality of resident relationships.

During the first few weeks of the field study, the researcher spent time in all of the ten homes, observing and talking informally with the residents. While the overall atmospheres of the homes could best be described as quiet and cordial, there appeared to be relatively few close relationships among the residents. Some roommates did appear to have close relationships. Most interaction occurred in the common areas of the homes, and there was little visiting in each other's rooms. Later in the study, some specific questions were asked to determine the degree of closeness residents felt toward others in the homes. When asked whom they confided in or discussed personal problems with, only four of the fifty-one residents named other residents. About one-quarter of the sample indicated that they did not have a confidant, while the rest confided in family, usually adult children.

While other residents were typically not named as regular confidants, about one-half of those interviewed responded that they did have someone in the home that they would tell if they received some bad news; however, about one-third of these named staff members, not other residents. Both interview responses and observations in the homes clearly reflect an important aspect of group life in these settings: talking about personal problems to other residents is viewed as burdening those who already have problems enough of their own. As one resident explained, "Everybody wants to share the good things—they keep the bad to themselves." In response to an interview question about sharing some good news, all but a few residents indicated that they would do so with other residents and staff.

Being in the homes on a twenty-four-hour-a-day basis naturally permitted the researcher some access to the backstage of life inside them. Consequently, she witnessed some encounters between residents that were neither quiet nor cordial. As expected, there were conflicts and disagreements, and sometimes these received open expression. Yet the researcher frequently observed instances of the residents telling either her or some other resident in the home, who was generally seen as a good sounding board, about their feelings concerning areas of potential conflict or situations involving others that upset them. There was, however, a general unwillingness to express those feelings publicly or take any action on them.

In the formal interview, the sample of fifty-one residents was asked what they would do if they were having a problem with their roommate or some other resident. The most common response, given by slightly over one-third, was that they would do nothing at all but just live with it. One resident's response was typical: "I'd ignore it; we aren't supposed to worry about problems."

Another one-third of those interviewed stated that they would go to the house manager or some other staff person with their complaint. Only four residents indicated that they would try to settle the problem themselves by talking to the individual or individuals involved and trying to work out the problem between them. The remaining residents replied either that they weren't sure what they would do, denied the possibility of such conflict ever occurring, or else declined to answer the question.

Part of the Share-A-Home ideology is that old people need and want a quiet and secure life style. Consequently, there was strong pressure from staff and from other residents to "get along" and to "keep the peace." In these relatively unstructured settings, there were no clear-cut and commonly understood procedures for dealing with conflicts and disagreements, and the potential for both in these shared arrangements was considerable. There were no house meetings, no grievance committees, no social workers, no nurses, etc. There was only a house manager who, after hanging out the laundry, cooking lunch, and driving people to various appointments, may have had little time to act as arbitrator/mother. Consequently, most people avoided confrontation, and some lived with a good deal of unresolved conflict—often over what others might see as trivial or minor issues.

The extent to which these settings might provide opportunities for the development of interdependence among the residents was a major question at the start of the research. In the formal interview, the members were asked to describe the kinds of help, if any, they gave to each other. While 75 percent said they gave help to others, only 48 percent said they received any. Those who claimed to give help most often mentioned helping ill or handicapped members. The following were typical responses:

I do as much as I can. I do lots of things for my roommate. She is in bad shape. . . . I look after her, help her get ready and find things. (a 75-year-old female)

I do lots of things for the ladies. I take some of them for little walks. I get help for them if they get sick at night. (an 82-year-old male)

I help out the sick ones. One lady had cancer and I did lots of things for her. (a 73-year-old female)

Those who said other residents helped them most often mentioned small tasks, such as sewing on a button or just "little things." Few mentioned receiving help during illness. One resident responded:

They do small favors for me . . . like rubbing my back. One lady cared for my plants while I was away. (an 82-year-old female)

The researcher observed considerable mutual aid, more in fact than responses to interview questions alone would reveal. For example, one woman told the researcher that, while she gave considerable help to others, she received very little help herself. She said it was not that she wouldn't be helped if she needed it, but she didn't need it. In reality, this same woman was the recipient of all kinds of help, including being helped to maneuver a tricky walkway with her walker, which she had to manage to get to the dining room. Some resident helped her at every meal. This and other incidents are evidence that such mutual aid is part of a taken-for-granted world that only an outsider would note as significant.

It must be recalled that the sample interviewed was a select group, tending toward the healthier, more intact members. Therefore, it might be expected that these individuals would be more often on the giving than on the receiving end of help and support. However, denying that one receives help from others, except for very minor kinds of help, also reflects the desire to retain the claim to independence. The reality of this claim is, in fact, the very basis on which the person may remain in the group. Except for the domestic duties the staff perform, a resident is expected to take care of herself. Lots of people commented to the researcher that one must do for oneself or be forced to move to a nursing home.

Nevertheless, the residents are involved in both giving and receiving help, in spite of an important organizational feature of the setting—the presence of domestic staff. House managers perceive their major roles as providing domestic services and helping to keep the older person out of an institution. The result is that residents may be discouraged at times from providing certain kinds of help to certain others. The attempt to keep everyone functioning as independently as possible (which is highly valued by the residents, too) may conflict with the maintenance of a sharing, supportive, and interdependent group of peers. This contradiction is evident in the following quotes from the residents:

I do little things for people, but I'd do more, and so would the others, if we were allowed to. We're supposed to be a family. Well, family members help each other. (an 82-year-old female)

I help some of the old ladies, but then they [the managers] told me not to. I guess it's against the rules. (an 85-year-old male)

Such comments were not uncommon in a number of the homes. The researcher also observed several instances of the household staff's intervention in situations involving one resident helping another. In all of these instances, the staff explained to the researcher that such intervention occurred only when they believed the recipient did not really need the help at all. Sometimes they felt some residents asked for help because they were merely seeking attention.

The decision by the staff that the "mere" desire for attention is not enough to justify one resident helping another is based partly on the belief that independence ought to be maintained at all cost. Anything that encourages helplessness in a resident must be avoided because it will result in increasing the staff's workload and in an earlier than necessary nursing home placement for the resident. The staff also feel that the other, more able residents will become overburdened by the demands of those who are becoming less independent. All of these factors contribute to the staff's justification in intervening in certain situations involving residents helping each other.

Such staff intervention was not done with the goal in mind of thwarting what Hochschild (1973) has called the sibling bond between residents; it was done with the best of intentions. It is worth noting, however, as a structural constraint on the development of interdependence in these settings. At the same time a kind of "sibling collusion" took place; that is, surreptitious helping was not uncommon. For example, one woman quite regularly poured her tablemate a second cup of coffee at breakfast even though the latter's doctor recommended against extra coffee. Upon being "caught" by the manager, both women looked embarrassed, ceased the disapproved behavior for a couple of days, only to resume it again, this time more discreetly. Thus, although it may bring them into occasional conflict with the domestic staff, the residents in most of the homes do engage in considerable support of the more disabled residents.

VARIATION AMONG THE HOMES

The nature of the population in some of these homes made the development and maintenance of close ties between residents highly problematic. Observations in the various homes revealed a wide variety of interactional patterns and styles, similar to "natural" families. In most of the homes, both large and small, the researcher observed many instances of mutual help among the residents, frequent conversation and interaction, and expressions of liking and trust for other residents. Those interviewed in these homes also tended to express high satisfaction with Share-A-Home.

A smaller number of homes, however, were less "successful," both in terms of the kinds of relationships that occurred among the residents and also in the degree of satisfaction with Share-A-Home expressed by the residents. In these homes, the group members were observed to interact less, to provide less mutual aid, and to express fewer positive feelings toward other residents in both informal discussions and formal interviews. The residents in these same few homes were generally less satisfied with the home than were those in the other homes.

The most "successful" homes tended to be those with the most stable resident populations. In those homes with very unstable membership, it was difficult for residents to develop and maintain ties with each other. The reason for the higher resident turnover in some homes than in others is related in part to the natural aging process of the group. That is, the homes that had been in existence the longest tended to have proportionately more very elderly individuals. Consequently, one of the oldest and largest homes lost one-third of its membership in a four-month period because of death or permanent nursing home placements. These were individuals who had lived in the homes for several years. There was a feeling of constant and unsettling change by the residents of this home, as well as a feeling of loss of old friends.

New residents must be able to care for all their personal needs and to function independently in these relatively unstructured settings. Given the advanced age of the Share-A-Home population, however, this level of functioning may decline fairly rapidly for some of the residents. If the individual becomes incontinent or nonambulatory or becomes extremely disoriented or confused, there is no choice about making some other living arrangements, such as moving to a nursing home. When the impairment is not so severe or advanced, however, the resident may be able to remain in the home and function adequately with the help of other residents and staff. Thus, those who were exhibiting symptoms of mental impairment were generally supported and accepted by others. One resident explained:

There are some of us who are less fortunate than others, but we love them nonetheless. Sometimes I get asked the same question a hundred times by the same person and I lose patience, but we get along. (a 77-year-old female)

The difficulty arose in those homes in which more than just a few residents began needing increased assistance from others. In those homes, the degree of tolerance was markedly lower. In one home, many of those who were interviewed felt overwhelmed by the sheer numbers of impaired residents. Some felt the need to protect themselves by withdrawing from interaction; this is the kind of response that has often been documented in studies of institutional settings. Some residents referred to their own incapacities or their own needs as precluding the giving of extensive help to others. A quote from one resident illustrates the reaction that the demands for help can cause:

[The hardest thing about living here] is having to deal with people who are in need of help, and I don't quite know how to help. . . . They come in here to talk but I've had to close my door lately. (a 69-year-old female)

A resident from another home expressed her concerns about others withdrawing from those who showed signs of increasing dependency on others. Mira (a resident) mentioned that Arlene (another resident) was "going downhill fast" and that she always tried to give Arlene a few minutes of her time each day. Many of the other residents ignored Arlene, which Mira saw as "inhuman":

How can you live under the same roof with someone and eat at the same table with them and not care about them? (a 74-year-old female)

Yet even this resident, as shown in an interview several months later, had changed her behavior, if not her sympathies, toward the more needy of her fellow residents:

All but one or two of them needs compassion all the time. . . . It wouldn't be so bad if it was just one or two. I'm beginning to block it out or I might fall into their state.

RESIDENT-STAFF RELATIONSHIPS

The relationships that existed between the residents and the staff, particularly the manager of a home, were of special interest throughout the research. It was expected that, given the ideals of Share-A-Home, these relationships might have a different character than those ordinarily found between staff and client in institutional settings. In many important ways, this expectation was correct.

The managers were in intimate daily contact with those in the home, not in the sense of providing personal care kinds of services, but in the sense of actually sharing the same house. Unlike institutional settings where staff may reside in separate wings or floors, even separate buildings, the live-in domestic help in Share-A-Home ordinarily live surrounded by the residents, even sharing bathrooms. There occurs a great deal of informal contact and often the development of close friendships between manager and resident. In many of the homes, the residents and managers seemed to know a great deal about each other personally—their families and backgrounds. As was discussed earlier, however, this same intimate contact often presented difficulties from the point of view of the live-in workers who may have felt that they never really got away from their responsibilities.

The formal interview included questions dealing with the residents' perceptions of the role of the manager in the home. When asked what qualities, skills, or training a manager ought to have, the majority responded in terms of personality attributes such as warmth, understanding, and patience, and an ability to get along with people. Only a few mentioned skills in household management or other domestic tasks. This suggests that the residents do perceive the manager as more than just a domestic worker. Observations and interviews with residents show that a manager who did possess those traits of caring and warmth often became a confidant and a friend. Not all managers developed these kinds of close relationships with the residents. Some were aloof, tending to concentrate on the day-to-day running of the home.

It appears that the manager can add much to the positive atmosphere of the home, both by making the environment pleasant and home-like and by interpersonal style. Yet observations over an extended period suggest that the basic patterns of resident interaction are a consequence less of the manager's role as a catalyzing force than of those factors discussed previously, such as resident turnover. These patterns survived in the face of frequent changes in managers, and close, family-like feelings existed in one home where the manager was not particularly liked. Adapting to new managers and to new domestic help in general is a fact of life in Share-a-Home, and the basic characters of the groups changed little as a result.

In a few of the homes, a kind of parent-child relationship between staff and residents was observed, similar to that which has been noted in other old-age settings. These were the homes described earlier that had the more vulnerable residents—the most impaired and therefore those with the fewest alternatives. The more able residents in these homes often ended up assuming a defensive posture, withdrawing their support and involvement. Thus, Share-A-Home staff in these homes had to contend with individuals who made increasing demands on their time and energy.

OVERVIEW AND DISCUSSION

Share-A-Homes in central Florida are examples of one model of shared living for older people. The goal of the sponsoring organization is to provide "family" living in which people are free to express their individuality and are also cared about and, to some extent, cared for.

The administration's philosophy and ideals are extremely important in shaping the "families'" lives. The founder of the homes is committed to the belief that older people can create "families" inside these homes because these people are old and thus have somewhat the same concerns and outlooks on life. The administration and house staffs perceive themselves as providing protection, security, and some compensation for the loss of family and friends. They wish to provide what they believe older people want—a low stress, safe, quiet environment.

We were particularly interested in determining whether residents developed family-like personal interaction and confided in each other. The extent to which individuals define each other as confidants has often been used in gerontological research to indicate the existence of intimacy, that is, close emotional ties. We found that relationships in these shared homes are not primarily characterized by intimacy, for residents do not perceive each other as those in whom they would regularly confide. Yet intense emotional relationships do exist, and these are often based on the need for support by the frailer or more disabled members of the households. Roommates are especially likely to develop these nonsymmetrical relationships if one of the pair becomes increasingly unable to function in the home. The physical and emotional stress which sometimes results has been described.

The fact that many people are likely to become too dependent for this kind of living arrangement has important effects on the nature of social life in shared homes. While some residents stay for five or six years, most stay only a year or two and so relationships are inevitably short-lived. The element of permanence which characterizes natural families is missing here. Yet while intimacy is not sought, the residents do develop a sense of obligation toward each other and engage in considerable mutual aid. Perhaps the structure and organization of the Share-A-Home environments help to foster a sense of obligation and of responsibility which is difficult to escape. It is hard to ignore one's fellow residents in an informal, noninstitutional setting like the typical Share-A-Home.

While residents may avoid confiding in each other because they see each other as troubled, disabled, or otherwise incapacitated people, they also tend to "just live with" the problems that inevitably arise in group living. While some turned to house staff when problems arose, very few residents chose to confront each other with their complaints or disagreements. However, new residents who disrupted the tranquility of the home met with disapproval from residents and staff; in fact, this was one of the few situations which elicited open complaining and expressions of dissatisfaction from the other residents. While they rarely confront the new resident herself with their complaints, they expected staff to do something about the unacceptable behavior.

Residents who have been in the homes for some time may begin to lose their abilities to function at the level of independence required when they entered the homes. Other household members provide considerable help, but some of these individuals remained in the home longer than the other residents felt was appropriate. Residents were torn between their feelings of empathy for those who were declining and their desire to maintain the non-nursing home character of the household.

The administration believes that house managers must act as the catalyzers of the groups. They are seen as the organizers of the "families" and the focal points of group cohesiveness. They are, in effect, expected to assume a kind of parental role and are hired on the basis of possessing nurturing and caring qualities. Such demands, coupled with the requirements that they reside full time in the homes, share facilities with the residents, and generally be available at all times, have resulted in high staff turnover.

Observations in the homes suggest that residents and managers may like each other and may even share confidences. Managers, however, play a smaller role in enhancing the quality of relationships among the residents than do other factors. The natural aging of the group may result in times of high stress for both residents and staff. Individuals who begin to falter in their capacity for self-care or those whose "minds are going," as the residents often put it, are not necessarily asked to leave. Instead, other residents and the staff help those people in countless ways, enabling them to remain in their Share-A-Home a while longer. Only when the helping becomes an excessive burden to the more able residents and to the staff are more formal, bureaucratic solutions sought, such as nursing homes.

Just as in natural families where nursing home placement is usually made only after long periods of trying to accommodate the older person, the Share-A-Home "family" and staff expend considerable effort to delay the departure of one of their number. Thus, these shared homes have the same problem that plagues many families as well as other types of group living arrangements for older people: the problem of increasing dependence. This problem is particularly serious in these shared living settings where potential helpers, the other residents, are themselves quite elderly and at least marginally dependent.

The use of the family analogy to describe Share-A-Home is appropriate and meaningful in an important way. For these settings reveal the same tensions that the family in modern society exhibits, tensions that are created by the problem of retaining individuality and independence while still relating intimately with others. The research reported here has revealed both attitudinal and organizational constraints on the development of intimacy and interdependence among the residents. Yet describing some of the contradictions and ambiguities inherent in these settings does not deny that, for some older people, shared living offers a satisfying alternative to living alone, or to moving in with adult children or entering a more institutional arrangement.

CHAPTER FIVE

Diffusion of the Share-A-Home Model

Modern societies are characterized by technological developments and emphasis on change, the adaptation of new practices, and the spread of these innovations to the general population. In this chapter, we will examine the nature of shared living arrangements as one kind of social innovation in the handling of the housing and care of frail older people in an aging society. In our research over a five-year-period, we have studied the diffusion of the shared living idea as it spread from the first units in Winter Park, Florida, to adaptations in other states. We have gathered information on the new shared housing residences and recorded their experiences, problems, and "evolution."

There is a rich literature on diffusion, but most of this is directed to diffusion of inventions, or technical ideas, or to the diffusion of improvements such as hybrid seed corn. It is much more difficult to trace the more amorphous process in the spread and adoption of a social idea than of a technical innovation.

During our study of the first ten Share-A-Home units in Florida, we found that persons were interested in adopting the idea in other states. We realized that we had a unique opportunity to trace the spread of the idea, and we have attempted to record that process. One way to analyze the shared housing "movement" as a social innovation is to adapt the four-stage framework presented by Sandol Stoddard (1978) in her description of the diffusion of the hospice movement in the United States. Hospice, Inc. of New Haven, Connecticut, has been recognized and affirmed by the government and thus has reached the fourth stage. The four major steps in the diffusion process are:

1) A problem is recognized and a need perceived by an individual or a small group of individuals.

2) A small local experiment is initiated by these early innovators or by persons who adopt their practices.

3) There is an attempt to inform and enlighten the general public about the need and proposed means of fulfilling it. This stage usually has the explicit or implicit goal of attracting the support of public officials or government agencies.

4) Government bodies take action and pass legislation in support of the innovation and ultimately provide public monies to pay for the establishment and use of the innovation.

The first step in the innovation process—the awareness of the problem and a belief that there is a way to meet the need—is described in chapter 3, which records the early stages of Share-A-Home, and chapter 8, which describes the origins of the Abbeyfield Society in Great Britain. In each instance, a single individual had a strong feeling based on ethical concerns that some kind of communal living would be beneficial for frail, isolated, lonely older people. They believed that shared family groups would avoid the difficulties, impersonality, and expense of institutionalized care.

The second phase, small local experiments, is also described in chapters 3 and 8, detailing the first homes in Florida and London. The first homes, in Winter Park, Florida, and in London, were established by the change agent, thus demonstrating how this stage could be achieved successfully. The third phase, that of trying to inform and enlighten a larger audience about the need and how the innovation may provide a desirable response, is the stage at which shared housing exists at present in the United States. In England, this stage has been reached, for the basic information about Abbeyfield and its 900 shared homes is widely known, and Abbeyfield is recognized as a successful program (see chapter 8).

The fourth phase, that of the government supporting the endeavor, has occurred in only a few instances in the United States. In the United Kingdom, however, public recognition of this kind of shared housing has resulted in specified procedures in subsidizing low-income residents, and in making available low-income mortgage funds to the organizers.

In our research on the spread of housing alternatives for the elderly, we devoted attention to mapping out whether the Stoddard model was applicable. As sociologists, we believed that the study of the shared housing concept would provide us with an opportunity to understand the process of social change and the factors that may assist or impede the change process. Furthermore, it was our appraisal that since we began our research when the shared living experiments were just starting, we had a unique opportunity to see the change process unfold in some kind of time perspective if we continued observations beyond the few months that is typical for field survey research.

This chapter will cover the growth of shared living units in the Winter Park, Florida, area through the efforts of James Gillies, the founder; the role of the media is disseminating information about the concept; and the spread of the idea to other areas in the United States. Our data are derived from five different studies, which were directed to various aspects of the diffusion process (see appendix 1 on methodology).

As was mentioned in chapter 3, Share-A-Home began as the idea of James Gillies of Winter Park, Florida. Mr. Gillies, a devoutly religious man, developed the idea of several elderly people sharing a household, not only to meet what he saw as a growing need for some alternative form of living, but also to satisfy a deep religious commitment to helping others. While this religious commitment is still present, Share-A-Home has developed into a shared living environment that is nonsectarian and essentially nonreligious.

Since its establishment, the Share-A-Home organization has survived several crisis situations. In June 1971, the Orange County Commission filed a lawsuit charging that the Share-A-Home Association violated applicable zoning ordinances. The case was heard before the Ninth Circuit Court of Orange County and was decided in October 1971. At issue in this case, which is discussed more fully in chapter 9, was whether Share-A-Home, as a nonprofit association of private individuals, met the definition of family as defined in the zoning regulations, or whether Share-A-Home was indeed a boarding house and as such specifically excluded from residentially zoned areas. Another issue that the court did not decide in this particular case involved the fact that the property had previously been used as a private nursing care facility, with the approval of the county commission. There remained the question of whether the property could be grandfathered into a zoning classification that would render the question of family versus boarding house moot. Adding to the confusion was the zoning regulation's use of a relatively liberal definition of a family and the fact that the particular Share-A-Home had been in operation for two years.

The Share-A-Home spokesman argued that each individual house is a single housekeeping unit, and that as a family they should be allowed to remain in operation. In October 1971, court was actually convened at the Share-A-Home site and the judge inspected the residence. The court then ruled that Share-A-Home was not a boarding house, and that the association met the definition of family contained in the Orange County zoning ordinances. This decision has had a major impact on the spread of the Share-A-Home model. Based upon the decision and the county commission's failure to file an appeal, the facility remained as a Share-A-Home, and several other facilities were established in the Winter Park, Florida, area. This court suit resulted in considerable publicity in the local news media, so that many in the general public learned about Share-A-Home, its purposes, and its operation.

As other homes were established, it became apparent that a support organization was needed to deal with the issues of acquiring property, receiving donations, and otherwise promoting the Share-A-Home model. Furthermore, the founder of the model needed additional time to concentrate on the day-to-day operation of the houses. For these reasons a nonprofit corporation was formed in 1972. Although market conditions have caused a fluctuation in the number of houses and the number of people served, the new corporation, Share-A-Home of America, Inc., in 1982 operated ten homes in the central Florida area serving about 120 people. The founder remains the general manager of Share-A-Home and is accountable to the residents. His salary for administrative services is paid not by the corporation, but by the persons living in the various Share-A-Homes.

A more recent crisis developed when in 1978 the owner of one of the Share-A-Home residences housing eighteen elderly people announced that the property would be sold at public auction. The residents had been living in the home for almost six years, and finding other accommodations would be difficult at best. It was decided that the Share-A-Home Corporation, as a nonprofit entity, would attempt to raise enough money to bid on the property. Letters from Share-A-Home of America, Inc. were sent to organizations and individuals stating the situation and requesting donations for the purchase of the home. Between the time of the auction announcement and the day of the sale, the corporation received donations and loans in an amount sufficient to make a down payment for the purchase of the property.

Another housing crisis occurred when two Share-A-Homes lost their leases in homes rented from Rollins College, a small private college in Orange County. In 1979 the college announced that it was planning to phase out many of its rental property units and wished to demolish the two Share-A-Home facilities. There were twenty-eight people living in the two homes, and finding alternative arrangements for such large groups became a serious problem. One aspect of the problem centered around the family concept. The founder of Share-A-Home believes that each individual unit represents a distinct, autonomous family of people. There is indeed a strong affectional tie among many of the Share-A-Home residents for one another, and it would therefore be a stressful event should those who had lived together for some time have had to be separated because of lack of space. The residents decided that every effort should be made to keep the groups intact. This meant renting and renovating two separate buildings capable of housing fourteen persons each. Unfortunately, in the short period of time available, no buildings large enough could be located. As a result, several members of each group were forced to seek other living arrangements. In place of the two fourteen-member groups, two facilities were established, one with ten members and the other with eight members.

The experience of losing the lease on the two college campus buildings has pointed out a very serious limitation on the spread of the Share-A-Home model, namely, the scarcity of homes capable of housing an eight- to twelve-member group of people. First, high interest rates and the nonprofit nature of Share-A-Home have combined to make purchase of the property generally unfeasible. Secondly, in order to stabilize the cost of rent, Share-A-Home must seek owners willing to sign long-term leases. These economic realities have had a dampening effect on the spread of the Share-A-Home model. This is illustrated by the fact that groups attempting to start shared living facilities in other parts of the country have stated that the lack of suitable structures with enough bedrooms is one of the major problems they face.

THE ROLE OF MASS MEDIA IN DISSEMINATING INFORMATION ABOUT SHARED HOUSING

One of the most important vehicles for the dissemination of information on new social patterns in the United States is the mass media. Therefore, we tried to trace the principal accounts and publicity that appeared in newspapers, magazines, and on television.

Share-A-Home operated as a relatively invisible group of small shared living facilities for several years, from 1969 to 1972. In 1971, the circuit court case mentioned earlier brought Share-A-Home to the attention of various media representatives. The local press was most interested in this unique experiment in family living for the elderly and published many articles about it. It was not until 1972, however, that Share-A-Home received national attention when *Life* magazine published a five-page article entitled "A Commune for Old Folks" (James 1972). This was in an era when communes were considered new and exciting life styles, and it was thought that they would be important components of America's future social patterns. This article stimulated the establishment of at least two of the non-Florida Share-A-Homes. It also brought the model to the attention of the University of Florida researchers.

Another major media event in the life of Share-A-Home was its inclusion in a segment of a three-hour documentary entitled "The American Family," broadcast by the National Broadcasting Company (NBC) in January 1979. The broadcast crew spent ten days in the Orlando area and several days in one of the houses, filming every possible facet of life in the home. There were high expectations on the part of those associated with Share-A-Home that this publicity, as part of a special television show on the American family, would stimulate the establishment of many new homes throughout the country. Unfortunately, the mammoth effort involved in filming and interviewing resulted in only a twelve-minute segment that was presented at the end of a three-hour program, at about 10:45 at night, following segments on other phases of American families. While it was professionally presented and gave an upbeat portrayal of the frail elderly, it did not have the impact that was hoped for. No new facilities were established as a result of the program, although we assume it generated much interest.

In our electronic society, publicity is often equated with success. In terms of exposure, a twelve-minute segment on a national television program sounds like a public relations coup. However, though many people may have been interested, intrigued and entertained, they were not stimulated to duplicate the model. To start a shared living facility, there must be a great deal of local involvement and reinforcement. It must be added that with the prejudice against old age in our society, any mass media program that presents a positive view of the elderly is all to the good.

The publicity about Share-A-Home that generated the largest number of inquiries resulted from an article that appeared in *Modern Maturity* in March 1980 (Getze 1980). The article was based upon the research of the University of Florida team and its report to the NRTA–AARP Andrus Foundation, the funding agency for two years of our research. The Share-A-Home organization estimated that well over 3,000 letters were received requesting information as a result of this report on shared living. There may be several explanations for this extraordinary response. This article published the address of the Share-A-Home organization, whereas other articles on the Share-A-Home concept listed only the name and city of the organization, thus filtering out all but those individuals tenacious enough to discover the address. Another factor leading to a large response is believed to be the specialized readership of *Modern Maturity*. This publication is produced by the American Association of Retired Persons and the National Retired Teachers Association (AARP/NRTA). The fact that the *Modern Maturity* article was sent to precisely the population for whom Share-A-Home was established, i.e., elderly, middle-income persons who may need alternative living arrangements, resulted in many of these persons requesting information on how to start or become a resident in a Share-A-Home.

As mentioned previously, local involvement and reinforcement are major factors in expanding a shared living mode. Although the national exposure achieved by the *Life* magazine article and the NBC segment were certainly impressive, they were ineffective in generating new facilities. Share-A-Home, however, as well as other types of shared living facilities, have been successful in using a more localized approach to publicity, which has included church bulletins and local newspaper articles. These local efforts have been successful in generating interest as well as donations for the establishment of new shared living facilities. In table 5.1, we have listed the major media events responsible for the spread of the Share-A-Home idea.

TABLE *5.1. Major Media Coverage of Share-A-Home*

Year	Media Stimulus	Results: New Share-A-Home Units Established
1969–present	Local church bulletins	Spread from 1 to 10 houses in Florida during 1971–1980
1971	Orlando newspapers' account of court case	Spread from 1 to 10 houses during 1971–1980
1972	*Life* magazine	Ashtabula, Ohio Cleveland, Ohio
1974	*U.S. News and World Report*	None
1978	*The Episcopalian*	Greensboro, North Carolina Gainesville, Georgia
1979	*The Catholic Digest*	Cincinnati, Ohio
1979	*The Episcopalian*	None
1979	*Generations,* Western Gerontological Society	None
1979	NBC-TV, "The American Family"	None
1980	*Modern Maturity* magazine (AARP/NRTA)	Cocoa Beach, Florida Bethlehem, Pennsylvania

DIFFUSION OF THE MODEL TO OTHER STATES

Since its inception in 1969, Share-A-Home has expanded to encompass twenty-two units in eight states housing approximately 306 people. In addition, there are three facilities based upon the Share-A-Home model in three different states. Table 5.2 presents the current data on the Share-A-Home-type facilities in operation in 1982.

Although some convents and church rectories are being used to house Share-A-Home-type facilities, the majority of them are located in former single-family dwellings. This would seem to modify our discussion of the overall flexibility of the model. However, while Share-A-Home, as well as other shared living arrangements, could easily adjust to many different types of structures, it is also true that both economic conditions and the lack of other types of structures may direct organizers to single-family homes. Hotels, motels, convents, hospitals, and various other structures may indeed be well suited to the needs of Share-A-Home, but the deciding element is often the financial arrangements that can

TABLE 5.2. *Inventories of Share-A-Homes in 1982 (Cont.)*

NAME	House-holds	Residents	Vacancies	Average Age	Type of Structure	Staff	Monthly Charges* (January 1983)	Affiliation
Share-A-Home of America, Inc. Winter Park, Fla. Founded: 1969	7	94	8	78	Single Family (5) Duplex (1) Multi- (1)	23	$395–$450	Lutheran Episcopal Catholic
Madonna Home Norfolk, Va. Founded: 1977	2	25	3	81	Convent (1) Single Family (1)	4	$400	Catholic
Family Share-A-Home. Cleveland, Ohio Founded: 1978	2	14	2	76	Single Family (2)	4	$460	Episcopal
Hamilton City West Share-A-Home Cincinnati, Ohio Founded: 1979	3	35	3	84	Convent (1) Single Family (2)	9	$415–$550	Catholic
Share-A-Home of Guilford County Greensboro, N.C. Founded: 1979	2	13	1	75	Single Family (2)	4	$400–$600	Episcopal
Share-A-Home of Gainesville Gainesville, Ga. Founded: 1979	2	14	2	76	Single Family (2)	4	$375	Episcopal
Share-A-Home of Lake Region Ashtabula, Ohio Founded: 1975	1	7	1	83	Single Family	3	$360–$525	Episcopal

Organization								
Share-A-Home of Riverside, Cocoa, Fla. Founded: 1982	1	12	9		Church Rectory	2	$450	Episcopal
Share-A-Home of The Golden Triangle, Eustis, Fla. Founded: 1982	1	9	4		Single Family	2	$390–$425	Episcopal
Share-A-Home/St. Charles, San Antonio, Fla. Founded: 1979	1	10	2	83	Single Family	2	$500	None
Share-A-Home of Louisville, Louisville, Ky. Founded: 1981	1	10	1	75	Single Family	2	$600–$650	Episcopal
Share-A-Home/Academy, Watertown, N.Y. Founded: 1982	1	3	7	80	Single Family	2	$375–$750	Episcopal
Share-A-Home Albemarle, N.C. Founded: 1981	1	9	3		Single Family	2	$390–$450	Episcopal
Share-A-Home of Bryn Mawr, Bryn Mawr, Pa. Founded: 1981	1	8	2	77	Single Family	2	$400	Baptist
Suncoast Shared Living, Inc. St. Petersburg, Fla. Founded: 1980	1	8	1		Single Family	2	$400	Florida Gulf Health Systems Inc.

TABLE 5.2. *Inventories of Share-A-Homes in 1982 (Cont.)*

NAME	House-holds	Residents	Vacancies	Average Age	Type of Structure	Staff	Monthly Charges* (January 1983)	Affiliation
Share-A-Home of Upper Pinellas Clearwater, Fla. Founded: 1980	1	10	1		Single Family	2	$450–$800	Private foundation
Share-A-Home of Lehigh Valley Bethlehem, Pa Founded: 1980	1	6	1	84	Church Rectory	2	$475–$750	Ecumenical church group
Facilities Based Upon the Share-A-Home Concept:								
Wilbon Family Winter Park, Fla. Founded: 1979	1	8	0	70	Single Family	2	$475–$525	None
Parker Morrow House Groveport, Ohio Founded: 1978	1	4	2	70	Single Family	2	$269.50–$379.50	County government
Facilities Developed Independently that Approximate the Share-A-Home Model:								
St. Patricks House Wilmington, Del. Founded: 1978	1	7	6	70	Convent	2	$225	Catholic

Proposed Share-A-Home Facilities: Newport News, Va; Niagara, N.Y.; Tavares, Fla.; Stuart, Fla.; Lehigh Acres, Fla.; Binghampton, Vt.; Burlington, Vt.; Chapel Hill, N.C.
*Monthly charges are current as of January 1983. Where a range of costs appear, the most expensive costs reflect the most attractive living arrangements, i.e., private room, private bath, desirable location.

be made. Put simply, it would appear that the use of single-family structures by Share-A-Home type facilities is a more economical use of resources.

From table 5.2, one notes that Share-A-Home sponsorship comes predominately from Catholic or Episcopalian church groups. While it is true that local churches have become involved in the establishment and operation of local facilities, and indeed several of the projects could not survive without church assistance, in no case has there been a regional or national church effort to organize shared living facilities. This is not to say that there will be no such effort in the future, only that Share-A-Home, in its present state, is a local phenomenon organized by local churches for local residents.

DIFFUSION OF THE IDEA: THE DECISION-MAKING PROCESS

The establishment of a Share-A-Home-type facility involves a great investment in both time and resources. As a result, a number of decisions must be made before a facility is organized. The first decision is often whether to become involved in a venture that has no certainty of success, will surely occupy an organizer's "free time," presents many complex problems, and offers little in the way of personal benefit beyond the knowledge that it will help a small group of people. It is impossible to know or even guess how many potential organizing groups have never proceeded past this stage of decision making. We do know, however, that at least seventeen of these groups have responded positively to the challenge of organizing a Share-A-Home and that there are more than 300 people who are directly benefited by that response.

Between the decision to become involved and the first home-cooked meal, there are many decisions to be made and many steps to be taken. Figure 5.1 presents the major elements in the process of establishing a Share-A-Home-type shared living facility. It should be pointed out that one or two people are usually the initiators of such an ambitious project, and even if the decision not to proceed is made by the entire group, these individuals may find another group interested enough to continue. This has happened in several cases, and as one organizer stated: "If the group won't do what needs to be done, you have to find another group who will." We now turn our attention to the groups "who will."

This analysis of decision making as presented in figure 5.1 is based on repeated observations by the authors of groups that passed through the stages outlined. It is derived from the actual experiences of the organizers rather than being formulated as a theoretical model.

ELEMENTS IN THE ESTABLISHMENT OF SHARE-A-HOME-TYPE PROJECTS

As stated before, the mass media have played an important role in the spread of the Share-A-Home idea. Usually, one person hears about the model, from any one of several sources, and obtains more information either from the literature or from the Share-A-Home organization. This person then goes about contacting friends who may or may not be interested in proceeding any further. After a period of informal discussion, there begins to form a group of persons interested in the idea. This period may be anywhere from one day to many months or even years. At any time in the process of formation (stages A and B in figure 5.1), this group can lose interest, become attracted to another housing concept, or abandon the idea as unfeasible. If, however, they continue, new and more information becomes vital.

As the interested group becomes more defined, the need for information is focused on specific areas of interest. Since organizers tend to be from various backgrounds, each has questions about Share-A-Home that relate to these backgrounds. Lawyers, housewives, physicians, insurance salespeople, realtors, and any number of others all have important questions that must be answered satisfactorily before the decision to proceed can be made. It is here, in stage C, that potential organizers seek the advice of the founder of Share-A-Home. Either through correspondence or, more likely, through personal contact, the founder provides information on a wide variety of topics. His answers to the organizers' questions have a profound effect upon the decision to proceed.

If the questions raised by the interested group are answered more or less satisfactorily and the group decides to proceed with the plan, then a final purge is made and "working committees" are established. When the process reaches this stage (D), much information-gathering work needs to be done. Those willing to work are rapidly and easily identified and the others, the "watchers," are either tolerated or politely dropped

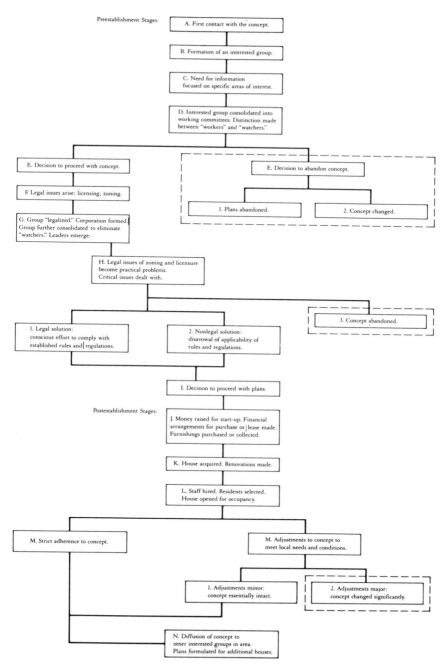

Preestablishment Stages:

A. First contact with the concept.

B. Formation of an interested group.

C. Need for information focused on specific areas of interest.

D. Interested group consolidated into working committees. Distinction made between "workers" and "watchers."

E. Decision to proceed with concept.

E. Decision to abandon concept.

1. Plans abandoned.

2. Concept changed.

F. Legal issues arise: licensing; zoning.

G. Group "legalized." Corporation formed. Group further consolidated to eliminate "watchers." Leaders emerge.

H. Legal issues of zoning and licensure become practical problems. Critical issues dealt with.

3. Concept abandoned.

1. Legal solution: conscious effort to comply with established rules and regulations.

2. Nonlegal solution: disavowal of applicability of rules and regulations.

I. Decision to proceed with plans.

Postestablishment Stages:

J. Money raised for start-up. Financial arrangements for purchase or lease made. Furnishings purchased or collected.

K. House acquired. Renovations made.

L. Staff hired. Residents selected. House opened for occupancy.

M. Strict adherence to concept.

M. Adjustments to concept to meet local needs and conditions.

1. Adjustments minor: concept essentially intact.

2. Adjustments major: concept changed significantly.

N. Diffusion of concept to other interested groups in area. Plans formulated for additional houses.

FIGURE 5.1. *Elements in the Establishment of Successful Share-A-Home-Type Shared Living Projects*

from the group. What remains is a "core" group that is committed to an idea and is willing to work hard to put that idea into practice.

After this period of information gathering, a decision to proceed or change plans is made. If investigation has revealed a more attractive concept, the organizers will abandon the Share-A-Home idea. If financial, legal, or other barriers exist, the group may abandon the plans entirely. However, if, from the organizers' viewpoint, the questions have been resolved and the barriers are not insurmountable, the decision to proceed is made. It is at this point when the aspects of zoning and licensure first emerge.

Usually, the group will decide to proceed regardless of any licensing or zoning questions (stage F). Perhaps this is due to an incomplete knowledge of the subject, or perhaps the group believes the issues do not present barriers to their plans. In any event, at this stage, licensing and zoning do not represent practical problems and therefore do not require immediate attention.

Shortly after the group eliminates the watchers from the workers (stage D) and decides to proceed (stage E), it legalizes itself by forming a nonprofit corporation. At this point, the idea of establishing a Share-A-Home-type facility ceases to be an amorphous dream and becomes an organizational commitment. Because of the seriousness of this step (stage G), it becomes necessary to allow those less committed individuals to drop out of the group voluntarily. This final purge, if successfully accomplished, leaves the organizing group with individuals who will work for establishment and who have, or can acquire, the required skills to bring the facility into being. It is this final group that bears the ultimate responsibility for the events leading up to that first home-cooked meal.

After the legalization stage (G), the group again is faced with the issues of zoning and licensure. What before were ill-defined problems, however, now are very practical issues with a potentially profound impact upon the organization. Usually, an organizing group will have at least three options with regard to the issues of zoning and licensing: it may avoid the issues by abandoning the plans; it may seek legal solutions by making a conscious effort to comply with existing rules and regulations; or it may disavow the applicability of existing rules and regulations.

In the authors' experience, all three solutions have been more or less successfully applied to the problem, and with certain exceptions, none of the three seems to be intrinsically better than the other two. One of the exceptions is that abandoning the concept, while removing the problem, also eliminates the establishment of a shared living facility. In that sense, either of the other two solutions is a better one. The other exception is this: by choosing to adopt what we have labeled the non-legal solution, organizers are putting themselves in the position of fighting a seemingly endless battle against regulatory agencies and municipalities. At the same time, they are basing the survival of the facility on the ability, or inability, of these regulatory agencies to enforce the established rules and regulations. Once the legal issues have been dealt with, in whichever manner seems locally appropriate, the group may then proceed with its plans.

Assuming the organizers have not decided to abandon the concept, they must now face the practical problems of renting or purchasing a structure, renovating that structure, furnishing it, and, last but most important, locating potential residents. That these problems are dealt with effectively is evidence of the talent, commitment, and fortitude of those involved. As we have discussed elsewhere, the flexibility of the Share-A-Home model makes the size and type of structure, the financial arrangements, and even the type of residents largely a matter of availability and what is needed locally. Indeed, one of the attractions of the model is that it allows local determination of needs and encourages local control of the individual households. That in itself, however, is the source of a problem area.

The problem can best be described by the simple question: When does local determination conflict with the concept, so that the facility is no longer a Share-A-Home-type facility? That question is the essence of the first major postestablishment conflict faced by these projects (stage M). Because the response is entirely dependent upon one's perspective, we shall not attempt to answer the question here. Suffice it to say, however, that among the existing Share-A-Home-type facilities, there is disagreement as to which projects are pure Share-A-Home projects and which are not.

Each local organizing group is faced with the problem of adjusting the Share-A-Home model to meet local conditions and local needs. Some groups have chosen to adhere strictly to the Share-A-Home concept as laid down by the founder. Other groups have found it necessary to adjust the concept to respond to local needs.

If the local adjustments are minor and the concept is essentially unchanged, the group may turn its attention to the next logical step. Assuming that the original household has been successful, the organizers formulate plans for a second house. In addition, the concept is transmitted to other groups with similar interests. Of course, such activities will also take place if the local adjustments to the concept are major, but here we are dealing only with the Share-A-Home-type facilities.

Thus, Share-A-Home and Share-A-Home-type facilities have spread from Winter Park, Florida, to eight other states. And although the establishment of only thirty-two units in fourteen years seems a modest response relative to the potential resident population, interest in the Share-A-Home concept has increased dramatically in recent years, such that new facilities and new concepts will undoubtedly surface. A concept such as Share-A-Home is consistent with the approach of "local solutions to local problems," which is gaining momentum in the United States. And that fact alone will probably lead to more facilities of this type.

TVA'S DESIGN FOR AN ENERGY-SAVING SHARED LIVING FACILITY

One of the more interesting and unique "spinoffs" from the Share-A-Home concept is a group home designed by the Tennessee Valley Authority (TVA). Although TVA's primary purpose is to produce electricity for a large area of the southeastern United States, the quasi-governmental agency has been involved in other projects affecting the life of the region, such as soil conservation and recreation. One of these projects is the Older Americans Initiative of the Community Resource Development Branch. The initiative was established to help older persons find ways to reduce their energy costs.

The director of the Older Americans Initiative, after hearing several presentations, including one by the authors, became convinced that one way for older people to reduce energy costs was to concentrate themselves in a single, energy-efficient environment. This common-sense assumption led him to explore the various models of shared living. The Share-A-Home model seemed to offer at least two advantages: it was organizationally simple, and it was flexible enough to include a wide range of potential target populations.

Having decided to pursue the Share-A-Home model, the director consulted with architects, solar design engineers, and others to produce plans for a structure that could house twelve people and would offer energy-saving design concepts not widely available in the current housing market. Although great effort was put into the actual physical design of the structure, interpersonal relationships and the overall social well-being of the proposed household were also considered. After several months of intensive effort, design drawings for a prototypical Solar Group Home were completed.

The director then assembled a panel of experts to make an assessment of the solar home. The experts, including one of the authors, made specific suggestions for improvements, and in 1981 the final drawings were completed (see appendix 3). Based upon the final drawings, it is estimated that the cost of construction, exclusive of land, would be approximately $275,000. (Estimates used here are for March 1981 in TVA's region of the United States.) Although no organizing group has yet been able to raise the funds necessary to construct such a facility, several groups have shown interest in the design.

A complete technical description of the design characteristics of the Solar Group Home is beyond the scope of this book,[1] but it should be pointed out that the design is based on state-of-the-art passive solar concepts to achieve what is an impressive energy-savings potential. In a computer simulation conducted by TVA with climatic and cost data for the Knoxville, Tennessee, area, the heating and cooling costs for the 6,750-square-foot structure were predicted to be less than $500 annually (based upon 1981 cost data). That amount, assuming full occupancy, is less than $3.50 per month for each of the twelve residents and represents a substantial cost savings when compared with other shared living facilities.

Given the extraordinary energy conservation properties of the design, it would appear that the only barrier to large-scale acceptance and development of such structures is the rather substantial cost of construc-

---

1. For technical data and descriptive material, contact: Solar Applications Branch, Tennessee Valley Authority, 300 CRU, Chattanooga, TN 37401. See appendix 3.

tion. Organizing groups have, so far anyway, found it easier to raise renovation money than the significantly larger sums required for purpose-built construction. It would seem likely, however, that if energy costs continue to rise, a design such as TVA's Solar Group Home will become more attractive, and that in the near future such a structure will be built (see appendix 3). Even if sponsors are not interested in the solar aspects of the plan, the house design in itself is functional and imaginative.

A SURVEY OF SHARED LIVING FACILITIES

In our attempt to locate shared living facilities, we were able to find many projects organized by persons who had no knowledge of the Share-A-Home model. In all, we located eighty facilities that offered what, broadly defined, could be termed shared living.

To obtain data about the facilities, a mail survey questionnaire was constructed. Fifty-eight separate projects operating eighty individual units were mailed the questionnaire. Follow-up telephone interviews were also used to obtain additional information or to clarify some answers from some respondents. Preliminary analysis indicated that ten of the projects would have to be eliminated from the survey. Five of these had either closed due to lack of residents or had never opened. Another four projects originally thought to offer shared living were in fact house matching services (see chapter 7), and one project was discovered to be a religious farm commune that was not a shared living environment for the elderly. Out of the remaining forty-eight projects, thirty-nine (81 percent) responded. These thirty-nine projects operated a total of seventy-three individual units of shared living for the elderly.

Kinds of Houses. As would be expected, the flexibility of these projects enabled them to utilize a wide variety of structures to house the individual units. There is a clear preference for the older single-family houses. Twenty of the projects reported using a structure that was formerly a single-family dwelling. Another eight stated that they used multi-family structures, apartment buildings, etc., and six reported that they had units located in former Catholic convents. Less frequently used to house shared living environments were university campus buildings, duplex structures, and former motels or hotels.

The preference for older single-family dwellings seems to be related to the fact that older homes tend to be more spacious than newer homes. Since economic viability is somewhat related to the number of rooms available for rent, the gracious old homes of a former generation are well-suited to the shared living model. While convents and hotels have large number of rooms, they also have an institutional or standardized character that may make them unappealing to the potential resident.

Licensure. Another issue that is becoming increasingly important to shared projects is whether the homes must be licensed. As with other issues, there seems to be a wide diversity among projects with regard to the licensing and regulation of shared living facilities by city, county, or state government agencies. The issue of licensing will be dealt with in detail in chapter 9. However, we should point out here that some organizers regard licensing as an intrusion upon what is believed to be essentially a family environment, while other organizers welcome or even seek government regulation as a means of legitimizing a particular model of shared living. In our survey of shared living projects, we found that about half of the projects involved in the survey were not licensed.

Because of the lack of uniform definition of shared living facilities, it is important to consider what licensing criteria and categories are used for these facilities and what government agencies are involved. Of the licensed projects responding to our survey, ten stated that they were licensed by their state government. Another four listed city or county governments as the licensing agencies, and three stated that both city and state governments were involved in the licensing process. When cities or counties are listed as the issuing agents, it is most often the county health department or the city building commission that retains the right of inspection. Where state governments are involved, the inspection agency most often mentioned is the state department of human resources. The obvious conclusion here is that counties and cities view shared living facilities from the standpoint of building structures and the state views the facilities from a resident or human perspective. There are many factors involved here, and lacking detailed and systematic research, we are not suggesting that either approach represents a better way of viewing the facility. We point to this only as an example of the diversity of government treatment of the shared living arrangement.

It is also important for us to consider the licensing categories under which the individual facilities are included. We have found that local and state governments tend to treat the facilities as being part of already existing categories for licensing purposes. While this has caused little difficulty in the past, it has caused some confusion in the formulation of a definition covering the wide range of alternatives. In many cases, it would be better to consider shared living environments as new categories of housing, or at least as special cases of the established categories. In our survey, eight of the seventeen projects that were licensed reported that the licensing category was "congregate care facility" and another five projects reported the category was "boarding home." Thus, almost 80 percent of the licensed projects fall into the established categories of "congregate care facility" or "boarding home." This reflects a tendency on the part of government regulatory agencies to define congregate care facilities and boarding homes in such a broad way as to include projects and facilities that in reality are only marginal to the categories that were established. In response to this confusion, at least one state has developed a category labeled adult group homes, which allows the state's interest to be served and at the same time is less restrictive than the other categories of housing already mentioned.

Requirements for Admission. Because shared living facilities offer no medical services, the requirements for admission are relatively simple. Beyond being able to afford the monthly payment, it is generally required that a potential resident be ambulatory, capable of personal self-care, and be able to manage his or her own medication. Obviously, within these categories there is some freedom of definition, so that one project might define ambulatory to include canes, walkers, and less frequently wheelchairs, while other projects specifically prohibit mechanical devices. There is similar latitude in defining the other categories, particularly in the case of the rather broad category related to personal care. In general, personal care relates to the individual's ability to dress, bathe, etc. In many cases, help with prescription medication is provided in the form of informal reminders at appropriate times. Because medically trained staff are rarely available, few facilities dispense medication. When medication is dispensed by a facility, it is usually in the form of one-dose packages prepared by medically trained personnel who are paid for that service.

While shared living environments exercise some freedom in defining the physical requirements for admission, most require that a potential resident be free of serious health impairments that represent a personal danger or danger to others. In our survey, almost 95 percent of the respondents reported that ambulation was a requirement for residency. Personal care was mentioned by slightly less, and almost 75 percent stated that they required a resident to manage his or her own medication.

Only three of our survey respondents listed mental competency tests as a requirement for residency. Many shared living environments do not have a formal means of determining the psychological well-being of an individual, but we have found that most if not all employ a face-to-face interview with the potential resident to determine suitability. It can be assumed that an informal nonprofessional judgment about mental competency is made during that interview. As with physical impairments, there is a wide range of mental states that will be accepted. Generally, however, a person exhibiting antisocial, destructive, or self-destructive behavior will be screened out as unacceptable. Since a major factor in the success of a shared living arrangement is the ability of the residents to live more or less in harmony, a potential resident exhibiting any signs of not being able to live cooperatively will be denied residency.

Our survey of shared housing revealed that the major problem facing many of them is recruitment of residents. Even a relatively small vacancy rate can present a most serious threat to continued operation. Part of the problem in recruitment of residents can be linked to the small size and newness of some projects. It is reasonable to expect some elderly to be resistant to the idea of moving from their present living situation into an environment about which little is known.

Another problem related to resident recruitment is that because of the small staff there is little time and often no money to allow for an active and rigorous recruitment effort. Many times projects are forced to rely upon free advertising and word of mouth to attract residents. Among our respondents, almost 75 percent said they used informal contacts as a source of potential residents. Another important method of attracting residents is contacting the manager of existing institutions, most notably acute care hospitals and nursing homes. The use of church bulletins was reported by about 54 percent of the respondents, and 45 percent said that they used newspaper advertisements.

Monthly Cost to Residents. The average cost of the shared living facilities in our survey (conducted in 1981) ranged from a minimum of $436 per month to a maximum of $465 per month. This means that without sources of subsidy a person would have to have an annual income of $5,232 to $5,480 in order to pay for shared housing. This amount pays only for housing, food, in some cases transportation, and the various staffing arrangements, but it does not include personal expenses or medical expenses. It can readily be seen that the average monthly charge for these shared living facilities is higher than most people receive from Social Security. This means, of course, that the potential resident of shared living facilities must have some source of income beyond what is provided by Social Security. If a person had sold her home before moving to a shared living facility, this would assist her in meeting the cost.

While subsidy money is not readily available, some projects have been very successful in locating and acquiring relatively stable sources of subsidy funding. In several cases, private foundations, businesses, community groups, and even private citizens have made financial commitments to local organizers of shared living projects. Another, although far less common, form of subsidy arrangement is where the funding source makes a commitment to an individual resident. The sponsoring of an individual resident is particularly suitable when only small amounts of subsidy monies are available or when a funding source has an interest in the welfare of a single individual.

Our survey of shared living arrangements in other states indicates that they include a wide and diverse range of projects designed to address local needs. The day-to-day operational issues are as diverse as the cities in which the projects are located. For this reason, it is sometimes difficult to define precisely what shared living facilities are; there are, however, some elements common to shared living facilities we have studied.

The Pattern of Daily Life. Perhaps the most important of these elements is the noninstitutional nature of these facilities. Organizers of shared living facilities strive to preserve the home-like environment. Since most facilities of this type were established to allow the residents to remain outside an institution for as long as possible, great effort is made to avoid the physical appearance of an institution. In some situations this has meant using the types of furniture, decorations, etc. found in private homes. Other efforts to avoid the stigma attached to institutions have been to eliminate schedules of activities, to involve residents in decision-making processes, and to locate the facilities in residential neighborhoods. Most shared living projects are nonprofit organizations that were established for the expressed purpose of providing housing in a homelike environment. Because of their nonprofit nature, the cost of living in various facilities is based upon the types of services offered and the cost of providing those services. In our survey, 87 percent of the projects included food in the monthly payment. In all cases, food services consisted of at least two meals a day, and often access to the kitchen was unrestricted. Eighty-seven percent of our respondents also reported that some type of housekeeping services were included in the charges. These services ranged from heavy housekeeping to cleaning the rooms of individual residents, and 79 percent provided personal laundry services. About half of our survey reported that transportation services were available. Other services reported by our respondents were shopping and recreation. The level of service provided is directly related to the abilities of the resident population, and the types of services are designed to prevent premature institutionalization.

Respondents in our survey reported that a variety of staffing arrangements were available. While staffing patterns are largely a function of the preference of the residents and the funds available, they are aimed at providing an atmosphere that is at the same time more independent than an institution and more supportive than living alone. Most facilities provided some sort of housekeeper or cook in addition to the administrator. In slightly over 25 percent of the projects in our survey, the cook is a full-time employee; 41 percent employ a full-time housekeeper. Another important staff position is manager or facilitator, with 47 percent of the projects reporting having a live-in manager and another 8 percent reporting having a live-in facilitator. Organizers believe that this live-in staff person provides an important source of security and a sense of well-being to the often frail residents.

In other cases, the manager went home at night and another person was employed to spend the night at the house. This person was given a free room and sometimes a small salary in exchange for "keeping an eye" on the residents and summoning emergency help, in case it was needed.

CONCLUSIONS

In summary, the major stages in the diffusion of the Share-A-Home idea and the establishment of a functioning Share-A-Home are described in figure 5.1. The figure outlines the steps in detail but the principal phases are: 1) initial contact with the idea; 2) formulation of a local interest group; 3) the group becomes a legal entity, usually a nonprofit corporation, and then copes with licensure and zoning; 4) money is raised for start-up and a financial plan worked out; 5) the house is located and rented, leased, or purchased; and 6) staff are hired and residents selected.

These major steps must be followed, and there is a logical sequence to their progression. However, several phases can be taking place at about the same time. For example, since the committee knows that a house must be acquired, an interested subgroup may be searching for a house before money is raised.

The formal chart and this discussion do not give an adequate or precise indication of the nature of the group dynamics involved in accepting the Share-A-Home concept and actually organizing a home. Our task here is to generalize about the major steps involved in the establishment of shared living. Obviously, each local situation is unique and requires ingenuity, adaptation, and imagination. There is a tendency on the part of social scientists to analyze and describe a process such as this in terms of an orderly model. This fails to capture the essential group dynamics—the disagreements and power struggles that have to be surmounted on a day-to-day basis.

CHAPTER SIX

Diversity in Sponsorship, Structure, and Cost: Fifteen Case Studies of Shared Living

The spread of the Share-A-Home model was discussed in the preceding chapter, with attention to how the idea has taken root through the efforts of the founder and the publicity in newspaper and magazine articles, television reports, and items in church bulletins. In the course of our research, we repeatedly received information about other shared group homes. When we reported some of our findings at conferences and professional meetings, often a member of the audience would give us a new "lead." We found that many sponsoring groups throughout the country had recognized the same housing need for the elderly in their communities and had developed similar projects to solve it. We learned of many group homes in other areas, and whenever we were in the vicinity of a shared living project, we would visit it and interview the sponsors and residents. Altogether, we visited forty different shared living homes in the United States and fifteen in Great Britain.

On first examination, the cases seemed very distinctive and diverse, with each having its individual characteristics: We asked: how can these diverse kinds of cases be organized into a framework for classification and analysis? What are the fundamental structural characteristics that can be used to make sense of the disparate materials? Are there any underlying properties that can be used to create at least a preliminary taxonomy?

First, it should be noted that all of the facilities share some basic characteristics: they have the goal of providing a noninstitutional kind of living arrangement for older persons in a homelike setting. Second, the population is characterized by the term "frail," for the median age in almost all facilities we have studied is over eighty years. The clientele are ambulatory and have a degree of independence that is not characteristic of the typical nursing home resident.

Our scheme for classifying the group homes (shown in table 6.1) employs two major variables: the nature of the sponsorship and the type of housing stock in which they are located. Since small group homes are almost never organized by the residents themselves, the sponsoring organization is of paramount importance. In our studies we found four main types of sponsorship: public, religious, secular-charitable, and proprietary. These categories have a degree of ambiguity because sometimes they overlap in their characteristics. For example, a category designated as secular-charitable may be composed of people with religious motivation.

In this chapter, we will present fifteen examples of shared housing established by groups that were unaffiliated with Share-A-Home of America or with each other. We have conducted site visits to all of the projects except Senior Village in Phoenix, Small Group Homes in Hawaii, and Home Close in Great Britain. These examples of shared housing show how the local initiative and community response in many different localities meet the needs of their older citizens.

CLASSIFICATION OF SHARED LIVING HOMES

Public Sponsorship. Most of the shared living projects have been started by individuals or small groups of private citizens, most of which had a religious affiliation. A small number, however, have been initiated by government bodies. The following two cases illustrate this category, for one is sponsored by a state agency and one by a local government. Both of these projects were started principally to save the costs of institutional care of older persons. Shared homes of this type are more apt to have professional guidance than homes started by individuals in the community.

CASE 1. SENIOR VILLAGE, PHOENIX, ARIZONA. A unique housing project was initiated in Phoenix, Arizona, by the Maricopa County Board of Supervisors in 1981. Called Senior Village, it consists of a cluster of

TABLE 6.1. *Classification of Shared Living Homes*

Type of Housing Stock	Sponsorship			
	Public	Private		
		religious	secular-charitable	proprietary
Built for purpose		Robineau Residence Skokie, Ill.		
Single-family homes	Senior Village, Phoenix, Ariz. Enriched Housing, N.Y., N.Y.	Wellsboro Shared Homes, Pa. Small Group Homes, Hawaii Weinfeld Residence, Evanston, Ill. Community Housing for the Elderly, Philadelphia Geriatric Center Group Homes, Washington, D.C.	Share-A-Home, Fla. Abbeyfield Society, England Shared Living, Boston Small Group Homes, Frederick, Md.	
Contained within a larger unit	Home Close, England (in old people's home)			The Shores Bradenton, Fla. (in retirement facility)
Adaptation of facility built for other purpose	Village Green, Greensboro, N.C. (built as a hotel)		Sunset Lodge, Ark. (old motel) Ithacare, N.Y. (Old hospital)	Mt. Vernon Lodge, Ocala, Fla. (old motel)

nine homes housing forty-five elderly people. The project received an impetus from a member of the County Board of Supervisors. This board also serves as the governing board for the County Flood Control District. As a result of the purchase of a number of tracts of land as a part of flood control operations, the county acquired the land and houses, which stood empty for a time. At this same time, the County Board of Supervisors (which, under Arizona law, is responsible for the health care of indigent elderly persons) had commissioned a study of nursing home residents whose fees were subsidized by the county. It was found that many people in the nursing homes really did not need nursing care, but had no other place to live. Thus, it was decided to search for alternatives, and the supervisor involved put together the two problems—what to do with the nine empty houses, and how to give supportive housing to frail elderly people. Senior Village was established with the conviction that this kind of an environment would give assistance and support, yet enable the residents to live an independent, noninstitutional lifestyle.

The residents are ambulatory and are provided with their main meal at midday, but are able to prepare their own breakfast and light supper. They are responsible for their own rooms. The specific day-to-day activities are under the direction of a manager, who lives on the premises. The County Health Department is the supervising agency for this project, and it employs an executive director, who oversees all operations.

As the county supervisor said,

The end result is keeping people who are mentally alert and who have all of their faculties together in one setting. In this way, they can enjoy the company of one another and not be subject to possible depression by being in close proximity with the senile and the physically impaired—i.e., those unable to take care of their personal needs. (Campbell 1981).

The houses had to be renovated and furnished. This was accomplished as a community project and involved the cooperation of church groups, civic groups, and neighborhood volunteers, who donated their time and also raised funds for the purchase of equipment, furniture, and appliances. The residents could bring their own furniture, but the first group, having come from nursing homes, was not well supplied.

The project was started through use of revenue-sharing funds from the Board of Supervisors and an Administration on Aging grant. The funds for the home health aides came from the Area Agency on Aging and one-time start-up costs from revenue sharing. Since the supervising agency for this project is the County Health Department/Long Term Care, the residents receive health services provided by home health aides, supervised by visiting RNs, plus visiting physicians, twice monthly. If a serious medical problem arises, the staff are able to refer the resident to the county hospital or primary care center for any assistance that may be required. Prescribed medications are also available.

The fees for housing each resident average $333 a month, which includes utilities, food, housing, maintenance, and staff. This cost is expected to increase to $415 per month when the project becomes self-sufficient. Senior Village has been operating since November 1981 as a demonstration project, and the current planning is to make the overall project as self-supporting as possible.

Those residents who may have income through social security or SSI are asked to pay according to their income, the size of the room, and the number of occupants in the house. The county is not responsible for subsidizing housing for income-eligible persons residing outside the nursing home.

The Phoenix project has kept careful statistics on turnover, which are of interest because they show how this population is subject to rapid changes, and how "solutions" to their problems may be of short duration. Since eighteen of the residents had come from nursing homes, it was obviously a very frail group of people. In the first fourteen months of operation, twenty-four residents were discharged from Senior Village: four died, eight went to nursing homes, seven to community/independent living, four to structured room-and-board care homes, and one to adult foster care. The turnover in this kind of housing demonstrates the necessity for a project supervisor. It would be unreasonable to expect volunteers to perform the functions of phasing residents in and out of the houses in a project of this size.

A rich array of activities has been organized, including monthly potluck dinners at a nearby church, bingo twice a week, a monthly birthday party for the residents, making and selling of pine cone wreaths in the months before Christmas, a weekly trip to the library with transportation by volunteers, assistance of residents in mailing out church bulletins, parties on holidays, and trips to the movies, theater, and museums. The Senior Village Activity Club raised almost $2,000 from craft sales and a rummage sale, which was used for ceiling fans and social events, such as birthday parties.

To illustrate the effects of this environment on some of the residents, we will quote four cases from the Senior Village quarterly reports (Pierson 1982):

Eighty-three years old, arthritic referred from nursing home. Family states she seldom got out of bed since 1969. She still moves slowly, but now takes care of own room and laundry, assists with minor chores, walks to meals and exercise program, beginning to attend Adult Center for bridge, arranges transportation on dial-a-ride, arranges weekly hair appointments.

Eighty-eight-year-old lady residing in nursing home until her assets were depleted. Multiple medical problems. Referred to Senior Village. Attended peer fitness training. Enjoys visiting a variety of Senior Centers. Is taking charge of planning a Senior Village Rummage Sale.

Seventy-nine-year-old bachelor, no family, referred from Maricopa Medical Center after suffering a stroke. Continues to be a loner, but no longer afraid of group activities. Participated in field trip to Prescott and Pinewood. Loves the outdoors and enjoys sitting under the trees in his backyard and reading. Has taken charge of the watering of the yards for all the residents.

Seventy-seven-year-old referral from Public Fiduciary. Was unable to ambulate without walker and lacked motivation to do anything except stay in her room. She now has taken charge of her house's kitchen duties and chores, on her own motivation, attends activities, has forgotten need of walker for ambulation.

The creation of Senior Village and involvement of many voluntary agencies and persons from the community not only got the project in operation and provided very satisfactory housing for the elderly, but had another effect—that of "consciousness raising." It focused an awareness in the community of the needs of frail older persons and resulted in a cadre of concerned, sympathetic community members. Volunteers come to the houses to assist in social events and holiday celebrations and to provide transportation. Thus a project that received its first impetus through fiscal considerations has had many other positive effects.

In summary, the executive director, Ann Pierson, told us,

Many of these people are enjoying a higher quality of life than they had in a nursing home. A number might be called the 'new poor'—those who have had their savings wiped away by illness, and who have needed some sort of public support for the first time in their lives. Now, living in their own little homes in Senior Village, they have their pride back again. (Pierson 1983)

She added that at first there was great wariness on the part of both professionals and people in the community as to whether unrelated adults could live together, but after a year of operation, everyone is enthusiastic. It is hoped that another village can be set up elsewhere in the county.

In conclusion, this project is an excellent example of the cooperation between public and private resources: the Board of Supervisors, the County Health Department, and community volunteers.

CASE 2. ENRICHED HOUSING, NEW YORK. The New York State Department of Social Services has developed a network of shared housing, called Enriched Housing, designed to prevent unnecessary institutionalization and, at the same time, take advantage of the positive aspects inherent in small neighborhood facilities. Of the ten approved projects in New York State, several are aimed specifically at frail elderly persons and all are based upon a realization that such small neighborhood facilities are less expensive than other alternatives.

Enriched Housing in Schenectady, New York, was established by the twenty-eight member churches of the Schenectady Inner City Ministry (SICM) to help frail elderly persons continue to live in their community. Seed money for the project came from a grant from the state of New York in the amount of $1,000 per resident and a $3,000 grant from the Cooperative Living for Older Persons (CLOP) program of the American Baptist Churches U.S.A. Other sources of seed money included grants from local churches and foundations and the United Fund. In addition, local churches, both within the SICM organization and nonmember churches, were instrumental in providing the furnishings for the project.

In December 1979, the authors were asked by the director of the CLOP program to make an analysis of the Schenectady program based upon our knowledge of other shared living facilities. At the time of our involvement, SICM had rented three-bedroom apartments in three separate locations in the Schenectady area. Each of the households is expected to be independent, and residents are expected to make whatever house rules seem appropriate.

Each apartment has the services of a housekeeper four hours a day, five days per week. The housekeeper helps with cooking, shopping, cleaning, and personal grooming, but the residents are encouraged to do whatever they can for themselves. Transportation is provided by SICM volunteers by appointment, and residents are visited by a registered nurse at least once a week. Recreation and outside activities are organized by SICM and the project director and include such things as concerts, movies, and social gatherings.

Enriched Housing has been approved by New York for Supplemental Security Income payments for low-income residents. This makes the program available to a large number of people who would otherwise not be able to afford such living arrangements. The monthly cost of Enriched Housing is $450 (1981), which includes a private room, food, transportation, housekeeping services, and a variety of SICM-provided social services. With state approval, residents are allowed to keep $55 of their SSI check for personal expenses, and the remainder is used to pay the monthly fees. Any deficit is paid by the state of New York.

One problem with shared living facilities is that, because subsidy funding is rare, organizers of such facilities must offer services based upon the potential residents' ability to pay for those services and not upon the potential residents' need for those services. This sharply reduces the number of persons who can or will move into such a facility. It is interesting that even though Enriched Housing seems to have developed a subsidy funding source, the program still has had difficulty attracting residents. The intriguing question is: why?

Probably the major reason is that Enriched Housing, like other forms of group housing for the elderly, may have a stigma attached to it that is similar to that attached to nursing homes. Because of the newness of these group projects, the general public does not yet accept or understand them. One might expect that there will be greater acceptance of this form of shared housing as the projects become a relatively stable part of the community.

Persons organizing group housing of this type are aware that it is important for the residents to be socially and personally compatible if the living arrangement is to work out. So, one of the problems of Enriched Housing is locating compatible persons who can live together in close proximity even though they are not related to one another and have not known one another before being brought together by the organizers.

The social worker managing Enriched Housing in Schenectady stated that probably half of the applicants for Enriched Housing do not have satisfactory interpersonal skills to live harmoniously with nonrelated persons in a small apartment. This situation, in her judgment, is not the result of the aging process but is a lifelong situation, and these persons have encountered interpersonal problems and difficulties throughout their adult years.

She noted that Enriched Housing, like other alternative living arrangements for the elderly, is one of the last housing choices people wish to make. Most persons would prefer to stay in their own homes and regard the sharing of bath and other facilities as a problem. Because of financial considerations, however, Enriched Housing has many positive features, and it is to be recommended from the standpoint of both the residents and the community at large. Still, there is a very strong emotional attraction to the idea of living independently even when that arrangement is inappropriate. Until, and unless, that attraction is overcome, by either increasing frailty or familiarity with group projects, elderly residents will continue to be disinclined to move to such facilities as Enriched Housing.

Another subject of some concern to the Enriched Housing organizers is the issue of integration of residents by sex and race. The social worker and the residents of one home told the authors they do not wish to have a sex-integrated home. The major reason for this is a feeling of modesty and privacy, which would be jeopardized if a man lived in the close quarters of a small three-bedroom apartment with two women. Racial integration is a possibility in some alternative living situations, but one would have to be careful in selecting the residents for a racially integrated home so that all parties feel comfortable in such a situation. Several houses have black staff, and it was the judgment of the social worker that some residents could live in an integrated household. Beyond the residents themselves, however, the question of a racially integrated home impinges upon the neighborhood and its residents, and also the landlord. In some neighborhoods, a racially integrated household might jeopardize the success of the project. Therefore, one would have to be diplomatic in organizing such a project in a neighborhood that seems hostile to racial integration.

Enriched Housing is interesting because it has, more or less successfully, combined public and private resources in order to establish a project that both sectors view as desirable. Because it is licensed by the state of New York, the government agencies may endorse the project as a money-saving venture; because it provides housing for the poor elderly, the churches of SICM may freely support the project as a "good Christian" endeavor. It is this support from both government and church, lacking in many other shared living projects, that has been responsible for the overall success of the Schenectady Enriched Housing program.

Religious Sponsorship. Group homes for the elderly have received considerable support from religious organizations that have taken the initiative in local communities to organize this form of housing. The illustrations in this section show how both large and small organizations with varying resources, with or without professional help, can successfully start and operate the homes. Local congregations, federations of social service networks with religious affiliations, and diocesan support enable shared homes for the elderly to get started. As missionary work overseas has diminished in many churches, there is interest in "missionary work at home"—projects designed to benefit people in the local community.

CASE 3. WELLSBORO SHARED HOMES, PENNSYLVANIA. Small-town living at its best is exemplified in the organization of the Lucy Austin Shared Home in Wellsboro, Pennsylvania. This was organized by members of the Baptist church with no knowledge of any other groups who were setting up shared living facilities. It was initiated through the efforts of a local physician who was also a member of the Baptist church. He had become concerned about the ability of some of his elderly patients to live alone. The gracious old mansion, over a hundred years old, had previously been used as a nursing home. When it was closed, the physician purchased it and made a gift of it to the church (for which he received a tax deduction). It was then remodeled by the Baptist church, and Wellsboro Shared Homes, Inc. was created as a nonprofit sponsor. The facility is not licensed. It followed the typical pattern in that applicants were slow in coming for the first few months. By the end of the first year, however, it was full, with sixteen residents. After two years of operation, it is still full and there is a waiting list.

Most of the residents are women, and they range in age from the early seventies to the nineties. The project charges a flat fee of $350 (as of 1983) regardless of the kind of room occupied (whether it is private or shared). The rent includes food, utilities, and housing expenses. Some residents are subsidized by the church because they cannot pay the full monthly fee, and several are on welfare.

The Lucy Austin Home, sponsored by Wellsboro Shared Homes in Wellsboro, Pennsylvania, was erected in 1881 as a private mansion. Located on the brow of a hill overlooking the town, it houses sixteen elderly people. The home is organized by the Baptist church, whose members take an active part in visiting the home and giving social supports to the residents.

The members of the Baptist church are active in the house, coming regularly to visit and take the residents for outings and church functions. The pastor and his wife bring new residents to the house to introduce them to the "family." They often come to eat a meal with the group, and they also explain the regulations to new members. There is a list of twenty volunteers to come and stay at the house if the evening staff person wants a night off. A member of the board of directors comes to eat lunch with the group once a week. The manager told us,

> They have a meeting afterwards, and have a chance to air requests about the physical structure—"We need a stair railing"; "I need a fan"; and the like. They also have a chance to air grievances or emotional problems, and complain about the staff. Recently they talked over their feelings about the death of someone in the house. Then the board member has a meeting with the staff the same day, so that if there are any messages to be communicated, they will be transmitted.

At first, the staff couple lived in the house, but the constant around-the-clock responsibility was too much of a strain. A teenager was then hired to sleep in an upstairs room and be on emergency call for assistance. The sponsors hope to hire a newly retired person for this responsibility. Two cooks are employed—one works from 7:00 A.M. to 3:00 P.M. and one from 3:00 P.M. to 7:00 P.M.

The first manager had formerly been a county commissioner for eight years and the county treasurer for four years. The involvement of the local physician (who is on call for the house), the pastor, and a former county official obviously gives the project great legitimacy and allays the fears of potential residents about moving into the house. Because the first manager was familiar with county government, he knew how to pilot the project through the bureaucracy when it was being set up.

Residents are urged to take part in the household tasks. When we visited the house, we observed that one elderly man was working in a vegetable garden, and a group was sitting in lawn chairs in the sunshine, chatting and watching him. It was a leisurely and companionable atmosphere. Everyone seemed glad to see us and exclaimed about their good fortune in living there. People strolled through the kitchen where the cook was preparing dinner, and one resident was setting the table.

The procedures for selection of tenants have been changed, for originally only one person interviewed the prospective residents. It was later felt, however, that perhaps the selection process had been too lenient.

Now three people conduct the interview to be sure the resident has the mental and physical health suitable for group living.

The Wellsboro home is another example of how older buildings can be adapted, for the sponsors renovated the large two-story mansion, which needed many repairs. The commodious character means it can accommodate enough people to make the project viable. In this way, the monthly cost can be kept at a very modest figure. On the other hand, the second floor and lack of an elevator pose potential problems. However, we were told that no one to date has had to move because he could not manage the stairs.

If space is available, this home also serves older persons who are discharged from the hospital and need a temporary place to stay, or older persons whose families are on vacation.

The Wellsboro Shared Homes project is an excellent example of grass roots initiative and community participation.

CASE 4. SMALL GROUP HOMES IN HAWAII. Small Group Homes in Hawaii is a project successfully mixing people from different cultures and ethnic groups: Caucasian, Oriental, and Filipino. Sponsored by Catholic Social Service, the project opened its first house in 1978. Within two years, six homes were filled, housing twenty-three people, with a waiting list of eighty. In 1983, there were eight houses and thirty-one residents. Most of the residents are on Social Security, SSI, or disability pensions. The residents are generally younger than those described in the other shared living groups, for they range from 51 to 72. The group includes displaced homemakers and men who have taken early retirement because of health problems.

The homes are former single-family dwellings located in residential neighborhoods. They are not licensed. Residents do their own cooking and shopping. The project director visits the group one or more times a week and has a weekly house meeting at which residents bring up any problems and plan five dinner menus—from Monday to Friday. The residents take turns in pairs cooking the five dinners from the menus they have agreed upon. Shopping is done by two or three persons, sometimes with the project director. Breakfast, lunch, and weekend meals are the individual responsibility of the residents.

Residents contribute their weekly share for the five dinners, and the average rental cost in 1983 was $210 a month, with a range of $180 to

$230. The cost varies according to the size and desirability of the person's room, and whether it has a private bathroom.

The leases on the houses are signed by Catholic Social Service. There have been so many applications to join the houses (150 in the first year) that the project director can select carefully and consider who will fit in most easily. The groups are chosen partly on need and partly on compatibility.

The project started after a group of community leaders in the field of aging met in 1977–78 to look at gaps in the field of housing and social services. According to Barbara Khurana, director of the project (1980), they identified a need for housing in a noninstitutional setting that was suitable for all of the ethnic groups. A local foundation assisted in providing seed money. The majority of referrals came from social workers in hospitals, nurses, home care personnel, and the Area Agency on Aging. People also heard about the project through newspaper stories, radio shows, television, fliers, etc.

Khurana (1980) reports that although most joined the group primarily because of economic reasons or ill health, they developed friendly relations and came to view the facility as their home. The organizers decided at the outset not to have a group home in a house owned by one of the residents, for they wanted everyone to feel equal ownership and pride in their new environment. They felt that owners would tend to exert too much authority about what was permitted in "their" house with "their" furniture.

This project is notable for its exceptionally good cooperation with community agencies and its successful mix of different ethnic groups. Because of the younger age of the residents, they have not needed a housekeeper or as many supportive services as the residents of other shared living projects we have studied. This results in lower monthly charges.

CASE 5. WEINFELD AND ROBINEAU RESIDENCES, ILLINOIS. Among the most notable successes in shared living for the elderly are the two residences in the Chicago area: Weinfeld Group Living Residence in Evanston and Robineau Group Living Residence in Skokie, Illinois, sponsored by the Council for Jewish Elderly, an affiliate of the Jewish Federation of Metropolitan Chicago. These houses bear some similarities to the other shared living facilities described in this book, but also differ in important ways.

The major difference between Weinfeld and Robineau and other experiments is that their sponsorship has deep roots in metropolitan Chicago and particularly in the Jewish community of the greater Chicago area. The Jewish Federation, founded in 1902, provides the fund-raising, allocating, and planning structure for the major Jewish social welfare, education, culture, and medical care for the Chicago area. It has its own annual fund campaign, and it is also a beneficiary of the United Way.

The Council for Jewish Elderly has a board of directors of 45 people and over 20,000 members as part of its corporate group. It has a staff of 320 full-time people, of whom 80 are professionals. In addition, over 400 volunteers assist in the programs. The council has a professionally prepared plan, which provides a general mandate for its activities. It has over twenty different services, including home health services, neighborhood drop-in centers, senior centers, information and referral, social and health assessment, casework counseling, legal assistance, home-delivered meals, religious activities, employment services, and a broadly based community education program. Day care for the elderly is provided in a specially designed facility. It also operates a 240-bed skilled nursing facility, which in effect completes the comprehensive long-term care system.

The funding for these many programs comes from diverse sources, including fees paid by the elderly and their families, rents, voluntary contributions, third-party payments, and funds available through programs administered by the U.S. government and the Illinois State Department of Aging.

Weinfeld Residence is the natural development of a social/health service agency that provides a multiplicity of services for older people, both in their homes and in the community. The agency is aware of the need for a continuum of care and living arrangements. Weinfeld is simply one phase of the continuum. Because the agency controls such a wide variety of service programs, it is possible to meet the changing needs of older people as they become more frail or more independent.

Weinfeld Residence was remodeled from six two-bedroom townhouses, and it houses twelve elderly people. Each apartment has two bedrooms, a living room, kitchenette, and bathroom. A small addition was constructed to combine the townhouse complex, and connecting walls were broken through to open the entire facility to the residents. A living room area was converted into communal space for all the residents, and another living room was converted into the communal dining room (see figure 6.1). This is another example of the flexible use of existing housing.

The project has a high degree of community support, financial backing, sophisticated planning, and highly trained professional staff who are knowledgeable about the kinds of services needed by the elderly. Weinfeld is only one of many services and activities of the Council for Jewish Elderly. It is important to keep this in mind when evaluating this facility in relation to other shared living models described in this book. Most of them have been started by single persons or small groups that had limited expertise in the housing and service field and often only limited professional backup. Weinfeld, however, had the financial and professional support of a large constituency who were supportive of the other programs of the sponsoring agency.

The residents of the house are very similar to those of the other shared living units we visited: most are women, and the average age is 82 (range from 79 to 92). Few of the residents are able to pay the full cost of the monthly charges, even those who have Social Security benefits and also income supplements from their families. The Jewish Federation subsidizes the difference between the monthly income paid by residents and their families and the true economic costs. In March 1983, the monthly charge was $875 per month. This includes room, board, and the full range of services provided by CJE.

The procedure for becoming a resident of Weinfeld is more formalized than for all of the other shared living arrangements that we studied. A person wishing to live in the home is interviewed by a social worker, who makes an evaluation of the social, emotional, family, and financial status of the applicant. The family is also interviewed. A nurse also meets the person and makes a judgment concerning level of physical functioning and ability to take his or her own medications. A letter from a personal physician is required, stating that the person is generally in good health. The person must state that she wishes to maintain an independent living status, and a summary assessment is made whether the person will be independent in all activities of family living and is

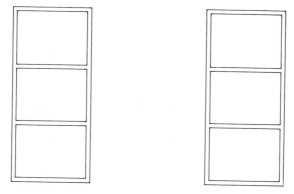

BEFORE: Six townhouses; Three 2-bedroom apartments in each unit, separated by a courtyard.

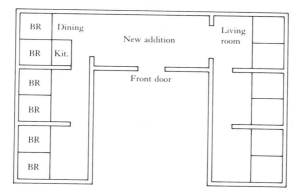

AFTER: Connecting structure joins two units. It contains kitchen, dining and living room. Doorways added to join all units together.

FIGURE 6.1. *Weinfeld Residence Remodeling*

capable of handling his or her own personal needs. The ability of the elderly person to "fit in" is one of the paramount considerations.

Financial arrangements and contracts are similar to those provided in a traditional landlord/tenant relationship. Residents have considerable freedom in coming and going. However, they are requested to alert staff to their anticipated time of departure and return. Three kosher meals a day are served on a schedule, but breakfast may be prepared by the person herself if she wishes. All other cooking is done by a staff

Robineau Residence in Skokie, Illinois, sponsored by the Council for Jewish Elderly, an affiliate of the Jewish Federation of Metropolitan Chicago, is the first purpose-built shared residence in the United States. Carefully designed to house twenty-four elderly people, it fits well into the neighborhood and avoids an institutional appearance.

cook. On occasion a resident may prepare some special dish, and residents have specific chores, such as setting the table, cleaning up after a meal, and helping with the dishes. Residents have responsibility for the upkeep of their own bedrooms, and they may offer a small amount of help in other rooms, but the major household chores, laundry, shopping, etc. are taken care of by a housekeeper or other paid staff. A staff coordinator is in the residence daily; at night a staff person, usually a student, is on the premises.

The day-to-day life of Weinfeld is very similar to that observed in Share-A-Home, except that there is more professional coordination. The residents share a common life and life style. They develop friends and rivals, share joys and sorrows. The achievements of children and grandchildren are part of the everyday conversation, and so many good times are shared that the loneliness of old age is reduced. As Judith

Wax quoted a Weinfeld resident in her lead *New York Times Magazine* article: "It's like your own home here" (1976).

The executive vice-president of the Council for Jewish Elderly, Ronald Weismehl, told us:

We first had a live-in "house parent" type of manager for the facility, but that did not work. Now we have a "coordinator" who is responsible for the operation of the house, oversees everything, orders the food, meets with the residents, answers their questions, and handles interpersonal difficulties. This person must be a "generalist"—specialized training in social work or in nursing does not lend itself to the role. It's hard to define this position. The main issues concern relationships with people and the need for objectivity about people and situations. A mature, motherly woman is best. (Streib 1980)

In addition, the house employs a cook and housekeeper and is visited regularly by a dietitian and social worker.

In 1978 the Council for Jewish Elderly decided that because Weinfeld was such a successful experiment in group living, it would erect a purpose-built structure in Skokie, the suburb adjacent to Evanston. Some funding for the project was obtained from the U.S. government through Section 202 of the Housing Law administered by the Department of Housing and Urban Development. A site was located and then the long and difficult process began to secure permission from the Village Board of Trustees to build a shared living facility for twenty-four elderly on five building lots. Two of the lots were zoned for commercial use and three for residential use. The staff of the Jewish Council prepared a very detailed plan for the building and the surrounding area to present at the public hearings held by the Plan Commission and the Village Board of Trustees. The report on the Plan Commission meeting of February 15, 1979, comprises twenty-three single-spaced typed pages and does not include all the supporting documentation: maps, drawings, brochures, photographs (including an aerial map), and newspaper reports about Weinfeld.

A group of experts attended the meeting to present the case for the zoning change: a lawyer, an appraiser, the architect, a social worker who administers Weinfeld, and the executive vice-president of the Council for Jewish Elderly. The members of the Plan Commission asked the sworn witnesses for additional details after the formal presentations.

Interested citizens and residents from the neighborhood asked questions or made statements about the perceived negative impact upon property values, the appearance, the setback from the street, the number and kinds of residents, the number of parking spaces, the number of employees and the number of cars they would drive, the amount of truck traffic, location of air conditioners, paving of the back alley and the increased width of the alley, the disposal of garbage and refuse, and the amount of kitchen odors that might be generated by a kitchen for twenty-four persons. One neighbor expressed the anxiety that residents might wander around the neighborhood in their night clothes. A reading of the minutes of the hearing suggests both skepticism and hostility indicative of ageism. It is perhaps surprising to learn that there were objections to such an admirable program for housing ambulatory elderly women—the grandmothers of a community.

The Skokie village trustees approved the zoning variance, and Robineau was constructed and opened in 1981. Its twenty-four residents have a program and activities similar to Weinfeld. Robineau is the only purpose-built shared living home in the United States that we have located in our research.

One of the residents stated in an interview with a newspaper correspondent:

This isn't a nursing home. You're free to go and do as you please. For a day or two I felt sorry for myself. . . . I gave up my home, and it was a nice home. But my friends are impressed. They say I sound more cheerful since I've been here. (Simons 1982)

This description indicates that Weinfeld Residence and Robineau Residence are excellent examples of how caring, well-trained professionals can develop coordinated shared living homes that are not institutionalized, operate as family-like groups, meet the needs of the elderly in an attractive setting, and are located in residential neighborhoods close to community services.

CASE 6. COMMUNITY HOUSING FOR THE ELDERLY—THE PHILADELPHIA GERIATRIC CENTER. Many older cities have street after street of run-down row houses in declining neighborhoods. This example shows how they can be remodeled and brought back to serve a new and important purpose. The Philadelphia Geriatric Center (PGC), as part of its many community activities, has developed intermediate housing adjacent to the campus of the center to provide shared living for the elderly. A federal subsidy aided in financing the conversion of ten inexpensive row homes in the area adjoining the parent geriatric institution.

The "236" Rehabilitation Program of the Federal Housing Administration also made it possible to rent 40 percent of the apartments at reduced rates to low-income tenants, as in public housing (Brody 1978).

Each home now contains three separated bed-sitting rooms, with a kitchenette and a toilet-shower. The three tenants share the front entrance and a common living room. They have a "hot line" phone to the nurses' station in case of emergencies, and they have access to many of the services and activities in the Philadelphia Geriatric Center. They can purchase optional services at nominal, nonprofit prices, such as frozen kosher meals, which are home delivered, or light housekeeping services from the PGC (Brody 1978). They can do their own shopping and housekeeping if they wish. The elderly people who chose to live here were persons who had lived alone, had fears about security in their original neighborhoods, and wanted more social contacts.

Social services included emotional support, mediating of disputes between tenants, and referral to community resources such as shopping services or medical care. The project office also was a focal point for socialization, and the tenants participated in the numerous social, recreational, and religious events sponsored by the PGC. Thus, the proximity of the housing to the large geriatric center was a definite asset (Brody and Liebowitz 1981).

The research team at the PGC kept a twenty-four-week log of the nature, number, and duration of the tenants' contact with the staff. The greatest number of contacts occurred during the first weeks of occupancy but dropped by half in later weeks.

According to Powell Lawton, intermediate housing has the advantage of keeping people in familiar surroundings because it is located in existing housing stock in the neighborhood. "Independence, security, social opportunities, and the group support of the sponsoring organization offer a rare combination of both support and relative autonomy," he stated (Lawton 1981:75). "Privacy is adequate, but can be problematic at times as a consequence of sharing of some space."

CASE 7. SHARED LIVING FACILITIES HOUSED IN HIGH-RISE BUILDINGS: GROUP HOME PROGRAM, WASHINGTON, D.C. Another example of the flexibility of shared living is the use of high-rise apartment buildings to house such arrangements. Although we know of no project that utilizes an entire high-rise building for "family" groups, there are several projects that have organized shared living facilities in one (or several) apartments within a single housekeeping unit. The size of the group is governed by the space available, but as a general statement, shared living facilities in high-rise buildings rarely have fewer than three residents or more than five residents per housekeeping unit.

Perhaps the best example of a high-rise shared living facility is the Group Home Program organized by the Jewish Council for the Aging of Greater Washington, Inc. (JCA). This group has sponsored several three-member housekeeping units in various locations around the Washington, D.C., metropolitan area. The JCA Group Home Program was established because the organizers were convinced that there were people in the area who, for a variety of reasons, were not capable of living alone but did not require institutionalization.

JCA was established in 1973 as a transportation service for elderly persons living in and around Washington, D.C. This was expanded to include an information and referral service for persons needing services from other agencies. The organizers noticed that many of the requests for information involved persons who were in need of housing or in need of housekeeping services. These persons were being forced out of their present living arrangements by condominium conversions, high rents, or simply increasing frailty. The JCA decided that it would be appropriate for the agency to rent an apartment and establish a group living arrangement.

The first apartment was rented in 1974 and was located in Washington, D.C. Since that time, JCA has expanded its project to include twelve separate apartments in Washington, D.C., and Maryland, housing a total of thirty-two persons. Residents pay $430 per month in Maryland and $450 per month in Washington (1980). Since only about a third of the original residents could afford the fees, HUD Section 8 assistance was applied for and received. In Maryland, the state also shares in the cost of subsidizing the residents. Thus, state and federal programs are used to help low-income elderly persons reside in group living arrangements.

However, the fees charged are not the full cost of the services provided. It was estimated that the actual cost of housing one resident in one of the apartments in Maryland in 1980 was $519 per month. While the state and federal programs help the resident pay the difference between a percentage of his or her income and $430 per month, JCA is responsible for the difference between $430 and $519 ($89) per resident per month. Grants from private foundations and other sources have enabled JCA to meet this financial responsibility with little difficulty, but the point is this: without the financial and organizational assistance of JCA, the entire program would be in jeopardy.

In day-to-day matters, the Group Home Program is much like New York's Enriched Housing program (although the JCA program predates Enriched Housing by six years). Each resident has his or her own bedroom, and each separate household has a housekeeper who works four hours a day, five days a week. Each of the residents is encouraged to be as independent as is possible, so the level of support provided by JCA varies widely among the different apartments. However, no medical services are provided.

One of the more interesting aspects of the JCA program is its approach to government regulatory agencies. With no state government to deal with, the apartments in Washington, D.C., are essentially without regulation. However, the Maryland state regulations require a professional staff (i.e., social worker, dietitian, etc.) in group homes with more than three persons over the age of 64. Since none of the JCA apartments has more than three persons, the project "falls between the cracks" of the licensing laws. To legitimize the project, however, the JCA has voluntarily submitted the program to review by the appropriate agencies and has received what is called "project approval" from the state of Maryland. Essentially, this process allows the state to endorse the organizational aspects of a program while not forcing it formally to license the practical aspects.

One of the most serious problems identified by the organizers is in the area of compatibility. The persons living in the apartment must be able to live cooperatively or the project will not be successful. The task of judging the compatibility of potential residents often falls upon persons who have little formal training in such matters. As the authors were told: "It is hard to find people who can live in close quarters without becoming irritable." Here again, attracting suitable residents and screening out unsuitable persons is one of the major organizational tasks performed by the organizers.

The JCA Group Home Program is interesting for a number of reasons. It houses residents in apartments located in more or less "high-rise" buildings. Thus, it has created a microsocial environment within the impersonality of the larger social environment of the building, and it has provided lower income elderly with housing that is better than what the person could afford if left to his or her own resources. In addition, it has dealt with the regulatory agencies in such a way as to enjoy the benefits of government approval without becoming bogged down in the restrictions of government regulation.

Secular-Charitable Sponsorship. Another form of sponsorship of small group homes is by nonprofit corporations and charitable community groups. Many of the Share-A-Homes and Abbeyfield Society houses in England would be classified in this category. The first example in this section is the Boston Shared Living Project sponsored by the Gray Panthers and the Back Bay Aging Concerns Committee–Young and Old, a civic organization composed of representatives of many groups. While we call this category "secular-charitable," the sponsors often have a strong religious motivation. In some communities, service clubs have also been involved in initiating and sponsoring small group homes for the elderly.

CASE 8. SHARED LIVING PROJECT, BOSTON. A unique experiment in shared living is found in Boston, where the emphasis is on intergenerational living. Another important consideration, however, is the fact that it is a small, successful part of a larger movement toward urban renewal and what planners have called "gentrification." Many cities have mounted such efforts to halt the decay of the central cities, and to keep the urban neighborhoods viable.

This project has been fortunate in being sponsored by two dedicated, involved, idealistic groups, the Back Bay Aging Concerns Committee (BBACC) and the Gray Panthers of Greater Boston. They have given a great deal of professional assistance, encouragement, and help in the fund raising.

The project was first considered when, in August 1977, the Department of Health, Education, and Welfare granted $15,000 to BBACC and the Gray Panthers of Greater Boston for the purpose of exploring the development of intergenerational cooperative living arrangements. After consideration of several alternatives, the present project was decided upon and the Shared Living Project began accepting residents in July 1979.

Seed money was provided by several funding agencies. In addition to the original grant for development of the idea, the other funding sources granted almost $45,000 to the project. The house was purchased by BBACC, a nonprofit corporation, with $118,320 in mortgage money loaned by the American Baptist Extension Corporation at a rate lower than the market level. In addition, a grant of $10,000 from an outside funding source was obtained to remodel the kitchen. Thus, the project has been assisted by financial support from a private foundation, a religious organization, and government grants.

The Shared Living Project attempts to provide housing for persons who would otherwise be pushed out of the neighborhood by rent increases and the limited availability of housing. The target population includes those persons "whose physical or emotional needs are more than they can provide for themselves."

Residents paid between $150 and $275 per month in 1982, depending upon size and location of the room. All bedrooms are single occupancy with shared bathrooms, living room, and kitchen facilities. There are no services provided by the project. The residents are responsible for all housekeeping chores, as well as the purchase and preparation of food. Residents are expected to eat one meal a week as a group. They must also attend a weekly house meeting where problems and interpersonal conflicts are discussed. The organizers of this project believe that group interaction and the use of a "house facilitator" may help keep intrahouse conflict to a minimum.

The Shared Living Project is a product of and is operated by BBACC. The residents are expected to take an active role in the day-to-day decision-making process, but policy and organizational decisions are made by BBACC. There is no live-in staff, since the residents are expected to perform household tasks themselves. The "house facilitator," in return for a free room in a carriage house adjacent to the main house, prepares an agenda for required weekly meetings and acts as mediator for in-house disputes.

As the project has evolved, several organizational crises have surfaced that have necessitated an adjustment in the original model. Originally, the project was to be completely autonomous of any organization. BBACC was to act in an advisory capacity, but the house residents were to be the "owners and operators" of their own house. After conferring with potential funding sources, it was determined that funds would not be granted for the purchase and renovation of a house unless there existed a relatively permanent nonprofit organization to take responsibility for the investment. BBACC thus became the owners and operators of the project.

Another problem developed when two persons living in the house when BBACC made the purchase refused to move. These two persons also refused to be a part of the Shared Living Project. An organizational dilemma surfaced because BBACC was formed, in part, to help those people forced out of their own neighborhoods by condominium conversions and new projects moving in. After considering the problem, the organizers decided to allow the two people to remain in the house as nonparticipating members of the project.

While the Boston Shared Living Project has received a great deal of national publicity as being intergenerational housing, only two persons under the age of 55 actually lived in the house in 1982. The two "facilitators" (a married couple who acted as managers) are also under 55, but they live in a carriage house studio apartment next to the main building. Furthermore, the term "intergenerational living" is subject to some question, since the group eats only one meal a week together. Because of the low rent and the very convenient location in the center of Boston, this project can easily find younger people willing to join the group. However, this is not "intergenerational living" as envisioned by family sociologists, even though residents are responsible for three chores a week and attend a weekly house meeting.

Another difficulty that the organizers faced which took a great deal of their time and effort was the attempt to obtain rent supplements under Section 8 of the Federal Housing Law, which provided for rent supplements for elderly, disabled, and handicapped persons. In this case, the law was strictly interpreted, and the Boston Shared Living Project could not obtain a waiver on its own, nor through the intervention of Congressman Edward R. Roybal. There were several reasons for this: first, the Boston project had sixteen residents, which exceeded the twelve-person limit stipulated by law. Second, some of the residents were younger, able-bodied people who were not covered by the law. The initial founders of the Boston project had an ideological and philosophical commitment to an intergenerational project and did not wish to change their goals. Finally, the Boston project was judged by the federal authorities to be essentially a rooming house and not a shared living fa-

The Shared Living Project in Boston is in an area near to the center of the city. Its convenient location makes it desirable as an intergenerational house. Originally a commodious single-family mansion, the house accommodates sixteen people, with the facilitator living in a carriage house behind (not shown).

cility, since the group did not eat together, except for one meal a week. The following year, in 1982, after a group of household members and sponsors made a trip to Washington, D.C., to seek eligibility of the house for Section 8 assistance, they finally obtained a waiver for this particular project. The Section 8 allocations for the Boston area were in short supply, however, and they were not immediately able to take advantage of the waiver.

The project in general has been very successful in providing low-cost housing to persons of mixed ages and in restoring a dilapidated old house to pleasant living conditions. Its population of elderly is not frail, as are those who live in other shared homes. This means that it has not had to provide services, for people are responsible for themselves and more or less "go their own way." One aspect of the age-integrated project is that the younger residents have their own private agendas and are more likely to be involved in outside activities than the older residents. This means that the facility has a centrifugal process at work, which tends to separate out the residents by age level.

The project has had strong ideological support and the advantages of subsidies and a low interest rate for the mortgage. The sponsors hope to start other projects if grants and suitable financial support can be obtained. In spite of the great amount of publicity this project has had as intergenerational living, we have not been able to locate any diffusion of the idea.

CASE 9. SMALL GROUP HOMES, FREDERICK, MARYLAND. Still another approach to housing the frail elderly has been initiated by Home Care Research, Inc., a private, nonprofit organization in Frederick, Maryland. As one of its many services offered in the health and welfare fields, it has developed several small group homes. Because the homes each contain only three elderly people, they are considered to be essentially private residences and do not come under the regulations for sheltered housing. Home Care Research is responsible for hiring the homemaker/health aides and other personnel needed, and it pays the house manager.

The homes do not intend to give twenty-four-hour-a-day supervision, for residents are expected to accept some responsibility for each other. Thus, no staff person stays in the home at night. Each person has a private bedroom, and there is a common living room, dining room, and kitchen. In short, the residents occupy a normal three-bedroom house that looks like any other house in the residential neighborhood.

The first house opened in 1978 with three women; a second one, which houses three men, opened in 1979. The monthly cost in 1980 was around $700, somewhat higher than some of the other shared living units we have described, but it must be remembered that this scheme uses paid employees and professionals, rather than relying only on community volunteers to organize and monitor it. Even so, it is about half the cost of many nursing homes.

Because existing homes are utilized in an age-integrated community, a comparatively normal family style is possible, according to Dr. Ruth Oltman, planning director. "The principle of 'minimum intrusion' prevails, so that the dynamic processes of the life cycle remain active, within individual limits, thus discouraging docility and passivity," says Oltman (1980:14). The homes allow the residents a large degree of control over their own lives and provide the supportive assistance of a semiprotected living environment.

Home Care Research, the sponsoring organization, hires a homemaker/health aide to come in four to five hours a day, seven days a week, to take care of planning and preparing meals, shopping, cleaning, laundry, yard work, and transportation. This is a private organization without outside funding; therefore it charges only what it costs to maintain the houses and contract other needed services. Home Care Research also maintains an ongoing evaluation of the program. Daily reports are required from the homemaker, a monthly report from the house manager, and there is frequent communication with the residents' families and physicians to promote preventive care.

The house manager coordinates the services, counsels residents, solves house problems, and arranges for needed services. A nurse-consultant visits the homes regularly to package prescribed medications so they are available on a daily schedule and serves as a liaison with the physician. The manager accompanies the resident to the doctor, if necessary.

Since Home Care Research is affiliated with Homecall, a licensed home health service which specializes in professional home services for older people, their small group homes have access to a host of services, many of which are covered by Medicare, Medicaid, group insurance, and workman's compensation. These services include nurses, a physical therapist, a speech therapist, and a social worker.

This is an interesting example of using formal business methods and procedures (such as the daily log) to foster and support "families" with an informal ambience. The sponsors wished to see if such experiments were cost effective. Although not designed to be money-making, they at least pay for themselves without public or private subsidies.

Proprietary Sponsorship. Sponsorship in which there is exclusive control or management in the hands of a single individual or corporation that operates for profit is classified as proprietary. To date, these types of organizations have not been active in the sponsorship of shared living for the elderly, largely because the profit possibilities are limited. If public monies should become available for shared housing, we would expect an increase of interest in proprietary sponsors, as occurred in the nursing home industry after Medicare and Medicaid funds became available. To date, there is no "shared living industry," and we expect that the very nature of the units—small, idiosyncratic and personalized— with "mom-and-pop" type of management, would preclude such a development.

In some states there are various kinds of small, profit-making adult care facilities similar to the shared living "families" we have been studying. However, research on private board and care facilities was not part of this study, although it is acknowledged that they often have similar characteristics in the day-to-day life of the homes.

Our examples of proprietary sponsorship will be discussed later in this chapter in the relation to the other variable in our chart—the type of housing stock used.

CLASSIFICATION OF SHARED LIVING HOMES BY HOUSING STOCK

The second dimension on the classification chart is housing stock. We have divided the cases into four categories: purpose-built homes, single-family homes, units within a larger institution, and adaptation of structures originally built for other purposes.

Purpose-Built Homes. We have found only one example of a purpose-built shared living home in the United States—Robineau House in Skokie, Illinois, described in case 5. However, plans for a purpose-built shared living home have been developed by the architects of the TVA and are presented in appendix 3. Plans for a purpose-built home were also prepared by the College of Architecture of the University of Florida by Yutaka Kodaira. The Abbeyfield Society in Great Britain has many purpose-built homes. Obviously, this type of housing approaches the ideal, for the homes are planned and constructed specifically for the purpose for which they are intended.

Single-Family Homes. This is the most common of type of housing stock in which shared living "families" are found. They are usually larger, older homes and may need a considerable amount of renovation to be used for shared living for the elderly. Cases 1 through 9 are examples of this type of housing.

Units Within a Larger Institution or Edifice. In a few cases, shared living "families" have been organized within a larger unit, usually to give more supports to persons who are already living in the larger unit but can no longer remain in their own apartment or room. This is a very new

kind of housing environment, and we can expect that it will be introduced in retirement facilities in the future as their residents age in place.
This approach is an example of retrofitting an ongoing structure to meet
the needs of a frail population. More recent developments in the retirement housing field involve a continuum of living in which several types
of housing are offered, including some kind of small group home, which
may be called assisted living, leisure living, enriched housing, etc. This
kind of living arrangement carries less stigma and is less threatening to
the resident than a nursing home, and it is more economical than a
skilled care nursing facility. It is expected that many more of these arrangements will be organized in the future.

CASE 10. LEISURE LIVING CENTER, BRADENTON, FLORIDA. An innovative sheltered housing arrangement, the Leisure Living Center, has been
organized within a retirement facility by the Retirement Corporation
of America in Bradenton, Florida. It occupies part of a floor in The
Shores, a large, full-service facility of 209 apartments. The retirement
center serves one meal a day, with the residents taking care of the other
two meals in their apartments. There are recreation facilities, lounges,
a beauty parlor, barber shop, library, and other facilities. A full-care
nursing home is attached to the complex.

Even in the supportive environment of a retirement facility, some
residents decline in health until they are no longer capable of independent living. They may become confused, forgetful, and unable to manage their breakfast or evening meal, yet they do not need skilled nursing care. For these people, the Retirement Corporation of America
organized a family-like unit housing eight to twelve residents with a
twenty-four-hour companion, observation, supervision of medication,
assistance in personal care, and provision of three meals a day. The unit
is located in a corner of the facility, between the nursing home and the
regular apartment units. Thus, the persons who move there are in a
familiar environment, near to friends, and often able to participate in
some of the activities they formerly enjoyed.

Richard Conard, M.D., a physician specializing in geriatrics who is
president of the corporation, states that people are reluctant at first to
join a group living environment. After they have been there a short
time and have adjusted, however, they are extremely secure and are
happier to be in a less demanding environment than living indepen-

dently. They settle down and enjoy the companionship of others in the "family" and appreciate having someone in charge, Dr. Conard observes. He believes that the stimulation of group living delays further deterioration and is important in preventing depression, which often occurs when the elderly begin the withdrawal process and reduce their social interaction.

Dr. Conard states,

If these patients are seen when they are entirely rested, they are very lucid, very competent, and very capable of reflective thought. Yet, after they have progressed through the day's activities, which may have included stressful elements, these patients can get into a state of emotional overburden in which their behavior will be absolutely like an atherosclerotic, senile-dementia patient. These steps of withdrawal, isolation, and situational depression often lead to the state of what I call circumstantial senility, and which fills many of our nation's nursing home beds—needlessly. (1982)

While many retirement facilities have nursing homes connected for residents who require skilled nursing care, the idea of small, shared family group living as an additional step in the continuum is novel and imaginative and can be added to the array of alternatives available in other settings.

CASE 11. HOME CLOSE: CLUSTERED FAMILY GROUPS IN GREAT BRITAIN. A related experiment in Great Britain should be reported here—Home Close, a facility which includes several clusters of small family groups. In Britain, old people's homes usually consist of forty to sixty persons residing in one institution. An experiment was undertaken to see if a home could be built to house several small "family groups" of elderly people. "The project was an experiment to see what might result from building a home in which residents would be encouraged to take part in purposive daily living," says Sheila Peace (1981:14). She describes Home Close, which contains five large flats, each of which houses groups of eight (mixed sex). There are six single bedrooms and one double room, a dining/sitting room, a kitchen, bathroom, two toilets, and two utility rooms. The structure includes a large central hall which could be used by all of the groups and is also used as a day care center for other elderly in the community.

Residents can bring their own furniture. They prepare their own breakfast and light evening meal, and a hot dinner is prepared in the central kitchen and brought to the apartments in heated trollies.

The success of Home Close has led to the construction of at least three other purpose-built group living homes in Cambridgeshire and its use as a model elsewhere. The DHSS (Department of Health and Social Services) issued a directive in 1973 suggesting that new homes built for small groups either adopt the Home Close model—i.e., self-contained units with bedroom, living and dining space—or create separate bedroom and living spaces, but continue to serve all meals communally. (Peace 1981:15)

Peace adds that the construction of new homes designed to accommodate small group living has been halted because of budgetary constraints. However, some social services departments have adapted their present old-age homes to incorporate "small group living." This kind of environment has been found to be "homier" than the traditional institutions. Residents are physically more active and mobile, make greater use of kitchen facilities, do more housework, and interact with each other more.

It should be added that not all of the residents welcomed the change, particularly if they came from other institutional settings. They found the new unstructured and permissive atmosphere unsettling, and some preferred to be looked after. Some complained that their new responsibilities were burdensome.

Peace concludes that in general, the results were very positive. Residents remain more active and retain greater control over their lives, regardless of disability, than do elderly people in a traditional old peoples' home. She believes that small group living provides one major way of improving the quality of life for the elderly in residential care.

Adapting Structures Built for Other Purposes. The ingenuity of concerned Americans in attempting to cope with a large, frail older population can be shown by the multiplicity of experiments in living arrangements that have been devised or adapted to the American situation. In this section, we will present examples of four other alternatives for housing the elderly. They involve adaptation of existing structures: remodeling of old hotels and motels for housing the elderly, and remodeling of an old hospital to provide housing for frail elderly who need supportive services. In discussing small group shared living, we have pointed out that one feature that reduces the expense is the use of existing buildings for a new purpose.

Just as there are many types of housing arrangements that can legitimately be called "shared" or "group" living arrangements, there is also a rich diversity of structural characteristics that are well suited to these projects. The renovation of old motels or hotels for use by elderly persons is an example of this suitability.

For many years, motels and hotels have been used to house people on a semipermanent basis and in arrangements that one would not expect to find in a "traditional" hotel setting. The single-room occupancy (SRO) arrangements in some large cities and the use of hotels to house homeless or "discarded" persons fit this category. Group living is only one of the nontraditional uses to which old hotels and motels have been put, and a clear distinction between the other uses and the group living use should be made. When we discuss the group living use, we are referring to an age-homogeneous group of people who have been brought together by what is usually a nonprofit corporation in order to establish a mutually beneficial environment where each individual has some responsibility to each of the other residents. The social element is the most striking point of differentiation between the group living use and other uses of these structures. Again, the common elements in the group living facilities seem to be that each resident shares in the cost of housing and each resident has a social responsibility to the group. The examples discussed below are typical of the wide diversity possible when group living facilities are housed in hotels or motels.

CASE 12. VILLAGE GREEN, GREENSBORO, NORTH CAROLINA. Village Green is a large, 347-room hotel located in Greensboro, North Carolina, and owned by a nonprofit corporation. Originally it was to be a traditional commercial hotel, but because of financial difficulties it was never opened. The Greensboro Housing Authority purchased the property and organized what is essentially a group living facility.

Village Green offers a number of services to its residents that are not available in more modest structures: an Olympic-sized swimming pool, a park, a sauna, a whirlpool bath, a billiards room, a branch of the public library, maid service, a coin-operated laundry, arts and crafts rooms, and a variety of shops and stores are all located on site. There is also a twenty-four-hour-a-day security system, and emergency summoning buttons are located in each room. For residents who want to cook for themselves, there is a kitchen on each of the six floors. Free transportation to a resident's physician is provided, and there is a medical consultant on call twenty-four hours a day. In addition, there is a health care center located on the first floor with space for twenty-six residents. This clinic is not a licensed nursing facility, but it does provide more care than an individual could get if living independently. The fee for residents in Village Green is a modest $295 per month, which includes all utilities except phone. For an additional $155 per month, residents are provided two meals a day (Village Green 1983).

Each of the rooms in Village Green is small, but care is taken to avoid a cramped feeling. One of the major structural changes made by the organizers was the installation of "pull-down" beds in each room so that the room could be converted into a living room with a minimum of effort. Bathroom safety bars were installed by the organizers, and three rooms on each floor were modified to accommodate handicapped persons. For persons who require more space, two connecting rooms can be rented for $545 per month.

Village Green has a full-time activities director who plans and conducts a variety of activities ranging from recreational to educational. In addition, the facility has a registered nurse on duty forty hours per week. Although Village Green was established to provide housing to persons who do not need the types of care available in nursing homes and "supportive care" environments, the facility does offer support services that go beyond what is available to individuals who choose to live independently.

CASE 13. SUNSET LODGE, HOT SPRINGS, ARKANSAS. A less luxurious although no less successful example is found in Arkansas. Operating under a statewide program called Attendant Care Facilities, Sunset Lodge is a shared living arrangement housed in a former roadside motel and located in a rural area of central Arkansas. According to the organizers, Sunset Lodge is aimed at providing room and board for elderly persons who need some help with daily living but who are generally able to manage by themselves.

Sunset Lodge is housed in a twenty-seven room, single-story structure. Although the structure is less luxurious than Village Green and some of the Share-A-Home houses, Sunset Lodge resembles Village Green organizationally. A separate nonprofit corporation was established to oversee the project, and the board of directors views each resident as a boarder. Much emphasis is placed upon social activities and and cooperation with other residents. Although Sunset Lodge has no activities director as such, there are two persons who act as managers.

The managers, a husband and wife, were the former owners of the motel. As in the case of the founder of Share-A-Home, these individuals are deeply religious and view Sunset Lodge as a manifestation of their beliefs. When, after two years, it became apparent that the operation of Sunset Lodge as a profit-making or even self-supporting venture was unfeasible, the two owners donated the physical structure to the nonprofit corporation. These two individuals have remained as the managers of the facility and are paid a small salary by that corporation.

One unique feature of Sunset Lodge is that the managers have been able to hold food costs down by growing some of the food used in the facility. In some instances, surplus food has been traded to local markets for foods needed by Sunset Lodge. This practice has been very successful, and the managers have purchased freezers and canning equipment so that the food may be preserved for the winter months. There is also another advantage to this practice. Although there is no requirement to work in the garden, many of the residents enjoy this activity as a recreational event. While this practice helps to hold down costs, it is also valuable as a social contact vehicle.

The residents in Sunset Lodge pay a minimum of $165 per month for a small room and food. Each resident's rent is based upon the resident's income so that some residents pay more than others. Any deficits in the operating budget are paid with state funds, and the entire program is administered through an Area Agency on Aging.

CASE 14. MT. VERNON LODGE, OCALA, FLORIDA. Although most of the facilities discussed so far are nonprofit corporations, that is by no means the only way such facilities may operate. Shared living facilities that operate for profit have also been quite successful, although the per-month costs to residents tend to be substantially higher than in nonprofit facilities. A good example of the use of a former motel as a shared living facility operated for profit is Mt. Vernon Lodge in Ocala, Florida.

Mt. Vernon Lodge is a former roadside motel with space for sixty-four persons on two floors. The owners have completely renovated and refurnished the building so that each room is a self-contained living environment, lacking only kitchen equipment. The facility is located in

a resort area and is surrounded by shopping centers, motels, and res-
taurants. The residents of Mt. Vernon Lodge pay between $550 per month
and $1,200 per month (1983), depending upon the occupancy (semipri-
vate or private), size, and location of their rooms. For an additional $15
per month, the management will do all of the resident's laundry. The
facility provides transportation to personal appointments, and there is a
registered nurse on duty at all times.

Former hotels and motels seem well suited to house most types of
shared living arrangements. For the most part, the three facilities mentioned above have been successful at meeting the needs of their target
populations. There are, however, some problems generated by the very
nature of the structure, and organizers would do well to keep some of
these in mind.

Most obvious among the disadvantages of using hotels or motels for
shared living facilities is the amount of money necessary to purchase
the property. In two of the cases mentioned above, the facilities are located in areas that are considered resort or vacation areas by the general
public. Were it not for extraordinary circumstances, neither of these two
structures could have been purchased by the organizers, except at a cost
that would have made the monthly fees paid by the residents prohibitive. In the other case, the property was actually donated by the owner
to the organizing corporation. Thus, under normal circumstances and
in more or less normal market conditions, none of the three hotel/motel
facilities mentioned here would have ever opened as a shared living facility.

High initial costs are a major impediment to this type of facility, and
maintenance costs are only slightly less important. Most hotels and motels have a bathroom in each room. What might seem to be an advantage from the residents' viewpoint is a costly luxury from the organizers' viewpoint. Put simply, three times the number of bathrooms means
roughly three times the maintenance costs. Although it is difficult to
locate comparative data, maintenance tasks for hotels and motels are
generally more costly than the same tasks for larger single-family
dwellings.

Another problem is that the value of the land upon which the structure is situated may increase so that the organizers will be tempted to
"sell out." Of course, the organizers would probably sell only if a new
facility could be purchased (especially if the organizing body is non-

profit), but this would at best be disruptive to the residents and would more than likely move them to a less desirable location.

Finally, a very practical problem, and one for which there is no solution, is the fact that the rooms in hotels and motels are usually designed for short-term occupancy and are characteristically small. In the three examples, the largest room is only 12 feet by 15 feet, and while that space is quite comfortable for short periods of time, to live there day after day for years could be quite unsatisfactory. Fortunately, it is also characteristic of these structures to have large public areas where residents may get out of their rooms and congregate. In the three examples, residents tend to socialize in the larger common areas and use their rooms as private areas. Indeed, it is not uncommon for one neighbor to meet another neighbor in the large public areas rather than in either person's room.

CASE 15. HOW AN OLD HOSPITAL BECAME A NEW HOME: ITHACARE, ITHACA, NEW YORK. Ithacare is a very successful and imaginative housing project developed in Ithaca, New York, by renovating an old hospital to provide a gracious, comfortable home for the frail elderly and for others who cannot live alone.[1] While this scheme is somewhat larger than the others we have discussed, it is such an excellent example of community ingenuity in utilizing existing structures and in surmounting bureaucratic obstacles that we decided to include it. It is also unusual in its close affiliation with the two institutions of higher learning in the community, Ithaca College and Cornell University, whose students play an important role in the daily life of the home.

The old hospital was set in an attractive residential area, surrounded by large trees and near one of Ithaca's famous gorges. It was about ten blocks from the downtown area, near the bus line. After a new hospital was built, it was bought by Ithaca College and used for some years as an overflow dormitory. When the college no longer needed it for this purpose, the question arose as to what to do with a spacious, sturdy old building with many rooms in a convenient, attractive, central location.

There were huge problems in securing HUD financing for the renovation, and officials of Ithaca College plus members of the board of

---

1. The senior author was on the board of directors of Ithacare during its first two years of operation.

directors worked many months putting together a proposal that could enable the project to receive government funds. The project was stymied in the planning and financing phases when it got caught between two bureaucratic agencies—HUD, the U.S. government agency, and the New York State Department of Social Services. These two agencies had contradictory policies and rules for financing a project of this character. First HUD preferred to fund only new construction, and this was a sixty-year-old hospital. HUD also specified that each room must be an "apartment," for it financed only apartments, not rooming houses. On the other hand, upon completion of the project, it would have to be licensed as a Residential Care Facility for Adults under New York State regulations, and these prohibit cooking facilities in the rooms. Since the project was designed for frail elderly people who could not shop and cook, all meals were to be served in the dining room.

It seemed like an insurmountable obstacle had been reached in the negotiations. Only when the organizers came up with an ingenious compromise could the project move forward. It was agreed that there would be a central kitchen and dining room where residents would eat their meals. Each room, however, would be provided with a small cabinet refrigerator (which looked like a bedside table), and on each floor there would be a kitchenette where residents could make a light snack if they desired.

The building was completely renovated, at a cost of over one million dollars, and all necessary safety features were installed, along with ramps, fire prevention apparatus, etc. After the project was finished, all of the state and federal officials involved were pleased with the outcome.

In March 1974, the first resident moved in, and by June 1975, 100 percent occupancy with seventy-three residents was achieved. The facility has continued to have an occupancy of over 95 percent. The average age is 81, with the range from 46 to 99. About one-third are men and two-thirds are women.

In an interview with the director, Mark Zwerger, in February 1983, we learned that the cost was about $23 a day for a private room, but that SSI pays only $17.50. Half the residents are on SSI, which means their income is not enough to cover the $690 monthly cost. To assist in meeting the deficit, the organization has started a day care center for the elderly, which helps to pay some of the overhead. Furthermore, a community fund-raising program brought in over $75,000 to the organization in three years. Zwerger added that with nursing home care costing about $65 a day in New York State, Ithacare is a bargain at $23.

This facility has one of the most outstanding programs of activities, lectures, and concerts that we have encountered, partially because of its setting in a community with two universities. Ithaca College has retained a special relationship with the home, and students are often assigned to do fieldwork there as part of their college course work or serve internships in the facility. This brings a constant stream of young people into the home. The School of Music sends students to perform almost every week. There are recitals, quartets, choral groups, dancing groups, sing-alongs, and regular exercise and physical fitness classes. Students in recreation are assigned to assistantships. In addition, there is a rich program of lectures, slide presentations, discussion groups, and Bible study. Each Sunday afternoon a different church in the community conducts a church service. In a facility as large as this, it is possible to charter buses to go to events in the community or on trips in the area, and many such outings are planned.

There is a greenhouse, with residents encouraged to take part in growing plants, and a craft and ceramics room with a kiln. There is an annual bazaar and yard sale to raise funds, and a gift shop staffed by residents. Another feature is a well-stocked library.

The day care program allows potential residents to "check out" the facility—see the daily life and make friends. They can then decide if they want to become permanent residents. This reduces some of the trauma of moving to a group facility such as this one.

This project has been marked by outstanding community support. Because of the involvement of so many college students, it has a liveliness and intergenerational atmosphere. Outstanding students have been awarded Ithacare scholarships, which are supported by charitable contributions.

CONCLUSIONS

We have gathered information on eighty different shared living groups in the United States and have personally visited thirty-five. In addition in the cross-national phase of the research, we visited fifteen of the nine hundred Abbeyfield houses in Great Britain. These will be discussed in detail in chapter 8. All of these projects have a common goal—the provision of small group living environments—and all have the aim of offering a place to live, meals, and a few services; companionship and a primary group atmosphere; and privacy and autonomy so that people can come and go as they wish.

The fifteen case studies presented in this chapter have many diverse characteristics in terms of sponsorship and use of housing stock. The reader can better understand their similarity and differences by studying table 6.1, which classifies the cases according to these two dimensions. However, sponsorship and housing stock are only two of the characteristics that distinguish the types, for one could sort out the cases in other ways: size, costs, social environment, type of group life provided, staffing, and professionalization. To highlight some of these differences and other special characteristics, we will give a brief summary of the fifteen cases and also of Share-A-Home and Abbeyfield.

Senior Village in Phoenix is unique in being started by the County Commission, partly because of the need to reduce the cost to the county of nursing home care for people who did not really need it but had no supportive place to live. It consists of a cluster of shared houses in the same area.

Enriched Housing, initiated by the Department of Social Services in the state of New York, has ten projects in various cities. Its management varies from community to community, but it is usually organized and supervised by professionals. Some of the projects are in public housing and some in rented private homes. The participation of volunteers is less than in some shared living projects although some churches have given financial support. This is an interesting example of how the sponsoring organization, a large bureaucratic agency, has permitted flexibility and autonomy by the local organizers.

Wellsboro was a grass-roots endeavor in a small Pennsylvania town, started by a local church and one of its members, a physician who saw the need for many of his elderly patients. He bought an old mansion and donated it to the church, which maintains a close connection with the house.

Hawaii's eight Small Group Homes are probably the scheme with the most economical cost. Because the people are younger and can prepare their own meals, they do not need a staff to supply everyday services. This project is unique in having an ethnic mix of residents.

Weinfeld Residence and Robineau Residence have probably the most extensive professional backup of any of the groups. Since these houses are part of the continuum of services of an old and well-established social service agency, the Jewish Federation of Metropolitan Chicago, organizers had an enormous advantage in getting started and funding their operations.

Community Housing for the Elderly in Philadelphia is a notable success, being associated with one of the outstanding geriatric centers in the country. By renovating old row houses and forming shared apartments for three persons, the project has enabled people to continue to live in neighborhood housing, yet be tied to many supportive services when needed.

Group Homes in Washington, D.C., uses apartments in a regular, high-rise apartment building. It has strong back-up services by the Jewish Council for the Aging. These three-person homes are integrated into an age-normal environment; however, this means the setting does not provide social programs and activities specifically designed for a frail population.

The Shared Living Project in Boston has received a great deal of public attention as an intergenerational experiment. Similar to the Hawaii program, the Boston project involves the residents in housekeeping tasks and the monthly costs are low. However, the residents eat only one meal a week as a group. It has strong endorsement from community groups and agencies.

Small Group Homes in Frederick, Maryland, is a project that uses the services of an independent social services agency to coordinate its activities. It is not licensed, as the houses have only three persons per home.

The unique experiment of a shared living unit within a high-rise retirement facility in Bradenton, Florida, probably indicates a pattern that will increase in the future. It represents the shared housing stage in the continuum of living arrangements as depicted in chapter 2. It is a step in between the residents' private apartments and the nursing home, all located in the same building.

Home Close, in Great Britain, is an innovative attempt to break up a large old-age home into small "family" groups.

The final four cases were included in the chapter because they illustrate the adaptation of housing stock constructed for purposes other than for housing the elderly. Although they are somewhat larger than the typical shared living units we have described, all seek to provide a family-like environment, and they have many similar characteristics to the other shared living models. Village Green in Greensboro, North Carolina, Sunset Lodge in Hot Springs, Arkansas, and Mt. Vernon Lodge in Ocala, Florida, are examples of how hotel and motel structures can be adapted to provide a sheltered housing environment for the frail elderly. The size of these facilities varies considerably, from an older 27-room motel to a modern 347-room hotel.

Ithacare, the final example, is the successful transformation of an old hospital into an innovative housing arrangement for the elderly, drawing on a rich array of community resources. These four examples emphasize both the social flexibility and the structural adaptability of alternative living arrangements for the elderly.

We have previously discussed in considerable detail the characteristics of the Share-A-Home houses. This scheme was founded by an individual with deep religious and ethical principles. He has been dedicated in spreading the idea of shared living and unstinting of his time and effort in visiting other communities who wished to start shared housing. He has deliberately chosen to minimize his dependence on all levels of government and has been able to involve individuals and religious organizations to provide financial and social support. Share-A-Home could be placed in both the religious and the secular-charitable categories of the classification scheme in table 6.1 because sponsorship varies according to the local community.

In a subsequent chapter a cross-national comparison is made with the shared housing developed by the Abbeyfield Society in Great Britain and the kinds in the United States. Abbeyfield is notable for its national spread in Great Britain—from one to 900 houses in twenty years. It has a strong and dedicated national organization, which gives assistance to new homes, helps them solve their problems, obtain funding, etc. It has cooperated skillfully with government authorities in getting housing grants. It has high prestige in Britain, for Prince Charles is one of its patrons. Abbeyfield can also be placed in two categories in table 6.1 in regard to sponsorship, for it has been organized by religious groups and professional or civic groups. In regard to housing stock, Abbeyfield uses both purpose-built houses and remodeled single-family homes.

To sum up, a common characteristic of all of these housing units is that they were started by a group other than the residents themselves. Such a "family" must have outside initiative, management, and funding. The initiating groups were both religious and secular: religious sponsors included a small local church parish, a large Jewish welfare federation, and a Catholic social service agency. The secular sponsors included a state unit on government in cooperation with local social service agencies, a county commission, a small home-service health agency, and a corporation that operates a full-care retirement center. The mixed sponsorship (Boston) combined an activist organization (Gray Panthers) with the Back Bay Aging Concerns Committee: a network of community people from church, corporate, commercial, government, and residential groupings.

The projects were urban in location except for the housing projects in rural Arkansas and in a small Pennsylvania town. The cities ranged in size from the largest—New York, Chicago, Boston, and Philadelphia—to mid-sized cities in the North (Rochester, Schenectady), to those in the sunbelt (Phoenix, Arizona, and Honolulu, Hawaii). There were also projects in smaller sized cities, such as Ithaca, New York; Ocala, Florida; and Bradenton, Florida.

Of the fifteen cases, most of the shared housing was located in former single-family structures, but these varied considerably in size and affluence from gracious mansions to small three-bedroom houses. Only one house in all of our studies in the United States was purpose-built. There was considerable variation in the costs charged to the residents, ranging from high costs ($800 or $900 per month) to very modest charges of less than $200. These costs to residents are directly correlated with the sponsor's ability or luck in obtaining private or public gifts, grants, or continuing subsidization to help underwrite the day-to-day expenses.

This brief picture of the diverse kinds of sponsors provides only a snapshot of the organizational contexts that give advice, support, resources, and understanding for creating this new form of housing in these different settings. All of these organizers and myriad organizations and networks are in principle democratically governed. They differ in ideology as to how housing and services should be provided by an affluent society. They all, however, adhere to some broad philosophy of public service and in their special ways try to combine resources for providing humane environments.

The social structures of the various types of living arrangements, whether truly shared living arrangements or group living arrangements, are as diverse as the physical structures in which they are housed. Common to all the facilities presented here, however, and to the true shared living facilities presented in other chapters, are a mutually beneficial sharing of housing costs and a concern for the social health of the environment. Other costs, such as transportation, food, and housekeeping, may or may not be shared equally among the residents. What costs are shared and the responsibilities of each resident to the other residents are determined locally, based upon what provides a better fit with local needs and local expectations. The very fact that few, if indeed any, of the facilities in our study are precisely alike is evidence of the adaptability of the concepts underlying alternative living arrangements.

In open societies like the United States and the United Kingdom, when a new service or facility is required, the imagination and ingenuity of humane persons is impressive, both in their separate efforts and viewed in a broader perspective. All of these natural "experiments" have sprung up individually with many thousands of persons in different communities all recognizing the same need.

CHAPTER SEVEN

Alternative Housing Using
Existing Households

The preceding chapters have focused on newly formed intentional "families." This chapter will consider supportive environments provided by existing households: house sharing, foster homes, and Granny Flats. While these were not the primary focus of our research, they are closely related, for they may deal with the same frail population and they also have the goal of providing a supportive environment for people who cannot manage to live independently and yet do not require institutionalization.

HOUSE SHARING

House sharing is an alternative form of living that has attracted great interest in recent years and has been the subject of grants, conferences, and professional reports. House sharing generally means living with nonrelated housemates in unaltered private homes. Almost any relationship may be worked out between the participants, ranging from eating meals together and sharing all chores, to merely sharing the front entry hall and the mailbox. Generally, the homeowner sets the rules and defines the terms—thus it is not true "sharing" but is somewhat of a modification of a landlord-tenant relationship. Often the agreement comprises the sharing of duties which the homeowner cannot perform, which means that the guest compensates partially in services rather than by simply paying rent.

House sharing is a new term for an old idea—boarding and lodging. This housing pattern was quite common in American towns and cities in the nineteenth century and the early part of the twentieth century (Modell and Hareven 1973). Families often took in boarders and lodgers to increase their income. By the 1930s the conditions that fostered these arrangements lessened because of the interruption of foreign and domestic migration and the development of a welfare state, which reduced the incentive for supplementing the family income in this form. The reemergence of this pattern of housing in the contemporary period results from the economic squeeze of older homeowners who see the need for income and have extra housing capacity. Many elderly also feel more "secure" if they have another person in the house.

House sharing for the elderly can be divided roughly into intergenerational—cases in which an older person takes a younger person into her home—and intragenerational—sharing one's home with a person of roughly the same age. The first pattern, while followed widely in earlier times, particularly to provide housing for unmarried persons, has largely disappeared from the American scene except in college communities, where there is always a large group of young people needing nonpermanent housing. In general, such arrangements have been handled privately by the parties involved and have not needed intermediaries or matching services.

Both of these types have captured the attention of gerontologists in recent years. The idea is that a frail older person who needs some extra income, assistance, security, and social supports, and has a large house with extra room, can "share" it with another person, perhaps more vigorous, so that the new resident can help to perform some of the necessary household tasks.

In an effort to stimulate such pairings, housemate matching services have been organized in different areas of the country: for example, Home Sharing for Seniors in Seattle, Washington; Project Match in San Jose, California; Project Share in Hempstead, New York (based in the Family Service Society of Nassau County and funded by OAA Title III funds). The concept was first studied by McConnell and Usher, who gathered data on existing programs and also interviewed people to determine their attitude about the idea (McConnell and Usher 1979; Usher and McConnell 1980). They found that most elderly people prefer to share housing with middle-aged people rather than with young people. Moreover, the older homeowners did not view house sharing as a social context conducive to intimacy. "This housing option is more appropriate as an instrumental arrangement for the homeowner who is in need of services or additional income" (Usher and McConnell 1980:165).

The fact that a number of social service agencies are successfully pursuing the model of shared housing suggests that a latent need exists that is yet unfulfilled, according to Lawton (1981).

Schreter (1982) has analyzed data collected in the National Survey of Housing Choices of Older Americans and also conducted a survey of seventy-nine clients of four home sharing agencies in the Washington, D.C., area (Schreter 1983). She reports that interest in house sharing is expressed not only by the elderly, for potential sharers (those who want to move in) and dividers (those who have a house with extra space) are more likely to be between the ages of fifty-five and sixty-four. In addition, persons who express an interest in house sharing are not necessarily the most economically disadvantaged. In fact, a reduction in SSI and food stamp allotments might result if they engaged in house sharing. Schreter points out:

SSI regulations require that all sources of income, whether cash or in-kind, be considered in the calculation of benefits. Thus, house sharing arrangements which involve cash payments or in-kind services (such as help with chores) to the homeowner could jeopardize the household's SSI benefits. Moreover, a house sharing tenant who receives SSI may be affected if he or she provides services to the homeowner in return for compensation such as reduced or free rent. The compensation can be deemed to be income received. (1982:18)

In Schreter's interview study, she divides her cases into self-initiated shared housing, agency-assisted (essentially a matching process), and agency-sponsored, in which the agency helps in setting up group households, securing staff, screening residents, and advising on management. Agency-sponsored group homes are the least common (Schreter learned of eighty-four in the United States), but they have been the most studied by gerontologists. She estimates that such arrangements house perhaps 1,000 elderly people in this country, while approximately 3,000 live in agency-assisted housing and 325,000 in self-initiated house sharing. The latter is essentially a landlord-tenant boarding house arrangement.

Schreter reports that the persons involved in house sharing were often in a transition phase of life, for 90 percent of the cases she interviewed had lost a spouse or a close relative, had suffered an economic change, or were recovering from a severe health problem. The majority of shared households in her study were intergenerational. She states that the housemate was usually a younger working person who got up, got dressed, and left for the day. This is clearly a very different pattern than the shared housing we have described in this book.

The shared house arrangements exist for a relatively short time and frequently dissolve because of personality conflicts. Involved in the transitory nature is the fact that if the householder goes to a nursing home or dies, the tenant usually must leave immediately.

FOSTER FAMILY CARE

Foster family care is another housing alternative for the elderly that has small group characteristics and seeks to duplicate family life. Like house sharing, however, it brings together unrelated persons. Foster homes can be considered to be a variant of house sharing, but they are under closer government inspection and scrutiny. Social workers usually inspect the home and negotiate the arrangement; public money often pays the fees. This represents a direct, bureaucratic intervention by the state, for usually the social worker monitors the situation.

Each state has its own definition of the foster home and sets up its specifications and surveillance procedures. However, we shall consider foster homes to be single-family households that incorporate one to four paying residents. Obviously, there is an enormous range in the quality of care and family life, for it can vary as widely as the characteristics of "normal" families. Lawton says, "It cannot be assumed that simply because they are in the community and small in scale that foster homes offer a style of life that is any richer than that offered by some institutions" (1981:78).

In an effort to determine whether foster family care for the elderly actually approximates family life or is really a mini-institution, Newman and Sherman (1979) conducted research on 100 foster family homes in New York State housing one to four clients. They wished to determine the "family nature" of the homes, the characteristics of the residents and caretakers, the relationships with the agencies, and the community reaction to the foster care program. They found that, although the primary purpose of foster care as defined in the state regulations is placement in a "family," only 58 percent of the caretakers were currently married, and only 29 percent of the 100 homes provided residents with an opportunity to participate in a family that involved husband, wife, and at least one child.

After studying the kinds of affectionate relationships within the home, the researchers observed: "Though the caretakers report they look upon residents as part of the family, they indicate that the residents do not often look upon each other as family, with one-quarter suggesting that residents view each other as 'friends' " (Newman and Sherman 1979:170). They added that caretakers often maintain contact with former residents, but former residents less often maintained contact with each other. This is similar to the situation we observed in Share-A-Home. In many cases, when a resident left the home, it was as if she had dropped from sight. It should be added that since a resident often moved because of a decline in health, perhaps it is too threatening for other residents to keep in contact, for they may contemplate their own decline.

The investigators measured social interaction and found there was a reasonable amount that could be observed: conversation between the residents, card games or other games, participating in trips or shopping, church, etc. They also used two indicators to measure the performance of ritual within the foster family household: how often cards or gifts were exchanged and how often residents said goodnight to each other. More examples of ritual were reported between the caretaker and the resident than among the residents themselves, as was the case with expression of affection.

Social distance was measured by finding whether residents eat with the family, use all of the rooms in the house, have access to the kitchen, and participate in chores in the house. In two-thirds of the families, residents often eat with the family; in about half the homes, residents have kitchen privileges and can use all of the rooms in the house; and in three-quarters of the homes, residents performed some chores, often at their own initiative. The researchers conclude that family integration and participation do occur in these foster homes, and that the majority of cases could be regarded as surrogate families.

GRANNY FLATS

One type of supportive housing in a noninstitutional setting which has received considerable attention in Great Britain and Australia is the

"Granny Flat." In Denmark they are called "Kangaroo Houses." The term was first used to describe a self-contained bungalow adjacent to a family house. Developed in 1940, it was designed to provide housing for an elderly person (usually a widow) who could no longer live independently and who needed some supports from relatives close at hand, yet who wanted to maintain a separate dwelling. In the Australian scheme, it was planned that mobile units would be rented and moved to a family's backyard. When the unit was no longer needed, it would be dismantled and moved to a new location to serve another family. In actual practice, this did not quite work out as expected, for many families were reluctant to give up extra space when the elderly person died. They preferred to keep it as a teen-age apartment, guest room, studio, or office, and thus the "mobile" part of the scheme was not realized.

In Great Britain, Granny Annexes were built adjacent to some new public housing complexes in an attempt to enable the elderly to remain in their normal environment and keep in close contact with their kin. A further aim of this scheme was to release underoccupied family houses and apartments, for often an elderly widow would continue to live in a family home after her husband had died, even though it was a burden to keep up, she did not need the space, she was too frail to live alone, and there were young families unable to find housing.

Dr. Anthea Tinker, in a research report on the Granny Annexes for the Department of the Environment, Great Britain, stated: "The idea is to enable the elderly to retain their independence, with their own front door, yet have someone nearby in case of need" (1976:2). Dr. Tinker reports an evaluation of Granny Annexes in a study of eleven local authorities where this housing was available adjacent to public housing units. Of the 240 units, interviews were obtained from 220 elderly residents of the annexes. The local authorities believed that the idea was successful, but there were some problems. For example, it was difficult to rerent both units together. If one unit became empty, often the family or person in the other unit would not want to move. "As a result only 20 percent of the units are now used by relatives," Dr. Tinker reported (1976:1). When the elderly person died, some authorities tried to persuade the family to move so that the linked units could be rerented to another family and its elderly relative, but this caused so much hard feeling that they abandoned that idea. Now they simply move in another old person on the waiting list for housing.

Dr. Tinker observed that the term Granny Annex is somewhat misleading, for a quarter of the residents were men, some had never married, and some had no children.

Because the annexes were new, compact, and easy to care for, they enabled many elderly to live longer in an independent household than if they had been in conventional housing. Even when the elderly resident was not related to the family in the adjacent flat, he still received neighborly support in many instances. In a sense, the resident really experienced a kind of "community care."

The idea of Granny Annexes has been explored recently in the United States. Leo Baldwin, housing coordinator for the American Association of Retired Persons, has suggested the name ECHO Housing, an acronym for Elder Cottage Housing Opportunities. Americans, in general, dislike the name Granny Annex.

A project in Lancaster, Pennsylvania, has stimulated the interest in ECHO Housing, or "Elder Cottages." Peter Dys, executive director of the Office on Aging in Lancaster, encouraged a local housing manufacturer, Coastal Colony Corporation, to develop a compact, factory-built, movable cottage for the elderly. He hoped that it would be possible to have a fleet of cottages that could be rented as needed (Hare 1982). The manufacturer built a model, which would cost about $18,000 installed on a site. It was on display in Lancaster and was visited by over five thousand people. As of October 1982, however, only two cottages had been sold, although there were orders for fifty more. The president of the manufacturing firm believes these units could be grouped in "cottage communities" in many parts of the country (*Modern Maturity* 1982).

The chief bottleneck to the spread of this form of housing is that zoning laws prohibit them in most communities. Baldwin hopes that an educational program planned by the American Association of Retired Persons will overcome this.

The modest cost of ECHO Housing is an important issue, according to Hare (1982). He states that HAUS, a West Coast group, is developing a unit that is expected to be similar in price to the $18,000 Pennsylvania unit. He adds that HUD estimates that the current cost of a conventional housing unit is $48,000. The planned units included an efficiency unit of 280 square feet, a one-bedroom unit of 508 square feet, and a two-bedroom unit of 702 square feet. These were intended to be installed either on treated wood pier foundations for easy removal or concrete foundations for more permanent housing.

According to Edward Guion, president of Coastal Colony Corporation:

We are currently working with a local land developer in an effort to get approval for placing a small cluster of Elder Cottages in a village community with its own winding streets, picket fences, shrubbery, etc., to effect a homogeneous blend of this type of housing in its own planned environment. Building in the cost of the land, streets, underground utilities and landscaping, we might add another $7,000 per unit to the above costs of $18,000 per unit. This would enable a party to purchase the Elder Cottage and the land on which it is placed as a compact home concept and secure a mortgage on the entire package. One local bank has reviewed this approach and has stated that they would currently (June 1981) finance such a home with a 15-year mortgage with 20 percent down and 15½ percent interest. If the total cost for an entirely self-sufficient house and land would now be about $25,000, the buyer would need $5,000 down payment with $20,000 being financed over a 15-year period resulting in a monthly mortgage payment of about $290.00 per month. (Guion 1983)

After considerable effort, the Coastal Colony Corporation finally obtained zoning permission for its first Elder Cottage Community, Swatara Village, located near Lebanon, Pennsylvania. Approval was granted by the township for placement of 240 Elder Cottages, a community center, and recreational facilities. In October 1983, two units were open for inspection. A one-bedroom cottage (508 square feet) would cost $20,200 and a two-bedroom unit (702 square feet) $24,890, installed on the property and connected to all utilities.

The village concept is an intriguing idea, and as a businessman, Guion presents a clear, concise picture of the economic considerations. But a sociologist would ask, "What about the intergenerational relations? Wouldn't this simply be another retirement village, away from kin and family supports?"

In April 1981, NRTA-AARP sponsored a Granny Flats Forum in Washington, D.C., in cooperation with the International Federation on Ageing and the Council of International Urban Liaison. It was attended by eighty-four people, and there have been many requests since then for information about the idea (NRTA-AARP 1981).

Barry Cooper, principal town planner and director of the Granny Flats Program, Victoria Ministry of Housing, Melbourne, Australia, said there has been a great demand for the units, which cost around $12,000 in

Australia. The waiting period for a unit through the Ministry of Housing is fifteen to eighteen months, but if the homeowners employ a private builder, they can have a cottage in about two months. He added that of five hundred units in place, only ten or twelve have been moved. It is estimated that it costs $5,000 to move one of the cottages.

Walter Benning, president of the Manufactured Housing Institute, told the forum that the manufacturers he represents have been building Granny Flats for over fifty years. He endorsed the concept and asserted that mobile home manufacturers could provide a 500-square-foot unit at a cost of $5,500, and the unit would be available in three days. However, he raised the question of zoning and restrictive regulations that prevent such units from being used as Granny Flats.

While contemporary gerontologists have considered the Granny Annex to be a novel and ingenious approach to the care of the frail elderly, Granny Annexes have been in operation in the Amana Colonies in Iowa for over 100 years. The large family homes often have an attached wing or small apartment for grandparents. What seems a new and fresh idea has been common practice for generations in the way of life of these religious communities (Shambaugh 1932; Streib and Streib 1975).

CONCLUSIONS

In summary, the first two alternates are forms of housing that have historical roots in American culture and have been used by other age groups than the elderly. From the standpoint of the community they are important in utilizing existing housing stock in an optimum way. They also provide affordable housing for persons on limited income and tend to be age integrated. House sharing and foster homes involve nonrelated persons, while the Granny Flat involves persons with a kinship tie.

The Granny Flat and ECHO Housing are a more ambitious and expensive alternative to traditional housing because they require the manufacture of a small housing unit located adjacent to an existing structure. Moreover, the British and Australian experience points out that this kind of housing has a limited life-span utility because, after a few years, the elderly person may need institutionalization or may die. Finally, the flexibility of the Granny Flat is questionable because when the facility is vacated, another elderly person does not move in.

One of the difficulties of house sharing is that it may not meet the needs of the population that is over the age of seventy-five. If the frail older person is the house provider, he or she may be able to negotiate an arrangement in which housing is exchanged for certain services that are needed. But if the frail older person is the one who is seeking supportive housing, the situation is less easy to solve. It is rare to find homeowners who are willing to rent to persons who need assistance and supportive care. They would generally prefer younger tenants who can cope with their own needs and perhaps offer help, not require help.

House sharing and foster homes enable single-family houses to be used to increase the variety of housing choices for the elderly. In a sense, they are variants of the old-fashioned rooming and boarding home. The interesting development in the housing of older people is that a process that used to operate in a market economy has been transformed into a semibureaucratic activity, in which an agency operates as a housing service for landlords and tenants. The agency acts as a broker or matchmaker in attempting to bring compatible parties together to increase the likelihood of residential stability. In market arrangements, it is up to the buyer and seller to negotiate the terms of the agreement. In the instance of house matching or placement in a foster home, we see how traditional exchange relations are modified in an urbanized welfare system. The use of third parties to arrange housing for older people is an instance of how a mediator or facilitator may be essential in an urban, impersonal society to meet the needs of the frail elderly.

CHAPTER EIGHT

Abbeyfield—Success Story in Great Britain

All developed societies have to face the challenge of the housing and care of lonely, frail older persons who can no longer live by themselves. Each society handles the situation in ways consistent with its culture and resources. In Great Britain, private and public organizations have developed a number of options for housing older persons (Butler et al. 1979). The three main types of public housing are designed for three different levels of self-sufficiency or frailty. Category I consists of self-contained dwellings for more active elderly. Category II, "sheltered housing," are grouped flatlets (small apartments, often adjoining each other) with a "warden" or manager for help in emergencies. Tenants do their own shopping and cooking. "Residential Homes," often referred to as "Part III Homes" from the section of an Act of Parliament under which local government is authorized to finance and manage them, are usually of a size of forty to sixty elderly residents in need of care and attention, but not full nursing care. Meals are provided in a common dining room. They are clearly institutional in their characteristics.

In addition, there are a number of privately organized types of housing for the elderly. The Abbeyfield Society is a charitable organization in the private sector which provides a special kind of accommodation for lonely older persons.[1] A typical Abbeyfield house consists of six to eight older persons, usually women, who live as a "family" group. Each person has a bed-sitting room, furnished with her own belongings. It contains a sink and minor cooking facilities (an electric tea kettle and

---

1. There are a number of other nongovernmental organizations that have been heavily involved in providing a variety of housing for older persons and other people in the United Kingdom, such as the Anchor Housing Association. See Heumann and Boldy 1982.

a hot plate). A live-in housekeeper shops, cooks, and serves lunch and dinner in a communal dining room. According to the Abbeyfield Society:

The aim is to give security and companionship to elderly people who would otherwise be living alone, who no longer feel able to lead a completely independent life in a private house or even an old person's flat, but do not want or need the full-time attendance provided by an Old Person's Home. . . . The aim is also to enable them to continue to live in a neighborhood and in the sort of domestic atmosphere to which they have been accustomed, with the support of a local group of kindly people and the fellowship of their fellow residents. (Members *Handbook* n.d.:6)

The Abbeyfield Society is a national voluntary organization with headquarters near London. In August 1982, the Abbeyfield Society had 534 local societies in England, Wales, Scotland, and Northern Ireland, and these groups operated almost 900 houses. The essential work of the organization is based in local communities and therefore the houses are acquired and managed by local Abbeyfield societies. These local groups are affiliated with the national organization and are bound by the principles of Abbeyfield. The local groups are autonomous and free to operate according to their own assessment of the needs in the locality. Except for the housekeeper and a few paid personnel, all workers are volunteers. In addition, community members voluntarily provide considerable professional consultation and advice.

HISTORY AND ORGANIZATION

The movement was founded by Richard Carr-Gomm, formerly a major in the Coldstream Guards. He began to study practical social work after retiring from the army and enrolled as a "home helper" in a bombed-out section of London. Particularly concerned with the problems of older persons, he called a meeting with other interested people in a house on Abbeyfield Road in South London. Subsequently he gave the name of Abbeyfield to the society. The group was especially concerned with the problems of isolated, lonely elderly in London, and it decided to bring them together in a "family" group. Mr. Carr-Gomm purchased an old house with his own funds and had it remodeled and redecorated. He then went around the area to the lonely old people he had heard of through his work as a home helper, inviting them to live together in his house. The first eighty people refused, but finally two people decided to "risk it": an 82-year-old woman who had lived by herself on a small old-age pension, and a 78-year-old man who had lived alone as a widower for twenty-five years and was going blind. Then two other tenants moved in, and a housekeeper was hired to assist.

Before long, Mr. Carr-Gomm was besieged by old people who wanted to join the group, and so he bought a second house, and then a third. According to the account related in the first bulletin issued by the Abbeyfield Society:

> And still the applicants came forward. Richard's money was running out: but by chance the next-door house in Gomm Road came up for sale, and it was too good an opportunity to miss. He bought it, and the two houses were run as one. He could just afford a fifth house, and this was opened at 279, Lynton Road in November, 1956. It was soon filled. In the meantime, though no appeal for money had been made, the venture had become known, and about £500 had come from many friends and well-wishers all over the country. Another house was for sale in Marden Road, nearby. The price was £750. Not knowing where the other £250 was going to come from, Richard read the letter concluding the purchase of the house with some misgiving. Then he remembered that he had not yet opened all his morning's mail. Inside the next letter was a cheque, from a complete stranger, for £250. (Abbeyfield Society n.d.:5)

By 1960, there were thirty local Abbeyfield societies, including groups in Portsmouth, Edinburgh, and Belfast. The young organization was fortunate in capturing the attention and support of several important business and professional men who were involved with charity work and who were exploring schemes for helping elderly, lonely people. The group made some wise decisions from the start, which helped insure the early success of the organization. According to Christopher Buxton, national chairman from 1964 to 1977:

> It was agreed that the central Abbeyfield Society should not open houses itself and that this responsibility should devolve on the incorporated local Abbeyfield Societies in towns and areas where sufficient interest and need existed. Perhaps this was the most important single decision which Abbeyfield ever took as it put the responsibility for setting up and running the houses firmly on the local group. One thing that working for 20 years in Abbeyfield has taught me is that the British are at their best if given a task and allowed to get on with it on their own, with a bit of help, but without interference. (1977:3)

Over the first three or four years, a serious policy disagreement occurred: namely, whether Abbeyfield should include students, ex-prisoners, unmarried mothers, and other lonely people in need of a family group. Buxton, in writing later about this disagreement, observed:

After long debate and, I am bound to say, painful personal conflicts, the majority view was that an Abbeyfield house was so small that it could not stand the strains of such differing ways of life, and that an Abbeyfield house should exist solely for the elderly. (1977:2)

This proved to be a wise decision.

During the early 1960s, the society developed its guiding principles and a constitution was written, which provided that representatives of the local societies would control the national society as a democratic organization. Another major organizational move was the division of the United Kingdom into fourteen regional councils with officers charged with developing their region. The regions are organized into areas, which encompass local societies. The local societies thus involve four layers of structure.

During the late 1960s, the young society almost expired because of the deteriorating financial situation. The fund-raising efforts were not successful enough to offset the deficits. For a time, it looked as if the headquarters might have to be closed because there was a deficit of £16,000. It was finally decided that each local society should send a gift of £50 to keep the central organization alive. The response put the organization back on its feet, and in the early 1970s, the headquarters was reorganized.

A national development fund was set up to receive gifts and legacies to be used in grants for new houses. In addition, a request was made to the government for grants to support the capital cost of new projects. The Housing Act of 1974 provided for Housing Association grants, which helped enormously to get local houses started. This act was designed to help the voluntary housing movement by providing substantial loans and grants from central government funds to "registered housing associations." If a project was approved, the grant would cover the greater part of the capital cost. Grants were also made to assist societies that found themselves in deficit in running of houses established before the act.

In order for the Department of the Environment to approve a grant, the project must supply a housing need, the accommodations must be of certain prescribed standards and the costs must be fair, according to the Rent Officer. Then if uncommitted grant funds are available, the project will be eligible for loans from the Housing Corporation for the entire amount. *(Manual of Information* 1976: appendix to section 2, 3:2)

By 1977, over £4 million had been received in housing grants to buy and renovate houses or build new ones. An inevitable accompanying frustration of securing government grants is, of course, the filling out of a multiplicity of forms and delays in securing approval.

THE NATIONAL ORGANIZATION

The policy-governing body of the national society is the National Executive Committee, an unpaid volunteer group which meets three times a year.

The headquarters are located in Potters Bar, a suburb of London. There is a small staff of about a dozen people, under the leadership of a general secretary. The three functions carried out by the headquarters are communication, representation, and collaboration. The staff at headquarters is the communications hub of the Abbeyfield Society—it collects and distributes information to the local groups.

In its representation function, the headquarters maintains contacts with departments of government, government agencies, and voluntary and charitable organizations working in the field of care of the elderly.

The collaborative functions involve working with the national officers and committees as well as the regional and local societies on matters such as developing new societies, advising existing ones, and providing information on topics such as finance, legislation, management, insurance, and investment. The expertise of the headquarters staff enables it to provide guidance to local societies in the complicated procedures of working with government and local agencies in financing houses. The headquarters also receive over two thousand requests annually for accommodation, which are referred back to local societies. It also produces publicity, booklets, a quarterly journal, and a number of manuals. Appendix 2 has a list of some of the major publications of the society.

One of the notable successes of the national organization is to encourage government bodies to fund projects they might otherwise be hesitant to support because of the cost. By using charitable donations in conjunction with public funding, the national society facilitated the organization of many new Abbeyfield houses and Extra Care houses. A total of £4,200,000 was provided in 1981 through government Housing Association Grants. The headquarters also provided £250,000 of charitable money to local societies over the same period.

The national organization emphasizes that the great strength of Abbeyfield is its ability to attract and hold willing volunteers. In their services to local societies, they have stressed this aspect, and they assist local groups by giving them information on recruitment, training, and utilization of volunteers. On the average there are between ten and twenty volunteers per society, which adds up to five to ten thousand throughout the country.

The national society recognizes that the problems of the inner cities have not yet been tackled. According to D. A. L. Charles, the general secretary, "Those Abbeyfield houses that we have established in inner cities rely heavily on volunteers from the suburbs. It will involve a reeducation program to form their own groups. I am hopeful that at some stage we may get Trade Union involvement in these social problems" (1982).

The Abbeyfield Society publishes a magazine four times a year which is sent to all local societies. It contains news of the local houses, notices of new start-ups, photographs of honors received by Abbeyfield groups, letters, articles, and helpful information, such as how to prepare a news release for newspaper or television coverage.

For example, in the December 1982 issue an article reports how a London house cooperated with a Youth Opportunity Program (similar to CETA in the United States) in offering training to unemployed young people who were placed in an Extra Care House. The trainee spends one day a week at a local college on a general subject course and also works shifts in the house on other days, altogether making a work week of about forty hours. The weekly wages are paid by the Local Authority. First results of this program have been very encouraging, and it is hoped that other houses will cooperate in the scheme. The Abbeyfield Bulletin is important in building a feeling of cohesion and esprit de corps so that the local societies feel they are part of a large, successful enterprise.

Abbeyfield has now spread internationally. There is a national society in Australia, and a society has been formed in Dublin in the Republic of Ireland.

LOCAL SOCIETIES

Local Abbeyfield societies are voluntary organizations in which the only paid employees are the housekeeper and her helpers. These local groups of private citizens are pivotal in the operation of the houses. "Volunteers, therefore, are the lifeblood of the society" (Members Handbook, n.d.:20). Each local society is an autonomous, independent, nonprofit, charitable organization which initiates the process of obtaining the house, hiring the housekeeper and staff, and selecting the residents. The work of the local committee is usually divided between two subcommittees, development and house. The former is concerned with organizing and funding of the local house, and it is often composed of newly retired business and professional men. It is recommended that this committee include a lawyer to handle legal matters, an accountant or banker to facilitate financial affairs, a builder to advise on property, and a physician to advise on medical matters and to be a liaison with the medical profession.

The house committee is involved in the day-to-day operation of the house itself and tends to be composed of women members. These committees are highly involved in the local society and give generously of their time, effort, and expertise in the management of the local society and the running of the house. For example, members of the house committee may take turns preparing meals on the housekeeper's day off or substitute in times of emergencies. The local committee is in close touch with the residents of the house and visits the house often, so that committee members are very knowledgeable about the residents' needs and the services they may require.

On occasion, the members of the house committee will help to raise money from the local community for aid in running the house or purchasing new furnishings, such as a new sofa or television. They organize morning coffee hours and craft sales. Such events have purposes other than simply raising money, for they enable community members to meet the Abbeyfield elderly in the house and thus become acquainted with the Abbeyfield idea in general. Such events also give the house residents a common goal and focus for cooperation. In addition to these committee members, who devote considerable time to the local societies' activities, it is recommended that a larger network of volunteers and helpers be developed who may assist on an intermittent basis.

RESIDENTS

Four out of five residents are women, with an average age of 81 years. The selection subcommittee personally interviews each applicant. Residents are expected to be able to look after themselves and come to the dining room for the two meals that are served by the housekeeper. Priority is given to residents who are judged to be persons likely to live in harmony with the others in the house.

While local societies evolve their own assessment of "need," the national organization holds the view that loneliness is one of the basic criteria, for this housing is organized primarily for the elderly who live alone.

It is desirable for residents to have a sponsor, such as a friend or relative who is ready to take responsibility for the resident if it becomes impossible to maintain her or him in the Abbeyfield house. The society realizes, of course, that persons who are really isolated may be unable to name a sponsor. In such cases, it is hoped that a church, service club, or other benevolent organization may be prepared to take an interest.

Residents are encouraged to join in social activities, especially those outside the house, but no one is forced to participate. Outings are often arranged by members of the house committee, or by Friends of Abbeyfield (an organization of contributors and supporters), and films are often scheduled for showing in the house. Most residents have a television in their room, although some houses also have a set in the lounge.

One of the basic principles of Abbeyfield is that each person has her own room and brings her own furnishings, rugs, bric-a-brac, etc. Residents are allowed to arrange the room as they wish, and they are encouraged to entertain family, friends, or other residents in their rooms for tea. There is a strong emphasis on individual privacy. It was explained to us that an Abbeyfield house is really six or eight "homes within a house."

In regard to drugs and their storage and care, houses that are registered under Section 37 of the National Assistance Act of 1948 are required "to make suitable arrangements for the safe keeping and handling of drugs." Headquarters offers guidance in the necessary procedures. Unregistered houses are not subject to legal statutory responsibilities, according to the Manual of Information:

> Medicines should normally be kept by the resident concerned, but common sense should prevail. Housekeeper's duties do not ordinarily include taking care of drugs, but if, for some good reason, it seems preferable for a housekeeper to look after a resident's medicines, this may be arranged if the resident and the General Practitioner concerned agree. (Section 7:12)

This sensible, flexible approach typifies the Abbeyfield way of doing things—and illustrates the family-like style of life.

Some Abbeyfield houses have "short stay" accommodation—usually spare rooms too small to be used as permanent residences, but often satisfactory for someone to stay for a week to two. For example, an elderly person who lives with family members could stay there while her family was away on holidays, or a potential resident could have a trial period to get an idea of what it is like to live in an Abbeyfield house.

HOUSEKEEPER

The housekeeper is of central importance to the success of an Abbeyfield house. In the Abbeyfield Manual of Information, it is stressed that without the right housekeeper, it can hardly become a home in the true sense. "Her job is comparable to caring for a good-sized family: and it should be regarded that way. Therefore it is essential to find the right person and make her happy and comfortable, giving her full scope for her own initiative and full support" (Manual of Information section 7:4).

It is not expected that the housekeeper be a nurse. Instead, she should have a talent for homemaking and cooking. It is hoped that she will look on the residents as her "family," while respecting their independence. In most of the houses, residents perform small chores, such as setting the table and other similar tasks.

The house committee has an important role in bolstering the efforts and spirits of the housekeeper. The senior author observed repeatedly how important it was for the housekeeper to hear praise and appreciation. Certainly a housekeeper's job must be discouraging and confining at times, but the constant support and consultation provided by the members of the house committee and other community volunteers help to solve the problems that keep arising.

In the early days of the organization, housekeepers had a bed-sitting room, but now at least two-thirds have at least two rooms. About half have private baths, and a third have their own kitchenette or kitchen.

Two-thirds of the housekeepers were fifty-five and over, and a few were even over seventy. About a third had a member of their family living with them—a husband or a child. Many of the housekeepers had pensions from previous employment and, although retired, preferred to keep busy, have a home, and earn wages in addition to their pension. Some local societies stipulate that a housekeeper has the privilege of joining the house as a resident when she becomes elderly.

There are paid helpers in about 85 percent of the nine hundred houses who assist in the cleaning, kitchen tasks, gardening, or act as relief persons on the housekeeper's day off. Very often, however, the members of the house committee take turns with this task and cook the noon meal. The residents themselves are often able to manage preparation of the evening meal.

"Salaries are not high," according to a report by the Abbeyfield Commission on Growth. "Fifty-one percent [of the housekeepers] were paid less than 19 pounds a week [in 1978] and only 18 percent were paid more than 22 pounds. . . . Those under 60 years of age were paid more than those who would also be drawing a pension." However, there are definite psychological bonuses—the housekeepers know that they are a vital part of an important service. Job satisfaction is high, with 96 percent reporting in the commission survey that they are very satisfied with their work (Morton-Williams 1979:14).

The national society, recognizing the difficulty of finding housekeepers, established Regional Housekeeping Registrars. As a result, over a hundred placements were made through this system in 1981.

THE HOUSES

Most Abbeyfield houses are converted from large homes in established residential neighborhoods. It is recommended that houses be near public transportation, shops, and churches. It is the policy of the national society that Abbeyfield houses be restricted to twelve members, although there are a few cases where larger houses were organized. Most groups consist of six to eight residents, which is considered the number most likely to produce a home-like atmosphere without being institutional.

It is recommended that the fire officer inspect the house, perhaps even before it is purchased, and that his recommendations be incorporated in the remodeling plans from the very beginning.

In some houses, there is a sitting room for the residents to gather together, in addition to the dining room. In other houses, there is a combination dining room–lounge, sometimes divided by a room divider or screen. If there is a good-sized entrance hall, sometimes it is used as a sitting room.

The residents' rooms are all fitted with a wash basin. Some residents have placed a screen in front of this area, so as to make the rest of the room look more like a living room. Often there is a cupboard nearby, with an electric plate for heating soup or light meals. In some houses, electric or gas heaters are provided in the rooms so that a person can increase the heat in her room to her own comfort, in addition to the heat from the central heating unit. Separate meters are sometimes installed. In Britain, these can be of a prepayment type, so that the resident inserts a coin when she wants more heat. The telephone is usually a pay phone, so that there is not a problem of dividing up the telephone bill.

FOUR EXAMPLES OF ABBEYFIELD HOUSES

To provide the reader with a description of the variety of Abbeyfield houses in local communities, we provide vignettes of four different Abbeyfield houses which were among the fifteen visited by the senior author while on a fellowship supported by the World Health Organization (WHO).

Colwyn Bay, Wales. We drove on a winding road through the estate grounds in Wales until we came to an impressive stone mansion, set on a little knoll. The huge wooden door was opened by the housekeeper,

In the British Isles, older, comfortable single-family dwellings are utilized for most of the nine hundred Abbeyfield houses. These houses accommodate six to eight people with private rooms, and a bed–sitting room for the housekeeper.

who proudly invited us in. The mansion housed eight elderly people, plus the married couple who act as housekeeper and gardener. The elegant, high-ceilinged living and dining rooms provide a gracious, attractive environment for the "'family." Several other rooms on the first floor were converted into bedrooms for persons who could not manage the stairs to the spacious second floor. Because of the concern over the stairs, an electric chair lift had just been installed. The "family" considered it to be quite a novelty but preferred to use the stairs.

The housekeeper showed us through the house, and we asked her how she and her husband happened to take this job. She replied that they had been caretakers for an estate of a wealthy family, but after some years had decided that they wanted to do something more "useful." She said:

The family who owned the big estate where my husband and I worked rarely used it and although the work was easy—much easier than this position—we got lonely and wanted to do something where we were 'needed.' So when we heard about this, we applied. It certainly is a great deal more work, but we know how important we are. Sometimes the pressure seems too much, as for example when someone gets sick, and I have to call the doctor at night. And then we have had trouble with the fire alarm—it is wired into the fire department downtown, and we had a malfunction two times last night. The people were in bed asleep, but they all put on robes and came down to the front hall. The fire department was here in a few minutes, but did not find anything. It must have been an electrical connection. After things got quieted down, and they went back to bed, it happened again. Oh, there is never a dull moment around here!

We learned that the family who owned the estate had given it to the local Abbeyfield Society, with the stipulation that it must be used for a home for elderly people. This certainly was the most elegant setting we visited. Some people, however, might prefer to be nearer to the town's life and activity, for the estate was quite isolated, being about eight miles from town.

Central Edinburgh. The Victorian brick row house looked just like its neighbor—except that the garden was probably neater and had more flowers. An elderly man was working in the garden, carefully and methodically, and inside the house, an elderly woman was watching his progress through the front living room window. We were informed immediately that Mr. Lewis was "such a wonderful gardener," and kept the house supplied with flowers. Everyone made quite a fuss over him, we were told, and the five elderly women obviously felt proud that they had a "head of household."

In this house, the bedrooms were quite varied in size and desirability, ranging from a large sunny "master bedroom" with a bay window to a small narrow room—perhaps the maid's room in former days. We asked if there was any problem or ill feeling because of the difference in size of the rooms. The housekeeper looked surprised and said no—residents took whatever room had become vacant and were glad that a place had opened up for them in an Abbeyfield house.

We were told of the very successful "morning coffee" that had been held the previous week. Organizing a coffee is a typical money-raising project in Great Britain (similar to what would be called a "Silver tea" in the United States). Announcements are made in the neighborhood and local churches that there is to be a coffee for the purpose of buying a new television set, for example, and tickets are sold for the event. There are often hand-crafted items for sale, made by both the residents and the sponsoring committee. It is obvious that such functions serve purposes far beyond simply raising money. They give a "purpose" to the residents many months in advance, as they sew and knit items for sale. Furthermore, such events bring neighbors into the house so that they become acquainted with the residents and get interested in their welfare. The sponsoring committee also becomes more involved with the residents as they work in a joint project.

Belfast, Northern Ireland. We drove cautiously through the narrow streets for a visit to one of the most unusual Abbeyfield houses in the United Kingdom. This was located in a huge, low-income housing project in the central "battle zone" of Belfast. We passed bombed-out buildings, piles of rubble, broken windows, "Brits go home" signs splashed on the walls. Finally, we came into a large, littered courtyard surrounded by gray high-rise buildings and rang the doorbell in a first floor apartment with a small sign, Abbeyfield.

The flat was neat, pleasant, and cheerful inside—in stark contrast to the courtyard. The good smell of meat cooking permeated the house. The housekeeper proudly showed us through the home and introduced us to each of the elderly residents. "Visitors from America!" she would explain. "From Florida!"

"Ah—from Florida!" exclaimed one elderly lady. "Now would you be knowin' my nephew in Tampa? If you ever meet him, you tell him how comfortable it is for me here. I had a flat in the big high rise, right over there, but I couldn't live alone anymore. It was too dangerous and I couldn't go out and shop. I'm glad to be here—it's safe and we get good meals. You tell him if you see him!"

This Abbeyfield house is unique because it is located in a large, low-income public housing project. Two adjacent first-floor flats were combined into one large unit, with doors cut into the walls between them, so that one housekeeper takes care of six residents. It was quite a feat for Abbeyfield to secure permission to combine flats for this unusual purpose, but the authorities finally bent the rules. In contrast to the Abbeyfields in manor houses, the rooms were small and modestly furnished. However, this is what the residents, who had always lived in the area, were accustomed to. They were near friends and family. They did not seem to be bothered by living in such a "troubled" section of Belfast, even though they could not walk any more in the little garden area behind the flat. The housekeeper told us, "People often throw rubbish out of the upper windows, and we wouldn't want anyone to get hit with a telly."

The unit is sponsored by an organization of business and professional women in Belfast. It was not possible to secure sponsors from the housing project itself. The women have been actively involved in money-raising activities for the benefit of this Abbeyfield house, sponsoring bazaars, bake sales, and rummage sales.

Suburban Edinburgh. A pleasant, upper middle class suburban neighborhood on the edge of the city was the location of this second Abbeyfield home that we visited. It was a large, attractive house—perhaps the former home of a banker or lawyer. It had a neat wall around the grounds with an attractive garden and a lawn like a putting green. The back of the house overlooked a meadow. The spacious living room had a fireplace, paintings on the wall, antiques here and there. An adjacent sunporch looked over the garden. "Mrs. Farley is the most marvelous cook!" exclaimed the director of the house committee. "She bakes something fresh for the residents every night, and they just love it!" (Mrs. Farley beamed.) We were told later that the residents "make such a fuss over her," for they claim that they never had such good meals in their lives.

We were taken around the house to meet all of the residents. Some were in their rooms, where they showed us the pictures of their families and told us where they had acquired various treasures and souvenirs that were displayed.

These four examples illustrate how local societies have taken existing buildings and converted them into Abbeyfield houses. As the movement spread, the national organization realized that in some areas, desirable older homes could not be found and specially built houses would be more suitable.

PURPOSE-BUILT HOUSES

It was originally thought that the elderly would prefer "old-fashioned" houses, for these would be similar to what they had lived in all their lives. Converted houses have some disadvantages, however, for maintenance costs are higher, bedrooms are of different sizes and desirability, and old houses are usually two or three stories high. The housekeeper's rooms are often not as desirable in regard to size and placement as one would wish. For example, in some houses, the housekeeper's rooms are on the third floor, which necessitates a great deal of climbing of stairs. Since many housekeepers are sixty years or older, this may be a real disadvantage. Furthermore, it is impossible to find a suitable house to convert in some areas.

In recent years, some societies have chosen purpose-built houses, which are like large, modern homes. These may be built in new housing areas, where elderly people want to live in an Abbeyfield house but be near their families, or in redevelopment areas of large cities. Although a larger capital investment is needed, the local housing authority mortgage on a new building can be repaid over sixty years, in comparison to thirty years for a converted house.

The purpose-built houses are neat and homey, and the housekeeper's apartment is comfortable, attractive, and well-placed in regard to the residents' rooms. The bathroom facilities are modern and include safety

These two examples of purpose-built Abbeyfield homes in Great Britain show variation in architecture and style, according to the requirements of the site and the wishes of the organizers. One is a single-story structure and blends into the neighborhood. The other is modern in design and can accommodate more residents, being two stories in height. Purpose-built Abbeyfield homes provide a comfortable apartment for the house-keeper.

FIGURE 8.1. Floorplan for Abbeyfield Purpose-Built House

features. The bed-sitting rooms are of approximately equal size and desirability. In appendix 3, plans are presented that illustrate various floor plans for purpose-built houses. The Abbeyfield Society has house plans available for local societies to consider in their planning.

EXTRA CARE HOUSES

One of the issues of concern to Abbeyfield in recent years is how to meet the problems of growing dependency and illness of the residents. The philosophy that an Abbeyfield house was a "family" became so completely accepted that many thought that when residents became too frail to take care of themselves, they should be cared for "at home," just as a normal family often cares for its older members. This led to the establishment of "Extra Care" units, similar to a residential home, for residents who are no longer able to care for themselves.

There is a considerable difference of opinion within the leadership of the Abbeyfield Society, and within the local societies, as to the need for Extra Care and the advisability of the Abbeyfield Society devoting its attention to this demanding problem. Some society members feel that it is difficult enough simply to operate an Abbeyfield house and that the already scarce resources should not be spread thinner by using them for more expensive nursing care. Furthermore, they feel that community volunteers could be used to greatest advantage in assisting the healthier ambulatory elderly, not the confused, invalid, or handicapped elderly.

Dr. H. Beric Wright, chairman of the Medical Advisory Commitee, wrote:

I took the view firstly that we had enough other problems to deal with and secondly . . . that Extra Care was a specialized activity which should be left to Doctors. . . . I have entirely changed my views and am now strongly in favor of our developing Extra Care facilities. Various changes and developments have contributed to this shift of attitude. The two main ones are our own strength and growth, and the sad inability of the social services to even begin to live up to their early promise. Additionally, my reading of the health care scene . . . is that in general terms the situation will get worse before it begins to improve. (Abbeyfield Extra Care n.d.:11)

Dr. Wright also argues that as residents move into Extra Care, the organizing group must be prepared to think flexibly, for the residents are frail, sometimes mentally disoriented, and perhaps incontinent. One adaptation that may be necessary is that residents may have to give up the privacy of a single room. Small wards of three or four people may make it easier for the staff to cope and also help to control costs. Dr. Wright observes:

Patients are easier to look after in four bedded wards than in single rooms. Indeed, to a degree they look after each other: they for instance sound the alarm when one falls out of bed or goes wandering. In addition it is easier for the staff to cope: and the availability and cost of staff is a critical factor in all this. (Abbeyfield Extra Care n.d.:12)

Residents in Extra Care may not be able to use all of their own furniture, except for a bed and chair.

Extra Care also means that some people will have to be moved from their houses. While some Abbeyfield houses have built Extra Care unit wings adjacent to their houses, in other cases, several societies have joined together to support an Extra Care home in their area to serve several homes. Dr. Wright points out that this means some people will have to move to be accommodated, but he adds that it is better to move to an Abbeyfield Extra Care than to a geriatric ward in a hospital or to a nursing home.

Finally, there is the question of medical services. Dr. Wright believes that one physician should serve an Extra Care unit instead of having each person engage his or her own physician.

The Abbeyfield Society stresses the need for residents to maintain a continuity in their lives and tries to avoid a sense of institutionalization. The society hopes to achieve the sense of a small community, akin to a family in its social and medical ties and in its internal organization and relationships. The society believes that this family sense can be achieved ideally with an average of fifteen residents, although there are also good economic arguments for larger homes with up to twenty-five residents.

The national organization has had great success in convincing the government of the need for Extra Care, and in the past year, many units all over Britain have been financed at the rate of £350,000 to £500,000 for units of about twenty people. Thus, residents can stay under the Abbeyfield umbrella, even when they become too frail to live in an Abbeyfield house.

THE ABBEYFIELD SOCIETY EVALUATES ITSELF

The application of social science research to assess programs has become widespread, particularly as part of public programs in the 1960s. Howard Freeman (1977) wrote that evaluation research in the United States had become a "growth industry." Evaluation research is part of the broad social trend to maximize rationality in the operation of human resources and human service programs, particularly those that are tax supported.

Self-evaluation is a process that most organizations find difficult to initiate. Thus, it is remarkable to find that a small, nonprofit British organization, the Abbeyfield Society, made a deliberate decision to evaluate itself after twenty years of steady growth and increased public service. This was a bold and significant decision, because as a private, voluntary body, it did not have the same statutory responsibility as does a public agency. The leaders of Abbeyfield made the decision, however, and a commission was appointed in 1977 to carry out the mandate.

The initial investigation focused on four areas of study: the need for Abbeyfield-type accommodation in the United Kingdom in the next decade; the relationship of this need to the present Abbeyfield geographical spread; the possible variations on the Abbeyfield-type accommodation in relation to the forecast needs of the elderly and the rising level of expectations for housing in society; and the need for more Extra Care accommodation and the suitability of the present types of Extra Care projects.

As part of this evaluation, the Abbeyfield Society Commission on Growth contracted for a comprehensive survey with Social and Community Planning Research, a nonprofit social research organization, which specializes in the design, conduct, analysis, and interpretation of sample surveys. This organization conducted a survey of 255 residents in 100 Abbeyfield houses, selected by random sampling methods, and also interviewed a random sample of 100 housekeepers. The survey of residents included 63 interview items and yielded a wealth of data on the health, mobility, leisure activities, and general satisfaction with Abbeyfield housing. In this section, we will summarize some of the results of both the survey of residents and the report of the commission on the future of the organization. The accurate, detailed information on residents is of interest because it indicated to sponsoring groups the precise nature of the target population and aided them in defining their goals and procedures in meeting the needs of this group. It gave a national perspective to the needs of Abbeyfield in relation to the local societies.

Characteristics of Respondents. The average age of the respondents was 81, and four out of five were women. Nearly two-thirds were widowed, and 28 percent had never married. Most were persons from middle-class status with extremely modest incomes. About 30 percent came from a family with a managerial or professional status. About one-third were white collar, and almost 20 percent were from a skilled category. The survey also asked questions about the person's income, and some persons were reluctant to reveal their income, as is characteristic of other industrialized societies. In all, about 18 percent of the respondents in the survey refused or were unable to give an answer about their income. Approximately three-fourths of those reporting their income needed government supplemental benefits to pay their Abbeyfield fee. This means that 76 percent had an income less than £34 a week. Abbeyfield fees varied according to the expenses in the house and the cost of the mortgage. They ranged form £15 to £37 in 1978, with the median charge being £22 (Morton-Williams 1979:74).

Health. The health of residents was rated by asking them about their illnesses and giving a score to each person. A major illness or ailment was scored as two points, and a mild illness was scored as one point. The scores were then added and respondents were divided into three health-score groups: 33 percent reported good health, with a score of 0 to 4; 42 percent had moderate health, with a score of 5 to 10; and 25 percent were rated as being in poor health, with a score of 11 to 42.

This method of health scoring was the same as that used in a community survey carried out by a British organization, Age Concern (Abrams 1978). When the Abbeyfield residents were compared to the community residents, there was approximately the same distribution of common ailments in the Abbeyfield residents as in the community sample of British over 75 years of age. Arthritis and rheumatism were reported to be the most common ailments.

A substantial minority (37 percent) said their health had improved since coming to Abbeyfield; 35 percent said it had stayed the same which, among the elderly, must be regarded as an achievement. . . . Of those who had been in Abbeyfield less than a year, 45 percent said their health had improved, suggesting that the change to Abbeyfield contributes to their well being. (Morton-Williams 1979:60)

In this context, it should be mentioned that the interviewers were asked to give an assessment of how lucid they thought the respondents were. The interviewers rated almost two-thirds of the residents as being lucid and clear thinking, and 29 percent as fairly lucid. Only 7 percent were rated as confused.

Happiness. One of the first questions asked by people who hear about alternative living arrangements is, "Are the elderly really happy there?" The Abbeyfield survey confronted this question directly, asking residents to say overall how they felt about living in an Abbeyfield house, what they liked about it, and what they felt could be improved. Over half (58 percent) said they were "very happy" living there, a third (34 percent) were fairly happy, and only 7 percent said that they were not really happy (Morton-Williams 1979:47). The residents were then asked what they liked about living in the Abbeyfield house, and a list of seventeen different advantages was compiled. The three most frequently mentioned attributes were, first, the house had a good atmosphere and was like a family; second, the freedom, for no one interfered and there were no strict rules; and third, the privacy of having their own room.

Many residents emphasized the importance of the housekeeper with such comments as "The housekeeper is marvelous; she makes sure that no one is left out and she's always cheerful" (Morton-Williams 1979:48).

A question was also asked about what could be improved in the house, and 47 percent replied, "Nothing." Only 6 percent complained about the food and thought meals could be improved (certainly a small percentage, if we consider that in any group there are certain to be some people who do not like the food). Three percent wished they could have a better room, and another 3 percent said the bathroom was too far away or in the wrong place. Those who rated themselves as "very happy" in Abbeyfield were much less likely to mention any criticisms. Only 8 percent said that they would consider moving if there were other options available.

Activities. Abbeyfield residents are by no means isolated from family and friends, for 62 percent saw one or more relatives at least once a month; 41 percent were visited by a close relative at least once a week. In addition, 44 percent had friends who came to visit them at least once a month, and 27 percent reported friends visited them at least once a week.

The residents, in general, were very active, for almost half (47 percent) went out at least five times a week. Attending outside activities or shopping is, of course, related to the age and health condition of the individual residents. When asked if they would want more organized activities outside the house, 77 percent said they would not want any more, and 85 percent said they would not want any more activities organized inside the house.

When queried about the indoor activities they enjoyed most, 47 percent said reading was something they did a lot, and an additional 21 percent said they read "a fair bit." Listening to the radio was mentioned by 27 percent and watching television by 16 percent as activities they engaged in a lot. Knitting, sewing, and crocheting were also popular activities.

Coming to Abbeyfield. What are the situations and circumstances that lead persons to become residents of Abbeyfield? One-third of the residents in an Abbeyfield house had lived there for one year or less, and only 8 percent had lived there ten years or more. The average age when a person entered Abbeyfield was 77, while at the time of the survey, the average age of respondents when interviewed was 81. Although over 22 percent of the residents were 85 years of age at the time of the survey, only 9 percent were that old when they moved in. About half of the residents were between the ages of 71 and 80 when they moved in.

At the time the residents moved into Abbeyfield, about two-thirds of them had been living alone, and over half of these people (55 percent) had been living alone for five years or more. Most of the residents came from the immediate vicinity of the Abbeyfield house in which they live; about one-half had lived within two miles of the house, and almost two-thirds had lived within five miles. In terms of their previous living situation, over half of the Abbeyfield residents had lived in an entire house by themselves, and another quarter had lived in a self-contained apartment.

How Do People Hear About Abbeyfield? Residents of Abbeyfield learn about the houses in a variety of ways. Informal social and community networks, that is, through a friend or relative, or through someone at a church, accounted for almost half of the means whereby persons heard about Abbeyfield. About 25 percent of the residents reported some previous connections with an Abbeyfield house, such as a relative, a friend, or someone who was a housekeeper. Another 15 percent of the residents had heard about Abbeyfield through the welfare system, and only 10 percent said they first heard about Abbeyfield through various kinds of publicity such as an advertisement, a feature article in a magazine or newspaper, or a circular that was mailed to them. There was usually a triggering factor that led persons to come to Abbeyfield, such as recent bereavement or illness, or some kind of crisis having to do with their residence or finances. But for many, the decision to move to an Abbeyfield home arose out of the gradual deterioration of their physical or emotional health. After a person applied to Abbeyfield, it was possible for 40 percent of them to move into an Abbeyfield house within one month; 63 percent, within three months. This is a remarkable responsiveness on the part of Abbeyfield in being able to accommodate persons who feel they should be in shared housing of this type.

The first use of the survey was for the leadership of the society to have a clear picture of the residents, their needs, capabilities, and satisfaction. In addition, extensive survey data were gathered on 100 housekeepers, their conditions of employment, training, their rapid turnover, and their "involvement" in Abbeyfield. A careful survey of this sort is of great value to management in evaluating their program and determining what components need to be strengthened or modified.

CROSS-NATIONAL COMPARISONS IN SHARED LIVING

The study of the Abbeyfield Society provides a unique opportunity to compare the way in which shared living is organized and delivered in the United States and in the United Kingdom. Let us first note the similarities between the two nations and then direct our attention to those aspects that differentiate the results. We should stress that this comparative assessment is not set forth to show that one form is superior to another, for the primary assumption that the student of comparative social organizations must accept is that a service program like shared housing is rooted in the social structure of a particular society and reflects its basic values and customs.

In two societies as similar as the United States and Great Britain, one would expect many similarities. It needs to be emphasized, however, that American and British culture also diverge in significant ways. For example, Britain is not as legalistic and adversarial as the United States, and it seemed to us more pragmatic about bending the rules to meet the needs of local groups and individuals. Perhaps because of their war experience, British seemed to be more patient, tolerant, and pragmatic—less concerned with speedy results. They know how to "dig in their heels" and keep working on an idea. For example, the founder of the Abbeyfield Society asked eighty people to join his first house and got eighty refusals before he found one person who said yes.

The fundamental similarity that strikes the observer is that the target population in both nations is identical and results from the same forces of modernization and the demographic patterns associated with urbanization, industrialization, and bureaucratization. Both the United States and the United Kingdom are developed societies that have a higher percentage of elderly than less developed societies. Within each, there is a growing percentage of frail persons who are in need of supportive living arrangements of the kind described in this book. Therefore, the need for the formation of organizations to deal with frail, lonely old people is similar in both countries. The organizers are from similar backgrounds, usually religious and humane persons concerned with a dependent population. It should be emphasized that in both countries, it has been private voluntary groups that provided the initiative for these organizations.

Other similarities include the selection of the residents and the attempt to create a compatible small group atmosphere. In both countries, there is a problem of locating concerned and competent staff and maintaining their involvement and commitment to the work despite its difficulties and lower pay scale than other occupations. Another common problem is that in both countries, the advanced age of the residents means there is increased frailty and incapacity, which makes it difficult after a few years for these persons to remain in the house and take care of their personal needs. There has been a tendency to use older homes and remodel them in both countries. Finally, and very importantly, because the sponsoring organizations are privately organized and supported, each local unit must maintain its economic viability.

One of the major differences between the situation in the United States and that in Great Britain is that there is a national organization in Great Britain, with a central office providing information, coordination, and assistance to the hundreds of local societies scattered throughout the British Isles. Indeed, the growth of the national organization and the spread of the Abbeyfield idea have made it necessary to regionalize the administration and coordination of the society's activities.

Although the Abbeyfield Society is only one of several organizations providing housing and care for older people, it constitutes a kind of "social movement" directed to the welfare of older people. One index of the prestige of Abbeyfield is the number of persons of high rank who have been associated with it, for the royal patron is Prince Charles, heir to the throne. Another patron is the archbishop of Canterbury, primate of England. The patronage of these persons of high social rank is impossible to duplicate in the United States because of the general cultural context—a republican form of government and a diversity of religious denominations. We have no single person whose endorsement confers such prestige.

Another contrast between the two situations is found in the strong local Abbeyfield societies, which include local community leaders—physicians, lawyers, accountants, social leaders, and others of high status. It is our observation that these local sponsors and committee members have long-term commitments to Abbeyfield and its purposes.

A major difference between the experience in the United States to date and that in the United Kingdom is the way in which the Abbeyfield sponsors have been able to utilize the resources provided by government agencies to expand and improve the work of Abbeyfield. The adroitness, statesmanship, and flexibility of the Abbeyfield sponsors, many of whom are more conservative politically than the supporters of the welfare state, have enabled them to put aside their political predilections and find ways to use government funds for the work of the Abbeyfield Society and for the benefit of the older people it serves. The pragmatic manner in which the agencies of the British government and private groups relate to one another is thus an important factor behind the success of shared housing in that country. This cooperation illustrates how a bureaucratic government can adapt itself to deal with the needs and problems at the local level.

Another difference between the two societies concerns cultural homogeneity and diversity. Britain has only 4 percent minority peoples, primarily from colonial areas. The United States, in contrast, comprises around 18 to 20 percent of ethnic minorities. Abbeyfield leaders are aware of their responsibilities to minorities. They recognize that ethnic groups have different cultural traditions and dietary preferences that may require special attention because the older members of these communities attach particular importance to them. The Abbeyfield Society is well aware of this fact, and it recognizes that adaptability tends to diminish with increasing age.

Abbeyfield leaders point out that people from similar social, religious, or ethnic backgrounds may integrate more readily and easily in a small housing arrangement than a mixed group from varied backgrounds. At the present time, ethnic groups are not involved in the Abbeyfield Society, and the leaders of Abbeyfield observe that perhaps such integration cannot take place in this generation. They realize that the question is not one solely of diet or other special requirements, for diet could easily be handled by the housekeeper, as other dietary problems are handled, such as diabetes. One solution could be to set up a special house to accommodate special nutritional preferences. In Edinburgh, for example, the society has set up a house for vegetarians. When one is dealing with ethnic minorities, the problems may become more complicated and may require considerable sensitivity in regard to ethnic differences that are based on national origin or religion.

Voluntary organizations such as Abbeyfield may have a special role in assisting minority communities to adapt special sheltered housing arrangements to their own requirements. In the commission report on the future of the society, Abbeyfield leaders wrote:

Where the ethnic minorities are concerned, we believe the broad idea of Abbeyfield may have a great deal to offer them during the period—which may be quite long—until they are so fully assimilated into the community that their elderly members can live in the intimacy of an ordinary Abbeyfield house without embarrassment, distress, or difficulty either to themselves or to others. We therefore recommend, that after consultation with the relevant statutory and other bodies, every opportunity and indeed encouragement, should be given to those concerned with the welfare of the older members of the several ethnic minorities to consider adapting the Abbeyfield idea to the requirements of the various groups. (1979:52–53)

The United States is much more diversified in its ethnic composition. It has a written constitution and statutes that explicitly state that there must be equality of opportunity and services, particularly when these involve public accommodations or funds. If shared family homes in the United States were to receive public funds, it is likely that there would be criticism and official inquiries about the lack of racial and cultural diversity within the houses.[2]

CONCLUSIONS: ABBEYFIELD LOOKS TO THE FUTURE

We have provided an overview of the Abbeyfield Society—its structure, organization, residents, and how they view their housing. This leads us

---

2. An integrated house, Ridgeview, has been opened in Largo, Florida, by Share-A-Home of Upper Pinellas County. This house adapts the concepts from milieu therapy to foster a mutual support system among the residents (Sauer 1983).

to a discussion of the society's analysis of its future, based on the survey of Abbeyfield houses in England and Wales. The thoughtful report, *The Lights Are Green* (1979), considered all of the major aspects of the society and analyzed the direction in which the organization is moving. The report focused on the need for housing of this type, the houses, and the rate of growth. The authors estimated that in the next twenty years, their target group of people over seventy-five will be half a million persons, and that 10 percent of these, or fifty thousand, would be well-served by living in shared accommodations such as Abbeyfield. Thus, the authors predicted a clear need in the future for a greatly expanded number of houses. At the time of the study, however, Abbeyfield was serving about five thousand people and was growing at the rate of forty to fifty houses a year. Thus, they concluded that there is an enormous challenge in helping the society to grow at the fastest practicable rate.

There are many limiting factors that may impede this growth, but four principal ones can be identified:

1) Money. The major source of growth for Abbeyfield has been grants from government authorities to build and renovate Abbeyfield houses. They anticipate that public monies will be their future major source of funds for growth. However, the society will continue to seek private funds through gifts, bequests, and endowments.

2) The voluntary principle. This is deeply embedded in the work of the Abbeyfield Society, but the use of volunteers can be a "chancy business," to use their words. They made specific suggestions to local societies as to how better leadership could stimulate the recruitment and use of volunteers. They suggested that each local society review itself every five years and recruit new people into the organization.

3) The national society's relation to the local groups. The authors of the report recognized that the regional offices and area chairmen were under "unfair pressure" and there was a need to reorganize their relationships. They suggested that the county become the unit of organization.

4) The need to strengthen the central office. The Society identified the importance of the Project Advisory Service, which advises local societies on the procedures to obtain government housing grants. They observed that the staff is overworked and that in order to obtain these housing grants, the central administration must have an increased staff.

In short, the Abbeyfield Society in Great Britain has shown itself to be a model organization in providing family-type housing for the frail elderly at an economical cost. Although there are cultural differences in the way in which services for older people are organized in Great Britain and the United States, we can learn a great deal from the British model. There is little doubt that the model of the Abbeyfield Society, with a national structure based upon local autonomy and a large cadre of volunteers, is an effective mechanism for providing this kind of service. Abbeyfield's leaders are aware of the limitations and the problems and have devised practical ways to meet them. Americans who wish to sponsor shared housing can be encouraged by the British success.

CHAPTER NINE

Problems and Dilemmas in Establishing Shared Living Facilities

We have shown in earlier chapters that a shared living facility "works" from the standpoint of the residents. Such a facility provides a comfortable home, a safe and secure environment, companionship, and nutritious meals at a modest cost. Now let us turn our attention to how a shared living arrangement "works" from the vantage point of the organizers. What are some of the factors involved in success and what are some of the dilemmas that may cause difficulties? These may be divided into two main categories: internal factors and external factors. By internal factors, we mean those that arise primarily within the houses themselves and are concerned with the services delivered by the programs. These include locating and acquiring the property, selecting the residents, and hiring and training the staff. Also included are such elements as keeping up the morale of the residents and the commitment and dedication of the volunteer organizers. The external factors include legal issues and constraints, zoning ordinances and regulations, and licensure and certification. The organizers and managers are constantly pulled in two directions as they respond to different pressures, priorities, and expectations from internal and external demands.

Because shared living environments are usually designed to approximate the home environment, many of the every day problems of the traditional household are present. Persons considering the establishment of such projects should be aware of both these problems and some of the external factors that naturally develop because of the unique structure of these living arrangements.

INTERNAL FACTORS

Location and Acquisition of Property. One of the major problem areas encountered by a group attempting to establish a shared living facility is the acquisition of suitable property. If a source of subsidy funding is lacking, then economic viability is related to the number of residents who may be accommodated. For this reason, structures with many bedrooms and large common areas are required. It is usually economically unfeasible for project organizers to construct purpose-built structures, so it is necessary for them to "retrofit" existing buildings. Among the existing projects we have studied, there is a clear preference for older, single-family structures. Due in part to space requirements and a limited amount of funds available, many groups expend large amounts of energy and time searching for a suitable structure. In most cases, the house that is finally located is in need of major renovation work before residents can move in. Because of these factors, the location of suitable property is one of the most time-consuming and costly activities encountered by an organizing group.

At some point in the establishment of a shared living facility, organizers must make the decision whether to buy or lease property. The purchase of property by an organizing group helps to stabilize costs over the long run, but it may also have negative legal consequences if the venture should fail. Purchase also requires that there be a relatively permanent legal entity, usually a nonprofit corporation, to take financial and legal responsibility for the property. Even though they may have no personal liability, many groups are unwilling to commit themselves to borrowing substantial sums of money when repayment is based solely upon their ability to attract residents to a new facility. One approach to this problem has been to have a particular church purchase the property and act as a benign landlord while the organizing group administers the project.

Since the purchase of the property is usually not feasible, most organizing groups have opted to rent the property. Since older persons usually have limited incomes, the stabilization of costs is important. By renting property, however, the organizers will probably face increased rental costs in the future. These costs are passed on to the residents. It is then difficult to attract residents from among those who own their own houses and, therefore, have more or less stable housing costs. The obvious answer to this problem seems to be a long-term lease, but here again organizers may be hesitant to commit themselves to any long-term arrangement.

Costs. Some of the more difficult questions asked by those who are planning a shared living facility concern the amount of money it will take to start the facility and the month-to-month costs. Because each facility is different, in terms of both service delivery and the initial cost of housing, and because the cost of living varies widely in different parts of the country, there are no simple answers. It is possible, however, to make a tentative estimate of the amount of money available for the operation of such a facility.

Before any calculations can be made, one must make two decisions. First, how much money the residents can pay for shared living, and second, how many persons are to live in the planned facility. The monthly charge to residents is based upon a number of elements, including the availability of rental housing in the area, the "market" rents of other structures, the location of the proposed structure, and the amount of renovation (or "retrofitting") that is required. Keeping in mind that any of these elements, or other elements specific to a particular locality, may require a substantial increase in the proposed monthly payment, a convenient starting point would be around $500 per person per month. Similarly, one should assume, for planning purposes, a facility designed to house from eight to ten residents. When making planning assumptions, it is prudent to underestimate the capacity and overestimate the charges. Therefore, in this example, we shall assume a population of ten persons and a monthly charge of $500 per person, providing the sponsoring group $5,000 per month with which to operate a shared living facility. At this point, a budget can be constructed that will give some indication of the costs involved.

The rent for a house capable of housing ten residents in five bedrooms is likely to be in the $1,000–$1,200 per month range. Again, assuming the higher cost, $1,200 per month would represent 24 percent of the budget. If the hypothetical planning group feels it is reasonable to spend 24 percent of the budget on housing, and if a house large enough for ten people can be located for $1,200 per month, then the group can proceed. However, if the planning group would like each resident to have a private room, or if local conditions require significantly higher (or lower) rents, then either the monthly payments must be increased (or decreased) or the plan must be modified. Modifications of the plan would include having a house donated by a church or other philanthropic source, locating the facility in a low-rent area, or purchasing the house with funds generated by the sponsoring group.

Assuming a housing cost of 24 percent ($1,200 per month), the hypothetical planning group should then consider the costs of food. Although existing facilities have been able to hold food costs down by buying in bulk and by very selective purchasing methods, local conditions have a major impact upon food prices. There are examples of shared living facilities where the total food expenditure is but 15 percent of the budget. However, the hypothetical planning group might consider 20 percent a more reasonable estimate. Thus, food costs would be approximately $1,000 per month. Each resident would receive ninety meals per month at a cost of $100 per person or $1.11 per meal. Obviously, breakfasts would cost less than dinners. Again, a decision must be made. If the sponsoring group feels these food costs are low for a particular locale, then the monthly payments must be increased.

The next major expense item that should be considered is the cost of staff. The questions are simple, the answers are not. The main questions are: how many staff persons will be needed, how many hours will they work, and what is to be their starting salary? A good way to avoid such questions temporarily is to start with an assumed budget figure and determine what can be afforded with the money available. If we assume a budget figure of 34 percent, the hypothetical planning group will have $1,700 per month to spend on staff. Although $1,700 per month for staff may at first seem to be a large amount of money, one must consider the duties of the staff. Again, local requirements are best determined by local planners, but the usual staff duties are cooking, cleaning, "social" duties, and "management" duties. Obviously, the last two categories are a bit amorphous and are subject to local definition, but they are, to many planning groups, at least as important as the other duties.

In a house of ten residents, it is reasonable to assume that one staff person needs to be on duty at any one time, and other staff persons could be part time. How the duties are divided and how such issues as hours, replacements, and stand-by personnel are dealt with are vitally important, but here the hypothetical planning group is considering only numbers of people and amounts of money. The realities involved represent an entirely different area of difficulty and are discussed in chapters 3 and 4. One important decision is whether a person will be on duty twenty-four hours a day. This varies in different houses, for some specify that the housekeeper must live on the premises, others hire a person (perhaps a student) to sleep in the facility, and others depend on the residents to telephone for assistance if it is needed. Local service requirements are the best determinant of the most efficacious path to follow, but the relationship of staff hours to services is contingent on local conditions, needs of the residents, and the involvement of the organizing committees.

So far the hypothetical planning group has allocated 78 percent ($3,900) of its budget on housing, food, and staff. The remaining 22 percent ($1,100 per month) must be divided among many different areas. If transportation is to be provided as a service, then a suitable vehicle must be bought or leased and insurance must be purchased. If 10 percent of the budget is spent for transportation costs (including vehicle, gasoline, insurance, and repair and maintenance), then $500 per month is available for these costs. If transportation is not to be a part of the services, then this money may be used to pay salaries or to reduce the monthly payment by $50 per resident.

It is likely that regardless of the area of the country within which the planned facility will be located, utility payments will represent about 10 percent of the budget. With expenses for telephone, water, sewerage, electricity, garbage pick-up, and the like, it is not unreasonable to expect a $500 total monthly utility bill for a house with ten residents. In any event, it would be better to overestimate this cost item than to underestimate it.

The hypothetical budget is now down to its last 2 percent ($100). With that remaining $100 per month, expenses such as administrative costs, liability insurance, renters' insurance (or homeowners' insurance), and maintenance costs must be paid. It is obvious that, assuming the budget categories and amounts above, any group planning a shared living facility must be very careful. The contingency fund is not great, and a group underestimating the cost of any one of the categories might be forced to seek financial help from outside sources if unexpected expenses occur. Table 9.1 is the final monthly budget for the hypothetical planning group. Table 9.2 presents the same information in terms of the cost per month to each resident.

TABLE *9.1. Hypothetical Monthly Budget for a Shared Living Facility Housing Ten Residents*

Budget Category	Monthly Amount	Percent of Total Monthly Budget
Housing	$1,200	24
Food	1,000	20
Staff	1,700	34
Transportation	500	10
Utilities	500	10
Insurance, administrative costs, and maintenance	100	2
Total	$5,000	100

It is relatively easy to design a planning budget; it is far more difficult to estimate the amount of seed money necessary for a particular group to establish a shared living facility. Because each situation is so different, one can only guess at the amount of money necessary to start such a facility. There are, however, several considerations that make this estimate more accurate. First, the amount of seed money required is inextricably linked to the acquisition and renovation costs of the house.

TABLE *9.2. Cost to Each Resident in a Hypothetical Ten-Member Shared Living Facility*

Budget Category	Monthly Payment	Percent of Total Monthly Payment
Housing	$120.00	24
Food	100.00	20
Staff	170.00	34
Transportation	50.00	10
Utilities	50.00	10
Insurance, administrative costs, and maintenance	10.00	2
Total monthly costs per resident	$500.00	100

Where the house is rented and the renovations are minimal, obviously the start-up costs will be less. Secondly, the number of residents expected to move in on the day the facility is opened has a significant impact upon the amount of money needed. If the house is fortunate enough to have full occupancy from the start, less money for paying deficits will be needed. Finally, lawyer's fees, real estate agent's fees, and incorporation fees (assuming the group is incorporated) all require the planning group to have a certain amount of start-up or seed money. Some groups are fortunate enough to have the required professional services donated by qualified persons within the organizing group.

The most common, and incidentally most expensive, start-up costs tend to be acquisition and renovation costs and budget deficits caused by vacancies. It is not at all uncommon for a planning group to spend $20,000 renovating an old house. It is also not uncommon to have only four or five residents in a newly opened house designed for ten people. The group planning to open a shared living facility would do well to accumulate as much seed money as is possible before the facility is actually opened. Here again, local requirements are best understood by the planning group involved, but a reasonable estimate of the amount of start-up money required may be estimated.

Using our original assumptions of ten residents and $500 per month per resident, the yearly income and yearly expenses would be $60,000 (ten residents × $500 × 12 months = $60,000). Five residents, however, would yield only $30,000. Assuming a renovation cost of $20,000 and an average occupancy for the first year of 50 percent, perhaps $40,000 would be needed in start-up money to renovate and support the facility for one year ($20,000 renovation costs plus $20,000 to make up for vacancies). It is obvious that the assumptions here are not precise, because the food costs and staff costs for five residents would be less than for ten residents. However, the rents or mortgage, utilities, insurance, etc. would be constant.

We were informed by one group that they determined their budget on the basis of five people in a six-person household. Thus, if a vacancy occurred, the finances were not disrupted, and if the house remained fully occupied, they were able to build up a contingency fund.

Of course, if no renovation is necessary or if some individual or philanthropic organization can be found to underwrite possible budget deficits, then the required seed money can be substantially reduced. What should be clear is that, although the precise amount of money required to start a shared living facility varies widely in response to local concerns, planning groups need more than good intentions to get such a facility started.

Organizers often wonder if they can receive income supplements for low-income residents under Section 8 provisions. Although some units have been able to get a variance from local officials, a strict interpretation of HUD rules presents obstacles, for each eligible resident is required to have private access to a bathroom and kitchenette. In addition, food stamps and SSI benefits are sometimes reduced if the elderly person moves into shared facilities, even though such housing would result in a net federal savings, in comparison to new construction. It will be recalled from chapter 6 that when Ithacare was organized, HUD officials finally decided that provision of a small cabinet refrigerator in each room would satisfy the private kitchenette specifications, and the project was able to receive Section 8 renovation subsidies.

In Great Britain, the more flexible regulations permit the subsidizing of low-income persons in shared housing. In the United States, shared housing is often not the best economic solution for the very poorest elderly, for they would lose other benefits.

Residents. Another problem area is the location and recruitment of potential residents. Because of the relatively small size of the sponsoring organizations, little time and money may be devoted to the recruitment of residents. In many cases, the primary responsibility for recruitment has been delegated to a general manager or project director. More often than not, these directors or managers are also responsible for the day-to-day operation of the individual facilities so that only a small amount of time may be set aside for recruitment purposes. As a result, some projects depend upon "at need" recruitment procedures, whereby they look for residents only when space is available. This policy of recruitment may have adverse effects. By not maintaining a waiting list of potential residents, the organizers are forced to deal with a vacancy as a crisis situation. By delaying recruitment procedures, the personnel involved must then devote all of their efforts to locating residents in the shortest period possible.

Another related problem is that organizers have to make an assessment of the compatibility of potential residents. It is difficult even for experts, such as psychiatrists or psychologists, to determine precisely whether personalities will mesh together harmoniously in an organization. To help ensure compatibility, many projects have adopted a trial period wherein new residents are slowly introduced to the day-to-day life of the house. This trial period may help in the selection process, even though some new residents may be on their best behavior during the trial period. The projects that have been successful over moderately long periods of time have also been fortunate in selecting residents who can and will live cooperatively.

Because of the lack of clear definition of the goals of some of these projects, organizers and those responsible for recruitment may also be unclear as to the target population to be served. Indeed, organizers may find that their facilities are attracting a potential resident population that is very different from the one envisioned in the planning stages. For example, in areas with large populations of low-income elderly, organizers may see the shared living facility as a cost-effective way of housing these individuals. Because of the costs of organizing a shared living facility, however, the lower income elderly person may not be able to afford the services of such a facility. Therefore, the organizers must seek potential residents from a higher income group, who may or may not need the services of a shared living facility. The fact that the target population envisioned in the planning stages may not be the actual population that is served has been a major source of concern for some of these organizers.

A somewhat related problem occurred when organizers confused the actual need for shared living projects with the general expression of approval for facilities of this type. For example, if one asks people if they think shared housing is a good idea and they answer affirmatively, this does not mean that they would be willing to move into such a facility themselves. Confusing these very different issues has caused several organizing groups to open a shared living facility only to discover that, while it may be true that many approve of this type of facility, they are reluctant to move themselves. A striking example of this kind of misperception of need by organizers occurred when one organizing group went so far as to conduct a needs assessment. These organizers took into account population data, migration patterns, present housing data, and a number of other factors, all designed to tell them precisely if a shared living facility was needed, and if so, how many people it should be designed to accommodate. It was determined that at least 200 people in this particular locale needed this type of living arrangement. The organizers were so sure that need existed that they purchased a house, renovated it, and hired a full-time staff. After two months, the organizers had not received a single application for residency. It then became necessary for the organizers to dismiss the staff and sell the property at substantial loss, to avoid defaulting on the mortgage.

Staff. Securing a qualified house manager and a house staff is sometimes another source of difficulty. Usually, a shared living project with more than one unit will employ what we have termed project staff in addition to the house staff. The project staff are primarily responsible for the administrative details of the project, while at the same time retaining overall responsibility for the day-to-day operation of the facility. The project staff also act as liaisons between residents and the board of directors or other organizing unit. The house staff, on the other hand, are primarily concerned with domestic duties such as cooking and housekeeping.

One of the main staffing problems in shared living facilities is locating qualified house staff. Because of the financial situation of most projects, the house staff members are paid a wage that is often lower than compensation for other, similar jobs. This reduces the pool of persons willing to apply for positions in a shared living facility. In emergencies, some project organizers have had to turn to volunteers, and in some cases they have had to perform housekeeping tasks themselves.

Because of the nature of the work and the financial situation, organizers also face the problem of attempting to attract job applicants who are compassionate, dedicated, and honest to fill house staff jobs that may pay minimum wage. These house staff jobs may be high in responsibility yet low in public recognition. And even though the house staff in a shared living facility may feel they are in the best position to judge the well-being of the residents, they are occasionally viewed as household employees by the residents, the project staff, and the organizers. Obviously, with this situation, it may be difficult to keep qualified, dedicated staff on the payroll for any substantial period of time. Turnover rates tend to be high, and organizers are in the position of often searching for applicants. The personnel situation in shared housing is comparable to that faced by the operators of nursing homes. In the shared living facility, however, house staff may be paid a low cash wage, but they are compensated with room and board, and this may provide a desirable working arrangement for some types of employees.

Organizers usually find it difficult to raise the wages of employees to a level at parity with market wages, because that would raise the monthly charges to the residents. The solution has been to accept some applicants whose qualifications are sometimes lower than the ideal. This is not as serious as it sounds, for most employees are caring, competent people. But in a few cases at some shared living facilities, standards of employee behavior and quality have been sacrificed to availability.

Viability. Another issue of great concern is the issue of long-term viability of a particular house. Because few of these shared living projects have access to permanent subsidy funds, and since most projects are nonprofit organizations dedicated to providing housing at the lowest possible cost, long-term survival becomes a simple proposition of taking in more money than is paid out. Organizers and project staff usually find themselves under great pressure to maintain a standard of living at stable costs in the face of a constantly increasing cost of living. In this difficult situation, it is obvious that either more money must be collected by the project or ways of reducing costs must be found. In times of financial crisis, most facilities simply raise the monthly costs to the residents rather than cut costs by lowering the standards of service. In many cases, temporary sources of income can be located to finance short-term deficits, but for the long term a more stable solution must be sought. Some projects have developed interesting and innovative approaches to cutting costs while maintaining quality, such as growing a portion of the food used in the house. In one case, surplus crops were sold to supplement the project income. Another widely used method is the use of volunteer labor, and sometimes even residents perform small repairs and do maintenance work.

Residents with specific skills, such as plumbing or carpentry, are usually grateful for the opportunity to practice their skills. These residents, assuming they are physically able, can be valuable resources for a project. Caution should be exercised, however, to ensure that the line between volunteer labor and forced labor is not crossed. It is one thing for an elderly craftsman to enjoy volunteering his skills for the improvement of the facility, but it is quite another thing for that elderly craftsman to feel an obligation to volunteer his skills.

Shared living projects offer a standard of living at a lower cost than a similar standard of living for a person living independently. However, the monthly costs are higher than some low-income persons could afford. Project organizers are often able to help very low-income residents, and they find subsidy funding for residents who cannot afford to pay the monthly fees. Some families of the residents assist with the fees, as they would rather help to maintain an elderly relative in shared living than take them into their own homes. Unfortunately, when subsidy funding cannot be located, project organizers must offer services based not upon the need for those services but upon the ability to pay for those services. Where subsidy funds are available, residents with very low incomes may view shared housing as a definite improvement in their quality of life. Some middle-income residents may see shared living as a more supportive housing arrangement, although not necessarily their first preference. Given the current economic situation of the age category most likely to live in a shared living facility, it would appear that a substantial proportion of these elderly can afford to pay the monthly fees required to live in a shared living facility.

Because shared living facilities are usually established by groups with limited resources, the offer of any financial aid is greatly welcomed. Some organizers, however, may resist the use of government grants or loans because they wish to avoid involvement by the granting agency in the day-to-day operation of the facility.

So that we may distinguish between funds given to a project and funds given to an individual, we have labeled the former as financial sponsorship and the latter as subsidy. Where financial sponsorship is available, it is usually in the forms of outright grants of money by churches, private individuals, or philanthropic organizations and foundations. These grants are generally used as initiating funds to acquire property. In some cases, churches are willing to purchase property and lease it to a group of organizers. Other forms of sponsorship have included materials for renovation, the provision of volunteer labor for renovation and, less frequently, mortgage money so that the nonprofit corporation may buy property.

Depending upon the type and amount of the grant, funding sources feel more or less involved in the shared living project. When a church or foundation becomes involved in these projects, there is a tendency for them to try to influence decisions affecting the operation of the facility. The understandable desire of funding sources to ensure that their gift is used effectively may be seen by some organizers as a challenge to the autonomy of the facility. This is especially true where autonomy and freedom are seen as essential characteristics of a particular project. This places the organizers, and sometimes the residents, in the position of either making decisions based upon the wishes of persons who may have little knowledge of the situation, or giving the impression of being ungrateful for the generosity of others. While this sounds like a minor problem, energy and time are spent to reassure the funding agencies or the donors.

"Burn Out" of the Organizers. Some organizers are surprised to discover that, as plans for opening a facility are finalized and opening day approaches, their investment of time and energy must increase. It takes an enormous amount of time and personal commitment to open successfully a shared living facility. Unfortunately, the time and energy required for such a task is not evenly spread out among the organizers. Indeed, it is usually true that the everyday worries and decisions are left to a small subgroup, sometimes one person. These caring, responsible people become in effect unpaid full-time employees of the project. They sometimes discover that what began as a group of concerned citizens with an idea has somehow been transformed into a complicated project that not only takes a significant amount of time, but may also infringe upon their personal lives. In facilities that have been successful, the leadership responsibilities have been shared among organizers. By sharing responsibilities and the work load, an organizing group may avoid the problem of "burn out."

Health and Medical Problems. There are several problem areas related to the nonmedical character of shared living faciltiies. Only a few of the projects have medically qualified staff as an integral part of the project. Individual residents are expected to arrange for their own medical and hospital care if needed, and many units require the resident to designate a personal physician who will be called if necessary. The role of shared living has been viewed by organizers as providing nonmedical supports to frail, but essentially well, elderly people. The physical state of the resident population makes it reasonable to assume that as the population ages it will become more frail. Because of this, most facilities have an agreement with each resident (usually written) that as soon as the resident's personal physician determines that shared living is inappropriate, the resident will leave the facility. This is the rule, but the practice varies from unit to unit.

Because of the strong affectional bond between residents that may develop over time, there may be a tendency to overlook and compensate for slight physical impairment which, if discovered, might lead to the removal of the resident. For example, if a resident becomes unable to dress himself or herself, other residents may help to perform that task. While helping an arthritic friend tie her shoes is no major problem, and indeed may be an indication of a caring and healthy environment, potential problems may develop when this helping behavior is expanded to include help in bathing and the like. In a few instances, residents have remained in shared living facilities after reasonable health standards required removal, just as many frail older persons remain in their own homes in a perilous physical or health situation.

Another troublesome aspect of the increasing frailty of the residents is when it is not other residents who provide a helping hand, but the staff or organizers of the facility. Since long-term viability for some units may be a consideration, there is an incentive to keep residents in the facility for as long as possible. By helping residents with an ever-increasing list of personal care tasks, some staff may be compromising the nonmedical nature of the shared living facility and may be performing tasks that are best performed by trained nursing personnel. Residents, who may be willing participants in this situation, have strong motives for wanting to stay in the shared living environment. In some facilities, a few residents have been known to hide serious illnesses and conditions so that they will not be "put away in an institution."

Shared living projects usually offer no medical services. Therefore, organizers and staff must rely heavily on the judgment of a resident's personal physician. Because of this, it would seem reasonable that care should be taken to ensure that the physician is sufficiently familiar with the project to make informed decisions about the patient's capacity to continue living there. In many cases, however, it is the resident himself or herself who becomes the physician's main source of information. Based upon information supplied by the resident (who obviously wants to remain in the facility) and the fact that the physician may know that there are no other alternatives to institutionalization, occasionally a resident may remain in the shared living facilities after medical considerations make the environment inappropriate. It should be pointed out, however, that remaining in a shared living facility saves a considerable amount of money for the resident, the resident's family, and the government because of the much lower costs of living in the facility compared with living in a nursing home.

Persons interested in the subjective well being and mental health of the elderly have often asked us: How have the residents adapted to this form of living arrangement? Are they happy? Do they like living in these kinds of households? The evidence we have, based upon our interviews and personal observation in these homes, information supplied by persons who operate these living units, and outside observers, is that the residents by and large are very satisfied with this kind of shared living. It is the best option open to many residents, and most of them very much prefer it to any other available housing.

Our research does not make it possible to assess the impact of shared housing upon the mental health or social adjustment of these persons in quantitative terms based upon social adjustment questionnaires. These studies were not designed to employ psychometric scales or other social psychological measures that have been used by other researchers of older persons.

Some of the organizers, both in the United States and in England, have expressed the opinion that people retain their health longer in shared homes, and that if they must finally enter a nursing home, it is only for a short time. We cannot present any overall statements about mortality and morbidity because of the short time these homes have been operating and the lack of precise information on a sufficient number of cases. Senior Village in Phoenix has the most detailed information, as reported in chapter 6.

EXTERNAL FACTORS

Legal Issues. A group of issues that has proven problematic to many organizers and potential organizers may be described broadly as legal issues. As stated before, most shared living projects are operated as nonprofit corporations or corporations not for profit and are chartered in their respective states. Some have applied for and received federal tax-exempt status from the Internal Revenue Service. Because of the nature of these projects, some states and some courts tend to view them as being somehow different from other nonprofit corporations.

The issue of legal responsibility and the possibility of lawsuits are troubling to some organizers. Some believe that if the group of residents is defined as a "family," no one person could be sued for negligence in case an elderly resident fell or suffered an accident. Recent events in other situations have shown, however, that even family members can now attempt to sue each other. Because there have been no cases to clarify the issue, the legal relationship between the residents and the manager, and between the residents and the organizers, remains unclear. But the good citizens who volunteer their time and energies to serve on these boards of directors must have some occasional moments of anxiety as to whether they could be held responsible for accidents that might occur to a resident.

Zoning. Of the many issues affecting the establishment of the shared living facility, perhaps none is more uncertain and ill-defined than zoning regulations. Municipalities tend to define family in such a way as to exclude most shared living facilities from residential, single-family neighborhoods. Few would argue against the common-sense assertion that small, family-like, noninstitutional homes would be beneficial for the elderly in a residential neighborhood. Many people, however, do not welcome such facilities in their own neighborhood, feeling that this paves the way for other group-living units, for example, group homes for delinquents, halfway houses, or communes. The exclusion of shared living facilities from the single-family classifications of many municipalities, and the fact that the type of home best suited to shared living is likely to be located in those areas, combine to limit severely the expansion of existing projects.

When dealing with zoning boards, organizers tend to present the facility as a group of elderly persons living as a single housekeeping unit. In some cases, organizers have made claims that a shared living facility was indeed not significantly different from a traditional family. The zoning boards, on the other hand, have tended to view shared living facilities as group homes consisting of several unrelated individuals living in the same structure. This difference of opinion has been the genesis of several court cases, but there appears to be no clearcut trend concerning the outcome of these legal actions. Few cases involving shared living and zoning regulations ever reach the litigation stage. Many disputes are resolved because the zoning boards issue variances to the projects. A number of disputes are resolved because the organizers choose to locate the facility elsewhere, or they choose to abandon the plans to establish the facility. There are, however, two very important court cases that have had an impact on the issue. The first case involved a shared living facility in the state of Florida, and the second case involved a private home in New Jersey.

CASE ONE: OPERATING A BOARDING HOUSE IN A RESIDENTIALLY ZONED AREA (SHARE-A-HOME, WINTER PARK). In this court case,[1] the facility in question had been in operation for two years. The owner of the property had operated the house as a private nursing home for a number of years. When the surrounding neighborhood was established, it was zoned as exclusively residential, but the nursing home was "grandfathered" in. It was understood that as soon as the property was sold, or if the nursing home ever ceased operation, the property would then automatically be rezoned as exclusively residential. The original owner retired, closed the nursing home, and transferred ownership of the property to twelve elderly individuals who wanted to live in the house. The twelve people formed what they called a cooperative association and remained in the house, unnoticed by the community for two years. After receiving complaints from several neighbors, the Board of County Commissioners filed suit in the county circuit court charging that the cooperative association was in fact a boarding house and therefore a violation of the applicable zoning regulations.

The residents of the house, through their paid manager, contended that their association constituted a family, albeit a somewhat unusual family, and that they should be allowed to remain in the house. For the purposes of zoning, family was defined in the county ordinances as: "one or more persons occupying a dwelling and living as a single housekeep-

1. *Orange County vs. Share-A-Home Association of Winter Park, Florida et al.,* Ninth Circuit Court, Orange County, Florida, 71-3319, October 19, 1971.

ing unit, as distinguished from persons occupying a boarding house, lodging house, or hotel." Unlike other definitions of family, we find here no mention of the legal or biological relatedness of the occupants. In this case, the court ruled in favor of the project, based upon the fact that, in the court's view, the use of the property fit the definition of family as described in the zoning ordinance. More importantly, the judge ruled that this shared living facility was not a boarding home:

The court finds that this occupancy is not that of a boarding house for many reasons, including but not limited to, the nonprofit nature of the operation, power to discharge the manager, and to exercise control over the operation by the members of the family association and the kitchen and ice box privileges extended by the family to each other.

Here we have the first articulation by a court of what a shared living facility may be. Without becoming overly concerned with the term "family," it would appear that the elements that distinguish a shared living environment from other traditional categories of housing, at least in this county ordinance, are that it is nonprofit; that the residents ex-exercise some control over the staff; that the residents have some decision-making power; and that the kitchen is open to all. Incidentally, this facility is still in operation and the county commission has made no further challenge to its right to occupy the structure.

CASE TWO: LIMITING OCCUPANCY BASED UPON BIOLOGICAL OR LEGAL RELATIONSHIPS. In this court case,[2] a state supreme court was asked to decide if a municipality could, through the use of zoning ordinances, place limits upon the number of unrelated individuals occupying a single structure in a single-family zone. Here, nine people had occupied a house in a single-family residential section. The county commission had successfully sought an injunction prohibiting that use of the property based upon a definition of family that explicitly prohibited more than four unrelated individuals from sharing a single housekeeping unit. The individuals involved appealed to the state supreme court on the grounds that since they were living as a single family, they should be allowed to remain in the house. Unlike the previous case, this was a very strict and narrow definition of what constitutes a family.

In this case, the court was asked to rule on the legality of restrictions

2. *State of New Jersey vs. Dennis Baker,* Supreme Court of New Jersey, A-59, September term, 1978.

on occupancy rather than, as before, on whether the individuals involved met the definition of a family. As in the previous case, the court ruled in favor of the residents. In the decision the justices stated:

As long as a group bears the generic character of a family unit as a relatively permanent household, it should be equally as entitled to occupy a single family dwelling as its biologically related neighbors . . . zoning regulations which attempt to limit residency based upon the numbers of unrelated individuals present in a single nonprofit housekeeping unit cannot pass constitutional muster . . . [therefore] municipalities may not condition residence upon the number of unrelated individuals present within the household. Given the availability of less restrictive alternatives such regulations are insufficiently related to the perceived social ills which they are intended to ameliorate.

Here again we find the elements nonprofit and single housekeeping unit in a judicial description of what is essentially a shared living environment. This decision goes far beyond merely helping us define a complex phenomenon, for it shifts the definition of a family from a biological definition to a social definition. Basically, what we have here is a judicial declaration that if a group of people looks like a family, lives like a family, acts like a family, and believes itself to be a family, then as far as zoning ordinances are concerned, it is indeed a family.

Twenty-four states have passed zoning laws in recent years which affect foster and/or group homes. The laws of all but two of these states, Florida and Idaho, remove the authority of the local governments to deny the establishment of small group homes of six to ten persons in any residential area. The issue has arisen because of recent federal and state laws and court rulings which require deinstitutionalization and relocation of persons with special living needs to residential neighborhoods.

The Department of Health and Rehabilitative Services of Florida, after several years of study, has prepared a pamphlet, "Guidelines for Zoning and Special Community Housing" (State of Florida HRS: 1983), to assist the counties in establishing zoning regulations for small group residential facilities. While emphasizing that planning and decisions about group homes must be made at the local government level, the HRS planners present the issues involved. The 1975 Florida Legislature passed the HRS Reorganization Act (S 20.19, Florida Statutes) specifying that a department goal is to prevent or reduce inappropriate institutional care by providing for community-based care, home-based care, or other programs of less intensive care. The planners refer to the "normalization principle" which means that the more a person with special living needs is exposed to the normal environment of society, the more likely the person is to reach a higher level of functioning.

The pamphlet discusses the problem of neighborhood resistance to group homes and cites a study in Jacksonville, Florida, "But Not in My Neighborhood" (Jacksonville Community Council: 1980). This report reveals that while persons commonly recognize the need for community-based residential facilities, they oppose them near their homes. The Jacksonville study highlights the need for more education of citizens in the community, and full and open communication with the neighbors by any organization or individual planning to locate a facility in a residential area.

Manatee County in Florida has developed what many leaders in the state consider to be a model ordinance. They amended their zoning codes to define the various categories of community-based residential facilities and provided for their placement. In a 1979 report (Manatee County Planning Commission: 1979), they identified more than fifty types of residential-care facilities that are licensed, administered, operated or reviewed by the Department of Health and Rehabilitative Services. They changed the Manatee County Zoning Ordinance to include six new definitions, shown in table 9.3.

TABLE 9.3. *Definitions of Community-Based Residential Facilities*

	Number of Clients	Length of Stay	Services
Family Care Home	1–6	long term	low intensity personal services
Group Care Home	7 or more	long term	low intensity personal services
Emergency Shelter Home	1–2	short term, less than 30 days	low intensity
Emergency Shelter	3 or more	short term, less than 30 days	low intensity
Recovery Home	1 or more	temporary	intermediate intensity
Residential Treatment Facility	1 or more	temporary	intensive diagnostic and therapeutic services

SOURCE: Jacksonville Community Council, 1980:9.

Persons who are involved in planning housing for the elderly sometimes lose sight of the fact that facilities for older people are only a small consideration in the entire zoning picture. In a pilot study in Tampa, Florida, Mangum (1983) has reported that the elderly are among the most preferred residents of special kinds of housing arrangements. Some citizens feel, however, that small group homes for the elderly may be the wedge which will lead to establishment of other special-care homes in their residential neighborhoods.

Licensing. An issue that is becoming increasingly important to the future of shared living is regulation by licensure. In our study of shared living facilities, almost three-fourths of all individual units were unlicensed. Among the projects that were licensed, we found that some organizers welcomed or in some cases even sought licensure as a means of legitimizing a particular model of shared living. To many of these persons, regulation by licensure represented a benchmark or minimum standard of operation by which performance of a particular facility could be judged. In other cases, meeting minimum standards, such as for fire and safety regulations, was seen as a means of limiting the liability of those responsible for operating the facility.

Among organizers who openly oppose licensure, there are many different reasons given for their opposition. There appear, however, to be two main types of arguments against government regulation. The two categories of arguments, while somewhat related, do have differences. For the sake of simplicity, we have labeled the arguments philosophical and restrictive. It should also be noted that while most unlicensed facilities can be neatly fitted into one or both of these categories, there remains a smaller, but significantly large, group of facilities that have other reasons for not being licensed. Some are unlicensed not because of any conscious effort or organized resistance, but because their small size and relative invisibility means state regulatory agencies have not discovered them. Still others remain outside government regulation because the agencies involved do not insist that a particular facility become licensed.

A few projects avoid licensure by "hiding from the system." A smaller number of projects openly resist regulation by government agencies. In the case of what we have called the restrictive argument, organizers who oppose licensure believe that government regulation restricts the successful operation of shared living by requiring unnecessary expenditures of funds. These people believe that in any regulatory situation, at least some money and resources will have to be used for the sole purpose of satisfying regulations and that these regulations will probably be of little benefit to the residents.

In one case in our study, a group of organizers was told that in a facility with more than ten people, the state required the kitchen to have certain equipment and that it be arranged in a particular way. The cost of meeting this one requirement was in excess of $25,000. The organizers believed that this represented a needless expense since other equipment would serve the same purpose at much less cost. This example is clearly representative of the restrictive argument. If regulations had been met here, the quality of housing (indeed even the availability of housing) would have been severely restricted by the fact that resources would have had to be diverted away from the areas that directly benefit the residents in order to satisfy what may have been unnecessary regulation. Put more simply: if satisfactory kitchen equipment for ten people could be purchased for less than $25,000, then the difference (if indeed a facility could have raised the original $25,000) could be applied to the purchase of food. Given the choice between better food or institutional kitchen equipment, it is believed the elderly residents will opt for the food. In this particular case, a variance to the state regulation was granted, and the facility purchased the less expensive kitchen equipment.

The philosophical argument against government regulation is perhaps more prevalent among those opposed to licensure. To this group of organizers, any government regulation and licensure is viewed as an undue intrusion into what is believed to be essentially a family environment. Residents in these facilities are seen as being individuals free to live as they choose within the limits of what their monthly payments will purchase. Any attempt by government agencies to tell the residents how to spend their money is viewed as an example of government interference in the lives of private citizens. It is not surprising to find that in facilities such as these, the organizers who do not seek, and in some cases refuse, any government funding. In the restrictive argument, the efficacy of rules and regulations is being challenged while those adhering to the philosophical argument against licensure are challenging the fundamental right of the government to regulate what they view as an association of private citizens.

Some states and municipalities seem disinclined to force the issue of regulation. Where the projects are operating without a license, the state regulatory agencies have so far taken no action. In fact, we know of no court action based upon the fact that a shared living facility is operating without a license. While the reasons for this seem to be a complex combination of bureaucratic incompetence, a conscious effort to look the other way, and a general confusion as to what agencies should be involved, there are some issues that are important and should be resolved.

Most important among these is the question posed by those who are philosophically opposed to regulations: If a group of people who are legally competent to manage their own affairs decides to live in a single structure, does the state have any right to regulate those people? This question gets at the heart of a more fundamental problem. Society seems to view the state as the ultimate parent of the young, the old, and the impaired. To many it is only those healthy people between the ages of eighteen and sixty-four who are capable of making their own decisions. However, the majority of the elderly people in shared living facilities are quite competent to make decisions affecting their lives.

The fundamental question of the state's right to regulate citizens in a shared living environment seems to rest on how the resident is perceived in relation to the organization providing the environment. Are residents of shared living facilities independent citizens capable of self-determination, or are they fragile beings who are more or less dependent upon the facility for their very existence? States tend to see the residents in terms of what activities they *cannot* perform for themselves, whereas organizers see them in terms of what they *can* perform for themselves. There seem to be no simple answers to these difficult questions.

CONCLUSIONS

In this chapter, we have described and analyzed the internal and external factors that are present in organizing and operating a shared living facility. Organizers and managers must face the fact that there may be competing demands generated by the nature of the organization itself and the goals it is trying to reach. Weighing and balancing these competing rules and regulations, both formal and informal, coming from inside a house and from the environment outside, forces the leader "to look inward at his organization and outward at his concentric zones of environment," as Merton has observed (1976:86). These organizational dilemmas must be considered as a form of "sociological ambivalence," which arises and operates on a social level and must be distinguished from psychological issues and problems rooted in particular persons and personality types.

CHAPTER TEN

Sociological Interpretations

THE CONCEPT OF FAMILY

In this book, we have described and analyzed several kinds of alternative housing arrangements for frail older persons. The demographic trends clearly indicate that the over-75 age category is the most rapidly growing segment of the population. Extrapolation of these population trends points to a growing number of frail older persons who will require some kind of housing other than the traditional individual home or apartment, or the use of expensive institutional arrangements, such as nursing homes. It is clear that there is now a population that needs social supports but does not need nursing care per se, and this will increase in the decades ahead.

The persons who organized shared living groups have had the goal of creating family-like environments for the elderly. Shared living groups are usually composed of small numbers of older people whom the proponents of such living arrangements believe can provide the kinds of close association and support characteristic of primary groups like the family. As sociologists, our task has been to discover how shared living groups might provide opportunities for the development of primary group ties.

Whatever the degree to which shared homes might serve as the setting for supportive and intimate relationships among their residents, the residents do not constitute a "family" in either everyday or scholarly senses of the term. The term "household," defined as a group of people who share a common dwelling (Leslie 1979:20), is a more appropriate one to use in discussing shared homes. While members of a household are often related by marriage, blood, or adoption, this is not necessarily so; households are defined by common residence, not by kinship ties.

Thus our description and analysis of shared living arrangements are contributions to what Ball (1972) has termed the emerging sociology of households.

The desire of organizers to create "family-like" environments is based on an ideal image of the family as a loving and supportive group. Although many natural families could hardly be described as either loving or supportive, this ideal remains and is an attractive alternative to the institutional model of living. It is attractive to practitioners, policy makers, and the public in general. Even those who do not envision a "family" of older people living together still hope for the development of microenvironments that may serve as alternatives to the nursing home for some older people.

ARE SHARED LIVING ARRANGEMENTS REAL FAMILIES?

One of the central research questions that guided our investigations is whether a family can be created from unrelated adults at the end of life. Are shared living arrangements genuine families? The simple answer is no—for alternative living arrangements of the kind we have been studying are more accurately described as households.[1] Many of these alternatives have a sharing and caring atmosphere and encourage behaviors that approximate what we think of as·primary group characteristics observed in some families. Indeed, some of these alternatives may have a *more* supportive and benign atmosphere than many natural families.

However, there are some basic features of these alternatives that dif-

1. Some sociologists attach considerable significance to the label or category assigned to a person or group. Shared living arrangements are labeled or categorized somewhat differently, for it depends on whom one asks—organizer, staff, or resident. There is also variation in labeling from project to project. Some arrangements are licensed, some are not; some consider themselves a "family," others do not. In the case of those in central Florida where the manager has a strong feeling about the homes as "families," we learned that in conducting the 1980 U.S. census, the local field team made the decision that the shared living arrangements were institutions, and people in the homes were listed as "residents" by persons who designated themselves as "institutional census takers." No attempt was made to determine the head of household or other family or household facts about the persons in the dwelling unit. The census employee did not go to each residence for enumeration but obtained all of the information about the residents from the office of Share-A-Home of America, Inc. The census enumerators did mail forms to the live-in staff persons, but no forms were mailed to the residents.

ferentiate them from natural families. First, they are formed and operated by other people—individuals or groups who are not themselves members of the households. Almost all of the eighty shared living arrangements in our study in the United States and the 900 Abbeyfield houses in Great Britain were set up by non–family members—persons wishing to serve or to help elderly people unrelated to them. The basic reason for this is that frail elderly people usually do not have the physical, emotional, or intellectual strength to organize such a group. Furthermore, their period of residence in the family group may be limited, depending on age and health. Thus the groups change in composition yearly—sometimes even monthly—and there is a need for ongoing, stable supervision by someone other than the household members themselves. This is in sharp contrast to the biological family.

Second, the economic viability of the household is crucial, for without it, the group dissolves, no matter how warm or caring the atmosphere. Since these residences do not have the cement of kinship obligations, the economic arrangements are the key to survival. The financial arrangements are usually cooperative with an equitable sharing of costs, but this is a limited kind of economic involvement, and group members do not have any economic responsibility for persons other than themselves. And in some cases, the payments are made by third parties who are not involved in the enterprise or do not have any tie to the living arrangement.

Third, members choose to live in these arrangements as a last resort in most cases, not as their preferred life style. The decision to move into one is basically because of frailty, which makes other forms of living precarious, dangerous, or undesirable.

Fourth, the sense of obligation is usually limited, and the persons participating may withdraw from the group at almost any time. In most alternative living arrangements, they have few financial or legal obligations and can decide to terminate the residence upon short notice with no risk or sacrifice. The organizers of the households assume the risk and financial obligation if a vacancy occurs.

Fifth, there is the possibility of governmental intervention. The entire area of certification, licensure, inspection, and rules and regulations is a murky one and varies considerably from place to place. The fact that many of these arrangements come under a variety of service or housing programs that may require some kind of licensure or certification emphasizes, however, that they are not families in a legal sense of the term. There have been instances where the authorities have treated these alternatives as "families" and they have enjoyed some freedom from government regulation, inspection, or certification. Share-A-Home, for example, was recognized by a court in Florida as meeting a county's definition of a family in a zoning dispute. The trend, however, seems to be in the opposite direction, with local, state, and federal regulatory agencies seeking to become involved.

The physical setting of the intentional family may take on more importance than that in a kinship-based family, not only because of the desires of the individuals and the wishes of their relatives and friends, but because city and government agencies may become concerned and involved. While a biological family can choose to live in almost any sort of conditions, as soon as a "family" is organized by others, standards may be set for fire safety, cleanliness, food standards, etc.

Sixth, certain kinds of individual foibles will not be tolerated in these living arrangements, as they are in a kinship group. In organizing a family for the frail elderly, one must be sensitive to the compatibility of people as to their attitudes, values, personalities, and physical and emotional health. Moreover, a shared living facility may induce conformity to certain manners and modes of behavior because of the threat of expulsion from the group.

Seventh, one other sociological aspect which is important is a conception of the authority structure—who has the position of leadership and the power to make decisions? Sociologists have done considerable research on family authority structures: matriarchal, patriarchal, democratic, "open," etc. In the kind of households we are considering, the authority structure (who has positions of leadership and the power to make decisions) may range from an explicit organizational arrangement—almost a chain of command, or a table of organization—to a very loose, democratic structure. There may be a formal authority structure and an informal structure that may exercise decisive influence or power on occasion or about specific matters.

Eighth, social integration by age, sex, religion, and race is an area of perennial interest to sociologists. The modal pattern is a home with an average age of over 80, of whom about 80 percent are women. The households tend to be integrated in terms of religion and cultural background, with a variety of religious backgrounds and affiliations. There is also a mixed pattern of socioeconomic status. While some organizers have tried to seek residents of similar educational and socioeconomic backgrounds in order to increase social compatibility, congeniality, and conversational interchange, in general, the desire to fill up the house has meant that most applicants in good enough health are accepted.

The one issue that most houses have not had to face is racial integration. Some of the projects in the United States are racially integrated in theory because of public support provided, but in practice, almost no black persons have applied for membership in a "family." It can be anticipated, however, that racial integration is an issue that will have to be considered by some groups in the not too distant future. In some parts of the country, this may be a particularly difficult issue and may result in problems of recruiting and keeping both white and black residents. The intimate nature of family-like arrangements—eating, sleeping accommodations, sharing of toilet facilities—could be a potential problem area.

Ninth, a shared living arrangement is not a family in that the members do not share a family history, other than the "history" that may be unfolding as they live together. Many natural families have a history or a sense of history, partly derived from genealogical ties or, perhaps more importantly, from remembering a common past from living together or hearing about events that occurred in an earlier generation. A family history involves family rituals and rites, family foibles, and family accomplishments, plus those secrets known only to some members of the family.

Finally, when we speak of alternative living arrangements approximating family life, we should realize there is a difference between family life in "good times" and family life in "bad times." It is easy for shared homes to approximate family life in good times—at holidays, birthdays, shared outings, recreations, bingo, shared meals, etc. If one looks at Share-A-Home family life during the good times, it is clearly a warm and caring environment.

However, a family life in the bad times is more difficult—when someone gets sick, senile, disagreeable, incontinent. There are not the feelings of obligation, of shared background, or of financial responsibility. The members of a shared housing group sometimes withdraw from each other when things get unpleasant. For example, it is too threatening to be around someone who exhibits signs of serious mental impairment. Members may feel that they have all they can do to keep their own spirits up, and they cannot cope with the more depressing aspects of someone else's confusion, personality change, or incontinence.

Thus, alternative living arrangements can substitute for the family mainly in offering a supportive environment for the good times in family life, but they are less able to approximate family supports in crisis conditions. The managers of shared housing can be important in *referring* the elderly person for help in times of crisis, but neither they nor the residents can act as long-term caretakers for the seriously impaired, as many families do.

It should be added that natural families also may find a crisis extremely upsetting and may not be able to muster the support that is needed. And because shared homes are not true families, it is perhaps unreasonable to expect a heroic response.

In conclusion, this discussion of shared living arrangements indicates that they differ in many ways from kinship-based households. However, they fulfill some of the functions of the family, particularly nurturance. Lasch (1977), one of the critics of our society, has pointed out that the nurturant function of the family has deteriorated in modern society. In his book *Haven in a Heartless World: The Family Besieged,* he emphasized that people need to have a place where they receive support, affection, and concern.

Lasch's critique of the family fails to discuss the effect of modernization on family structure and relationships for persons in late life. People who have never married, those who have never had children, or those whose children reside far away are particularly vulnerable, but it is not because of a "breakdown" of the family. The consequences of industrialized society and their effect on the reality of family life do not come within Lasch's perception. Lasch's incisive analysis of the brutalizing effect of the market economy and increasing bureaucratization in urbanized or industrialized societies overlooks the ingenuity and inventiveness of well-meaning people in their efforts to develop new responses and solutions, such as shared living.

SOCIAL ROLES AND SHARED FAMILY LIFE

It is our view that a shared living arrangement of older people is an emergent amalgam group that has some primary group characteristics but is closely related to a formal sponsoring organization. What roles are available for residents in this hybrid kind of social arrangement? The traditional family positions—spouse, mother, parent, home-maker—are not found in such living units, nor are there formal ap-pointive or elective offices. The formal structures are vague or non-operational.

Most persons observe that one of the major consequences of aging is the loss of institutional roles or a sharp decline in behavior associated with these roles. A person retires and gives up the work role; a woman moves to a nursing home and loses the homemaker role, to mention two of the obvious and dramatic role losses in late life. The role behav-ior of the frail elderly is, of necessity, characterized by reduction and declining participation. Disability tends to cause a limitation of ability to function in social roles.

In his trenchant analysis of role change through the life span, Rosow (1976) provides a novel typology in which informal roles in old age be-come an important focus for study. Informal roles are those that are not connected to a particular status or position but serve group func-tions, unlike formal or institutional roles, which are linked to positions or attributes, such as professionals, manual workers, and public offi-cials. Rosow argues that when informal roles occur, "they involve pat-terned activities that have perceptible consequences for a group and the relations among the members" (1976:467). The emergence of informal roles occurs in the variety of shared housing projects we have studied.

Those who advocate keeping the elderly in their homes as long as possible do not address the fact that when an increasing array of ser-vices are supplied, the elderly may gradually assume the social role of "recipients"—persons to whom much is given and from whom nothing is expected—a dependent role that has only rights and no duties.

In shared living arrangements, the residents have informal social roles. They must get up in the morning, get dressed, come to meals, and in-teract with other family members, and they are expected to participate in at least some of the family activities. They have certain "duties"—to cooperate, be friendly, keep up a certain standard of "good manners" to other residents, to guests who come into the home, and to the house-keeper or homemaker, who sometimes assumes a surrogate parental role. In short, the normative expectations are those of *participation*. Shared living keeps an older person's interaction mechanisms intact, and he or she is not as likely to withdraw. We have been informed of residents who were withdrawn and depressed, absorbed in their own misery, but, after a few weeks of shared living, began to relate to other people in the home and take an interest in their surroundings and in the on-going parade of life.

A thoughtful analysis of roles, attachment, and social supports throughout the life course has been presented by Kahn and Antonucci (1981), who introduce the concept of the "convoy." They observe that the life-course perspective, their interest in transitions, and the concept of aging itself call for the temporal extension of the network concept to include changes over the life course. They state:

It seems useful to designate these dynamic networks of social support with a unique term. We suggest *convoy* as an appropriate term, and propose its use for studying the process of aging and other life-course changes. By choosing this metaphorical label we imply that each person can be thought of as moving through the life cycle surrounded by a set of other people to whom he or she is related by the giving or receiving of social support. An individual's convoy at any point in time thus consists of the set of persons on whom he or she relies for support and those who rely on him or her for support. These two subsets may overlap, of course; there are relationships in which one both gives and receives support, although all relationships are not symmetrical in this manner. The convoy is a structural concept, shaped by the interaction of situational factors and enduring properties of the person, and in turn determining in part the person's well-being and ability to perform successfully his or her life roles. (1981:393–394)

It is our contention that shared living groups can become the elderly person's convoy. When former networks and support systems have diminished—loss of spouse, relatives, or friends through illness or death, loss of the work role and its associations, loss of special interest groups through inability to participate any longer—the shared living group takes on significance as the new convoy. It is not only the other residents who form the convoy, but also the housekeeper, staff, and organizers who give important supports.

In their discussion of social supports, these authors propose that they can be defined as interpersonal transactions that include one or more of the following key elements: *affect*, which means expressions of liking, admiration, respect, or love; *affirmation*, or the expressions of agreement or acknowledgment of the appropriateness or rightness of some act or statement of another person; and *aid*, in which direct aid or assistance is given, including things, money, information, time, and entitlements.

All of these kinds of social support have been observed in our research, and they have been reported to us by organizers of many of the projects in shared living. Thus the focus of our research—the shared living arrangement—becomes the observable means to link two concepts: the informal roles of the frail elderly and the importance of the convoy as a supportive mechanism. The convoy is a surrogate family group wherein individuals who share similar norms and expectations can enact informal roles. We have only impressionistic evidence, but it appears that the development of a convoy has a positive social and psychological impact upon the older resident.

THE AMALGAM OF FAMILY AND BUREAUCRACY

Sociologists who study shared living arrangements find one of the most intriguing aspects to be the fact that these living arrangements combine two important social categories: primary groups and formal organizations. Most sociologists tend to demarcate clearly primary groups from secondary groups. The history of sociology is replete with typologies that have focused on the dichotomy between primary and secondary groups, *gemeinschaft* and *gesellschaft,* mechanical and organic solidarity. Collins (1975) reminds us that Max Weber, the doyen of the study of formal organizations, did not make this error, for he realized that within formal organizations there are informal networks that arise, operate, and influence the manner in which the organization carries out its activities.

Our initial approach to the study of shared housing was to consider them as family-like structures. Very early in our research, however, we realized that the very use of the word "family" was somewhat of a fiction, and we labeled shared living facilities as *amalgam groups* with family-like characteristics (Streib 1978).

By an amalgam group we mean a social structure that combines the salient aspects of a primary group—one with intimacy, face-to-face association, emotional bonds, and informal rules—with linkages to a formal organization, which is characterized by written procedures, a formal chain of command, a hierarchy, communications that follow the hierarchy, universalistic standards, defined duties and obligations, accountability, and formal sanctions. An amalgam group combines in one setting in a unique manner the key characteristics of these two different styles of operation, the primary and the bureaucratic.

In summing up our research, let us first turn to the primary group aspects of the amalgam. We found that shared living has definite family-like characteristics. There is helpfulness, concern, bending of the rules, affectional ties, and informality of daily routines. There are shared meals, holidays, outings, celebrations. Activities are scheduled in an informal way according to the preferences of the residents. The size of the group is small, usually from six to ten people, and the physical structures generally are "normal" homes in suburban areas, not institutional types of buildings.

Unless shared living facilities give high priority to cultivating these kinds of relationships, their attractiveness as a place to live will be reduced for the residents, family members, and their physicians (who are often the individuals who recommend a shared living facility for the older patient). In short, the attractiveness of this kind of a living environment lies in the fact that it is *not* an institution, that is, a formal or secondary group.

Turning to the other component of the amalgam concept, the bureaucratic, we observe that shared living organizations, unlike families, must have certain attributes if they are to survive as on-going social entities. Without the ties of kinship to hold them together, they must have other attributes that insure social bonding over time. Since most of the persons who organize and operate shared living facilities expect their organization to continue beyond the first group of residents, they must be aware of the importance of the procedures that will insure continuity over time. This means a corporation must be formed. The corporation is a social invention that is a "person" in the eyes of the law, but it is also an organization that may live and carry on beyond the lifetime of any individual. Thus, in the fields of government and business, the use of the corporate device is standard practice to insure continuity of the organization. The corporation as a social body that lives through time operates also in the fields of education, health, and welfare through the creation of nonprofit corporations. Shared living organizations such as Abbeyfield and Share-A-Home have used the nonprofit corporation as a means of increasing the probability of their survival.

In this amalgam group, the formal or bureaucratic assumes dominance, first because nonkinship groups have a limited life unless they have some pattern of organiztion in a corporate manner to provide for survival. Second, the primary group aspect is subservient because it requires support and resources from persons outside the group—the organizers. The residents themselves are not able to organize their own "family" because of their limited health and resources. At this phase of life, they must depend on the good will and efforts of others.

As we pointed out in chapter 1, the allocative process in modern societies is carried on by formal bureaucratic structures. These permeate the society—in production, technology, government, education, communication. Therefore, organizations that are amalgam groups must be skilled and versatile in tapping the resources and personnel that are controlled by the dominant institutions in the society, whether they are financial, governmental, legal, or communicative.

The organizers and operators of shared living facilities should keep in the forefront of their commitment and practice the primary group nature of the service they are providing. The very nature of the service may be one of the most attractive characteristics that elicit support from the power structures that control resources. This suggests that the methods for tapping the allocative process may vary from one shared unit to another, from one community to another, and from one nation to another. Tapping the resource network is thus a process that requires considerable imagination, knowledge, persistence, and adroitness.

THE TARGET POPULATION'S PERCEPTION OF SHARED HOUSING

An idea like shared housing may be approved by the experts, endorsed by social workers, recommended by families, and encouraged by planners, but if the elderly themselves—the target population—have no interest in the concept, the "movement" will not progress very far. We have no information on how the current cohort of older Americans viewed the idea of shared housing. For this reason, we included questions on shared housing in a 1982 survey of residents of two large Florida retirement communities (Streib and Haas 1983). The respondents were of higher income and education than the average, and in this respect, they may not be typical of the average American elderly person. These individuals represent those who have planned ahead in earlier phases of their lifetime, resulting in successful careers, higher incomes than average, a move to a retirement community, etc. Thus their ideas and perceptions of housing-service needs as they age carry a connotation of realistic planning, which may not be characteristic of older persons in general. Their education, experience, and present situation indicate that they are a segment of America's elderly who are thinking beyond their present involvement and activity in their communities. So the plausibility of these data is enhanced by the special nature of the survey population.

The average age of these persons was 72, most of them were in good health, and their average annual income was over $15,000. Sixty-four percent of the respondents reported they had already visited a comprehensive life-care community, probably to consider whether such a move was a future possibility for themselves. We asked them a hypothetical question about shared living facilities, stated as follows:

In this section of the questionnaire, we would like to ask you about an alternative to traditional life-care facilities called Share-A-Home. Share-A-Home consists of eight to fifteen retired people who live together in one comfortable household and share expenses. A paid live-in staff does all the cooking, housekeeping, and maintenance. Bedrooms are either shared with one other person or, at extra cost, one may have a private bedroom. Bathrooms are shared. All meals are taken in a common dining room. The cost for a shared room (in the Florida Share-A-Homes) is about $400 per month. Share-A-Homes currently exist in Florida, Georgia, Ohio, and North Carolina. Is this kind of a shared living arrangement something you would consider if you were not able to cook or shop, or maintain a home yourself?

About a quarter of the respondents answered yes, they would consider this kind of housing, over 40 percent said maybe, and only 30 percent gave a clear negative, no. The responses to this question are significant because they suggest that a substantial proportion of the survey participants realize that it will probably be necessary for them to consider at some future time the necessity to live in a more supportive environment.

Gerontologists who stress the importance of the family as a means of support in times of frailty overlook the fact that the kin network of a substantial number of people is relatively small. This is indicated by the results of our survey, for most of these people were migrants to Florida, having moved from other states. Moreover, 21 percent had no children; of the remaining group with children, 84 percent of the children lived in other states.

We have further data on the need for shared housing and the interest in this kind of environment. When an article on the Florida shared living facilities appeared in the February–March 1980 issue of *Modern Maturity,* a publication of NRTA-AARP, 2,500 persons throughout the United States wrote to the Share-A-Home Association asking for further information. We conducted a content analysis of these letters and determined that about 75 percent of the total came from older people who were seeking, or anticipated seeking, new living arrangements. The remainder of the letters came from family or friends of older people, physicians and other professionals, and individuals and groups who were potential sponsors of new shared living arrangements.

We then selected a random sample of 20 percent of those 1,899 letters written by interested older people and sent each person a detailed questionnaire. We asked them to share with us their perceptions of the advantages and disadvantages of shared living for them personally. Of the 379 in our sample, 64 percent responded to our questionnaire. Of those who responded, three-quarters were females whose average age was 71 years; the 62 male respondents had an average age of 72.6 years; 60 percent of the females and one-half of the males were living alone at the time.

About 65 percent of our respondents (153 persons) gave reasons for dissatisfaction with their present living arrangements. The largest percentage of those expressing dissatisfaction (43 percent) mentioned problems with the maintenance and upkeep of their homes, while 30 percent felt their housing was too expensive. Less frequently, reasons for dissatisfaction included inconvenient locations of present housing, dislike of the neighborhood, loneliness, and heating problems in the home.

We asked the respondents to describe what might be the advantages and the disadvantages of a shared living arrangement if it were available in their communities. The advantage mentioned most often (by 44 percent) was that of having companionship; the next most frequently mentioned (21 percent) was provision of meals and housekeeping services. Other advantages listed included the lowered costs and lessened responsibilities as compared to maintaining a home alone.

The loss of privacy was the most commonly perceived disadvantage of these shared living arrangements; about one-fifth of the respondents said this aspect of shared living concerned them. About 16 percent of the sample described what we categorized as potential problems in interpersonal relationships. Next to their loss of privacy, the respondents most feared incompatibilities of interests, personalities, and backgrounds which could make life difficult in a shared living arrangement. Other perceived disadvantages included having to share bathrooms and having a roommate.

The respondents to this survey and the residents we interviewed in the Florida Share-A-Homes were alike in some ways—the majority were women who were living alone or had previously lived alone. The respondents to the mail survey were somewhat younger and had slightly more years of education. The residents we interviewed in the homes and the respondents to our mail survey agreed that having others around and not having to live alone is the most valued aspect of shared living. The convenience of having meals prepared and housekeeping chores performed was perceived as secondary to having the companionship of a household.

IMPLICATIONS OF DIFFUSION: WILL SHARED LIVING SPREAD?

We have shown in previous chapters that there is a growing need for housing frail older persons who can no longer live in private homes but do not need nursing care and do not need to be institutionalized. The various forms of shared housing described earlier indicate that these varieties of arrangements have met the needs for this kind of housing and have been accepted positively by the residents, their families, and the community, and by some professional gerontologists. Yet the movement remains small in scope, with only a few units scattered throughout this vast country. Britain, in contrast, has over 900 Abbeyfield homes, and a new one opens almost every week.

What are some of the factors that appear to have slowed down the diffusion and adoption of the idea to other communities in the United States after the establishment of the first ten units in the Winter Park/Orlando area of Florida?

First, this kind of housing has been a nonprofit arrangement as currently defined and organized, and at present, there is little possibility that these kinds of experiments could be part of the profit-making sector of the American economy. There was a limited and unsuccessful effort on the part of the founder of Share-A-Home to develop a franchise arrangement with other, similar shared living models spawned by the parent group. However, since shared living is essentially an idea that anyone can initiate, it is difficult to control or regulate the spread of the idea. It has no unique franchise possibilities, particularly when one must depend on volunteers to do the organizational work. Furthermore, other groups have independently organized very similar living arrangements. While the name can be copyrighted, the idea is not a patentable process and can be worked out by many different groups. Thus, shared living for the elderly, as constituted at present, is not compatible with the main thrust of a profit-making society. Having said this, we must quickly add that American society is replete with many examples of organizations that started as volunteer groups and now operate successfully in the health and welfare fields, such as the National Cancer Society, National Society for Muscular Dystrophy, and countless others. It also should be pointed out that the mass media of communications may play only a limited role in the spread of an idea like shared living arrangements. A nationwide television program or a multi-page article in a national magazine may bring attention to a need and possible solution to a social problem. As we have shown in detail, however, the actual organization and operation of a shared living unit is a local project that demands considerable time and energy for it to be established and for it to continue in operation. Programs like this involve commitment over an extended period of time. The number of persons in a society who have the interest, dedication, and time for this kind of work is, unfortunately, small.

THREE AVENUES OF DIFFUSION

There are three avenues through which an idea of this kind may be spread: 1) increasing the involvement and commitment of large numbers of citizens in creating arrangements such as these in their local communities; 2) transforming the concept and service into a profit-making industry; and 3) obtaining public resources to subsidize the initiation and continued support of the movement.

The first approach—that of increasing volunteerism—runs into the problem of competing organizations. There are already a multiplicity of groups attempting to tap the interest and abilities of volunteers. The number of demands for the support of "good causes" proliferates: saving the environment, promoting education and the arts, reducing religious and racial prejudice, aiding children, migrants, etc., fighting various diseases, and supporting political causes, to name only a few. All are seeking the time, talents, commitment, and financial backing of the limited number of concerned citizens who support such causes. If shared living grows in the future, however, it will receive its greatest impetus from concerned and committed citizens who decided that this particular volunteer focus is their means of commitment and fulfillment through community service.

One might ask what motivates the organizers of shared living facilities for the elderly. While our research was not directed specifically to this subject, we can say with assurance that the major motivations are ethical, religious, and humanitarian. The rewards for most people are certainly not economic, or personal prestige, but are rather those of giving service, concern for older people, and a desire to make their community a better place. This motivation-reward pattern is probably both the strength and the weakness of the organizations providing shared living. The strength of this kind of a reward system lies in the fact that people who are committed to this ideal are more likely to provide concerned, caring service as compared to those who may be more oriented toward profit-making. This same motivation system, however, is sometimes a weakness in terms of the widespread growth of the movement. In most societies, the number of persons is small who will consistently and effectively volunteer their services to others, particularly those with whom they have no kin ties. Hence, unless the pool of benevolent citizens motivated by noninstrumental values can be increased, we cannot expect an extensive spread of shared living arrangements and other forms of service that depend on philanthropic motivations.

Yankelovich (1982), in a thoughtful analysis of American society, sees the drift of our culture to an emphasis on self-fulfillment. He asserts that a well-functioning society must also have a commitment to one's community, and that self-fulfillment should include aspects of community involvement. It is our belief that newly retired healthy adults constitute one of the principal pools that can be tapped to achieve this goal.

The second approach, which is directed to the possibility of transforming shared living experiments into an integral segment of the profit-making economy, has more dangers than advantages at the present time. On the negative side, turning idealistic experiments into businesses means that the costs would immediately rise, thus eliminating one of the big advantages of shared living. Thus, units would be available for only high-income people. Since affluent persons already have other options, these small-scale living experiments are not a realistic possibility in the profit-making sector. The use of community volunteers would be greatly diminished if the projects were business enterprises. This, in itself, would reduce one of the chief attractions of the model.

In discussing the possibility of profit-making shared living, we should mention that board and care homes and adult congregate living facilities are similar to shared living in some respects and would be the chief competitors of such housing. These alternatives, which are sometimes called "rooming houses," connote a negative image in the minds of some people, primarily because of publicity about the abuses that occasionally occur. There is a constant effort by government agencies to enact rules and regulations, so that helpless, frail elderly people will not be exploited in such establishments. If shared family homes were to become profit-making, stricter rules and regulations would certainly be enacted. This would also result in higher costs to the individual resident, so that two things might result: the individual would not be able to afford shared housing, or public funds would have to be supplied to subsidize them.

The third approach is through subsidization by the government. This is also a way in which shared living might become profit making, similar to the way in which 80 percent of the nursing home industry in the United States is profit making—by receiving the greatest percentage of patient's fees as payments from government sources. It is possible that various forms of government subsidies could create the possibility for profit-making groups to consider and to organize such living units. This would, of course, demand increased government expenditures and higher taxes, which usually accompany such expenses. In the present fiscal situation, it is unlikely that a new program of this sort would be able to capture a significant amount of tax money.

In the long run, given the nature of the American political economy, the realistic probability is that spread of shared living arrangements will probably involve some combination of all three of these strategies—volunteerism, profit making, and government subsidies.

CHAPTER ELEVEN

Shared Housing and Its Policy
Implications

SHARED HOUSING AS INCREMENTAL CHANGE

We will now consider where shared housing for the elderly fits into a broader context of social policy. Some gerontologists have advocated that society must be restructured in fundamental ways to insure that more of the elderly receive proper supportive services and living conditions. Estes, for example, states: "Thus a services policy treats the problems of the aged, their illness and needs independent of their social causes while positing solutions in the consumption of services" (1979:238). She continues the argument by stating: "At the first and most important level would be major shifts in perceptions and structural alignments altering both the objective conditions of the aged and the social processes by which polices are made and implemented" (1979:240–41).

Olson pointedly states her position:

Liberal accommodationist reformers focus on remedying deficiencies of the established order without addressing the roots of the problems they identify. They demand not major structural changes, but instead, limited improvements to mitigate and treat symptoms of social ills. Their proposals, which do not question the basic logic, or resolve the inherent contradictions of monopoly capitalism, are shaped to conform to the requisites of capitalist production and values. (1982:223)

From Olson's perspective, the inadequacy of housing for the elderly and poor is caused by the structural constraints imposed by a private housing market. She writes: "The most fundamental issues related to housing deprivation are inextricably linked to the problems of poverty and the unequal distribution of power and income in society. These cannot be solved through housing policies alone" (1982:186).

A contrasting position to that of Estes and Olson regarding housing services for the elderly is put forth by Struyk and Soldo, who state: "It is important, but often forgotten, that any program resulting from a new policy initiative must be designed to mesh with existing programs" (1980:287). These housing experts believe in incremental changes in the housing and social welfare systems. New programs must be consistent with existing services.

Does shared housing simply deal with an existing small problem—propping up what some have called an ineffective social welfare system? The answer to this question is yes. The organizers and advocates of shared housing do not claim to be reshaping the system. Fundamentally, they accept the system as it exists. These organizers and advocates may question the day-to-day operations and some outcomes in terms of services and use of resources. But there is a basic acceptance of the fundamental premises and values upon which the society and the major institutions rest. This is true of both American organizers and the persons in Great Britain who formed and maintain the Abbeyfield Society. Their position is quite the opposite of that presented by Jeffrey H. Galper. He would argue that the kind of living arrangements and services described in our research "acts to subvert the welfare concept by organizing the role of social services so that they support and reinforce conformity, among both clients and workers, to the very institutions and values that generate the problems to which the services were addressed in the first place" (1981:168).

The persons who advocate a radical restructuring of society, rather than an incremental approach to the delivery of services to older people are vague as to how this restructuring would take place. Their discussion stops at the point where specific steps or means might be offered for initiating the restructuring. One can only presume that there is an acceptance of the electoral system in which democratic procedures are used to elect representatives who would vote in favor of radical restructuring. The current and near-future political climate and reality offer little evidence for such a possibility within the electorate, not to mention the elected. Olson proposes, for example, that there must be "progressive changes" that move a society toward democratic socialism and "instead of focusing on the requirements of specific social groups, such as the elderly, radical proposals crystallize issues around class" (1982:228). She argues for greater worker control of financial institutions, for example, by controlling the billions of dollars in pension funds.

The majority of older Americans do not agree with Olson, for they tend to accept the system as it is, and they look for programs, policies, and organizations that are congruent with their value system and also able to meet their needs. The "radical restructuring of the aging enterprise," as recommended by Estes, Olson, and others, has such long-range implications that it is not a consideration for the present cohort of elderly. In the shorter term of five, ten, or fifteen years, frail older Americans seek realistic possibilities to solve their problems. They expect that the situations they confront in the near future will be solved by means that are practical and possible in terms of economic and political realities. This means that the elderly in general are in favor of incremental changes that will make a difference in their remaining years. In the field of housing, shared living is one such possibility.

CONSEQUENCES OF INCREASED BUREAUCRACY

Irrespective of whether one is a structuralist or an incrementalist—that is, whether one wants to make radical reforms or incremental changes—there is usually a common consequence of either kind of change, namely, each results in more government involvement in the provision of housing for older people.

One of the characteristics of modern society is the increase in bureaucratic organizations and their influence in every facet of life. Bureaucracies are necessary for the integration of the major institutional arrangements serving large populations and attempting to achieve efficiency, predictability, cost control, and universalistic standards.

One of the problems, however, is that bureaucratic organizations, because they have formal rules and fixed structures, are often resistant to change. Bureaucracies are particularly effective in dealing with standardized, uniform tasks. However, as we have pointed out, the needs of frail older people involve many nonuniform tasks, so the dilemma that faces the practitioner and policy maker is how to blend the basic contradictions that stem from the nonuniformity of daily service and supportive activities with the requirements of formal organizations, particularly governmental bureaucracies.

In earlier decades, the housing and care of the frail elderly were matters that were handled by family and kin, neighbors, and private charitable groups. The transformation of our family structure and the development of a social welfare system have resulted in new expectations. Concerns that were formerly considered private and familial are now matters of public policy, public administration, and public funding. At the same time, however, the United States retains a highly individualistic value system, linked to a profit-making economy that assumes a high degree of individual responsibility.

When public monies are involved in meeting the needs of the frail elderly, it is inevitable that bureaucratic procedures will enter the picture. A bureaucracy, however, is often unable to deliver services to the homebound frail elderly at the time when they need them, for offices are usually open for a specified period of time during the working day, but the need may occur when the offices are closed. Furthermore, bureaucratic organizations are impersonal because the patrons or clients may be treated in an efficient but cold, indifferent, rationalistic manner. In addition, formal organizations are often inefficient because they are constricted with rules, procedures, chains of command, paperwork, and "red tape," which hamper the delivery of service or assistance. Also, budget cuts may reduce the staff and cause cuts in services.

In contrast, the organizations involved in shared housing are accessible and operate around the clock. They try to personalize their services, with employees encouraged to treat the residents as if they were relatives and friends. Their manner and demeanor are usually warm, concerned, and helpful. And finally, the organizations involved in shared living try to reduce rules, written procedures, and orders.

Some persons in the United States who are concerned with housing and care of the elderly regard public funding as the way to provide more service to the elderly, and to raise the quality of care. However, public funding, of necessity, also brings specifications, rules, regulations, evaluation and accountability, and a rigid time schedule. If there were public funds for the purchase and remodeling of a house for shared living, for example, there would have to be detailed specifications of room size, window ratio to floor space, plumbing, stairways, bathrooms, ceiling height, and so on—specifications that only an institution built especially for the purpose could meet easily. Most older homes would need so much remodeling that the cost would be prohibitive.

Such regulations were drawn up to prevent some of the very distressing conditions existing when helpless people are "warehoused"— especially those discharged from mental hospitals in large cities. There have been a few exposés of shocking living conditions when profit-making entrepreneurs have crowded too many people into a small space and kept them virtually prisoners, while receiving large amounts of public funds. Despite such occasional abuses, most people needing sheltered housing are not helpless, and they are not treated as prisoners.

Another area in which public funding and the accompanying rules and regulations would affect shared housing is staffing. The trend in bureaucratic organizations is to set up regulations that specify and describe staff positions and determine the training or experience required for particular staff positions. Most shared living facilities, however, do not require highly trained staff with academic credentials. In fact, the type of manager who is most effective in Share-A-Home and Abbeyfield is a mature, motherly woman with compassion, common sense, but often limited formal credentials.

Bureaucratic rules and regulations may inhibit the development and operation of shared living facilities by specifying the manner in which volunteers are involved in the care of older people. Volunteers can provide many needed services and play a meaningful role. Under the regulations of one state, however, it is specified that each person giving service to the elderly, including volunteers, must have a tuberculosis screening test, and the test must be on file.

Regulations such as this were placed on the books with good intentions and for a sound purpose. When carried out to the letter, such regulations could prevent the founding of alternative living arrangements or discourage volunteers from trying to enrich the program and improve the residents' quality of life.

Safeguards Against Abuse. Some of the first questions people ask when they hear about small group shared living are: "Are they inspected? Are they licensed? What safeguards are there that frail elderly people will not be abused?"

It is true, of course, that there have been serious instances of abuse in the nursing home industry, and it is pertinent to ask whether there is potential for such scandals to occur in shared living homes. We would emphasize that there are several major differences in the two housing environments. First, there is little opportunity for profit making in shared living homes, as operated at present. Organizations that have sponsored group homes have expended a great deal of time and effort without compensation, and in many cases they have donated their own funds or raised money for the start-up costs.

It cannot be predicted whether profit-making groups might enter the shared living scene in the future. Some motel chains, for example, have considered whether they could sell older motels to be used as small group homes for the elderly. Given the laissez-faire nature of the American private enterprise system, there is always the possibility that some profit-oriented persons might establish group homes and initiate cost-cutting procedures, which might result in exploitation of residents. In such a case, however, the residents could move out if they were not satisfied.

The second important characteristic of small group homes that differentiates them from nursing homes is that the residents are in a stronger state of mental and physical health than nursing home patients. Residents of group homes must be ambulatory and able to take care of their daily personal needs, such as dressing and bathing. Many are able to function independently and have contacts with persons in the outside community. They are more aware of their rights and the responsibilities of management than the typical nursing home resident. Some residents write letters and use the telephone and are more involved in day-to-day activities than persons in nursing homes. They could voice complaints to outsiders.

The third factor is that most shared living homes are sponsored by religious or charitable organizations, whose members have become involved for humanitarian reasons. And finally, the "visibility" of shared housing arrangements is an important safeguard against mistreatment of its residents. In most shared living situations, committee members frequently visit the house and interact with the residents. We believe that when a housing arrangement is open to public observation and scrutiny, there is far less danger of exploitation or mistreatment.

Of course, there is the possibility that abuse of the elderly could occur in any setting—even in private families, according to those who have studied "granny bashing." We are aware of this possibility but have not received information on a single incident during the course of our research in shared living arrangements. The degree to which added regulations and inspections would obviate the possibility of abuse is a matter of speculation.

Financial exploitation is another kind of abuse organizers should consider. In Share-A-Homes in Florida, the organizer was sensitive to the fact that financial exploitation might be possible in some cases. For example, if a confused elderly person sought help from the housekeeper or other staff in managing her checkbook, it is possible that an abuse could occur. Therefore, he requires that residents select someone not affiliated with Share-A-Home who has a power of attorney and who manages their finances, if necessary. The staff is instructed not to be involved in any financial arrangements.

To summarize, the combination of factors of healthier residents, religious and charitable sponsoring organizations, lack of a strong profit incentive, and the openness and visibility of the homes reduces the risk of neglect or abuse in comparison to the situation in nursing homes.

There is a related basic question that should be addressed: How much risk should society tolerate? The answer is complicated and cannot be covered in a few sentences. This is another one of those areas in which our society finds itself in a cultural bind. In some areas of life, Americans are excessively cautious, but in others we are unconcerned about the risks to ourselves and to other citizens. Most people accept risks on our highways with equanimity: there is general disregard of the 55-mile-an-hour speed limit, even though it has saved thousands of lives. In houses used for shared living, however, we are quick to demand expensive sprinkler systems when the same house used for a biological family would attract no such demand.

Some people believe that if we write better and more regulations to protect the elderly, we can prevent any accident, mishap, or exploitation. In reality, such a goal is impossible. Moreover, the American public will not pay the necessary taxes to enable all older citizens to live in the conditions specified in the laws. In fact, many of the general public do not live under ideal conditions in their own homes.

Another arena where bureaucracies create blockages in the operation of nontraditional facilities is the requirement of reports and paperwork. Low-cost, family-type living arrangements do not have the additional staff needed to maintain the records required by some states. If one is trying to maintain a family-like living environment, bureaucratic red tape has to be kept to a minimum. The greater the amount of record keeping and the longer the reports that are required, the more institutionalized the home becomes. Some record keeping and monitoring of persons is required because of the notion that this information will insure compliance with the law and thereby result in better service. However, record keeping and report writing are not necessarily correlated with better service delivery and happier elderly people.

In Share-A-Home and other arrangements described here, the underlying philosophy is that staff are more than cooks or housekeepers; they are friends, confidants, and part of the "family" themselves. It is considered more important for a staff person to talk to a resident, if that is what the resident needs at the particular moment, than to complete a specified household task. If a living arrangement is to function in a family-like manner, it cannot be formalized by over-rigid rules and requirements for reports.

British planners and practitioners, in attempting to provide sheltered housing for older persons, have established small projects averaging 30 units in size (Heumann and Boldy 1982). They report that there were 327,000 sheltered housing units provided in 1976. They are located in areas convenient to community services such as shops, transportation, and medical facilities. Most importantly, they are staffed by a live-in person (called a "warden" in Great Britain) who coordinates the social supports and activities, yet is on the periphery of the lives of the individuals in the housing units. In British terminology, the warden is defined as a "friendly neighbor." While the term has a different connotation in the United States, in Great Britain a warden "implies a resident counsellor, organizer and family proxy for such facilities as youth hostels, college dormitories, day care programs, summer camps or elderly sheltered housing" (Heumann and Boldy 1982:126). This is a nonbureaucratic approach to the complex administrative situation of housing older persons, for the warden, as a family proxy, uses her judgment to do what is necessary for the residents and refer them for more specialized services if they need them. With the aging of the residents, however, the burden and responsibilities of the warden increase, and the problems of the frail elderly take on the same character as in Abbeyfield and in the small group homes in America.

When gerontologists urge the establishment of a coordinated policy of housing for the elderly, they do not acknowledge the bureaucracy necessary to carry out that policy; to fund, to monitor, to promote, and to enforce. The trend toward bureaucratization—an inevitable facet of modern life—creates certain dilemmas when it intrudes into the regulation of small, family-like environments such as shared living homes.

POLICY IMPLICATIONS OF FINANCING SHARED HOUSING

The policy considerations of financing shared housing are a topic of primary interest to sponsoring groups. The shared housing movement for the elderly in the United States has been primarily a local, small-scale operation initiated with private funding. If the movement is to spread and serve more elderly who need this kind of supportive services, greater sources of financial support will have to be found in either the public or private sectors. Most persons interested in organizing shared housing have been ingenious in using whatever available limited resources they could muster to start each project. There has been some exchange of ideas and suggestions to avoid pitfalls and to enhance success of new shared housing endeavors.

A major policy consideration is whether public agencies at various levels of government—local, state, and federal—should encourage the development of more shared living projects. One of the most effective ways would be through financial support or inducements that would stimulate and facilitate persons and groups who are concerned about the housing and services for older people. Once a policy of public support has been established, there are a series of questions relating to the most effective financial mechanisms that might be utilized. The following criteria must be considered: The environment provided must be safe and comfortable; there must be prudent use of public monies; and there must be a minimum of red tape and bureaucratic specifications.

These criteria may seem somewhat contradictory, but a flexible policy could encourage people at the local level rather than frustrate them in securing access to funds. The financial devices that have been used to finance schools, hospitals, and nursing homes could be adapted to shared living units. One of the unique problems involved in the public policy aspects of shared housing is that the actual operation of the housing facility is a local, small-scale project in which local persons are involved in the initiative to start the houses. However, government agencies and private funding groups such as banks or insurance companies prefer to deal with large-scale, established organizations. Such groups employ lawyers, lobbyists, accountants, and public relations experts to promote their financial interests and pilot them through the funding process, such as securing tax-free bonds. The persons who have organized shared living facilities usually have not had the resources to hire this expensive kind of talent and professional expertise.

Another financial consideration is the way in which public resources could be made available to the residents and organizers of shared living facilities to meet the deficits of daily or monthly operations. Some of these financial problems arise from the declining income of the older female residents, who sometimes cannot afford an increase in the monthly charges. Some people have asked whether food stamps and SSI payments are made available to individuals of low income to contribute to the cost of running the house. There is no clear policy on this matter, for there are varying interpretations in different areas.

In some shared homes, especially those sponsored by a religious organization, supplements are made available for low-income individuals from charitable funds of the sponsoring organization. However, this source of supplements tends to be small scale and erratic and cannot be relied upon as a basis for sound financial support. In Great Britain, there is an established government policy to supplement the income of persons so that they can meet the charges of the Abbeyfield house in which they live. This varies according to the person's pension and the fees charged in the house in which they live. In the United States, there is no established provision to enable low-income persons to meet the costs of a shared living home.

The problems of the Shared Living Project in Boston in trying to get a variance for Section 8 rent subsidies were reported by Susan Stockard before a hearing of the Subcommittee on Housing and Consumer Interests of the Select Committee on Aging of the House of Representatives, November 17, 1981. She stated:

I think HUD is stuck on a standard of living that doesn't reflect the needs or the resources that exist in housing for older people today. You who make the policies for this country need to recognize and affirm the lifestyle changes that economics and longevity are precipitating. We grew up with an image of independence and self-sufficiency that centered around our single family homes and our nuclear family identity. We literally can't afford to keep perpetuating this image. (Stockard 1981:16)

The difficulties of financing and renovating an older house for shared living were emphasized at the hearing by Reverend Day-Lower. He noted that commercial banks are quite conservative in their practices, and public monies have been available in very meager amounts and often involve a very competitive process. He said that nonprofit groups would be interested in remodeling HUD properties to use for shared housing, observing that at present, such properties are purchased by private bidders for speculation. He emphasized that if such homes could provide housing for six, eight, or ten people, at a very cost-effective level when compared to new construction, there should be some means devised to assist them (Day-Lower 1981).

Another basic policy matter in the field of shared housing, as in so many service programs, is the degree to which public agencies should continue valuable experimental programs that are often started by local private initiative. In this field there is a need for information networks that operate in an ad hoc, informal way. One might recommend that state and local offices of aging should be designated as clearing houses for information on this subject. This would mean, however, that large amounts of public monies would have to be appropriated to meet the costs of operating an effective information network, and legislatures are reluctant to appropriate funds for such purposes.

In recent years, some sponsors of programs have demonstrated a lack of realism about costs. The fiscal approach has often been that of the cost overrun—"if we get the program started, it will be impossible to close it down, and somehow, the funds will be found." There is a tendency to raise expectations higher than it is possible to satisfy, for the cost of the program has been understated and its efficacy overstated.

Discussions concerning costs must be placed in the context of public attitudes. Many persons believe that there is enormous waste in government and that public agencies are not as "efficient" as private ones. There is a growing skepticism about how public agencies spend money. Whether or not these attitudes are valid is beside the point, for when people believe them, the attitudes take on a self-fulfilling aspect. To bring together these points, let us assert that the development of alternative living arrangements for the elderly must be understood in the context of attitudes and beliefs about government programs, public funding, and the need for fiscal restraints.

Considering these trends in public attitudes toward funding of housing programs and the reductions in financial support resulting from economic stagnation, it seems that provision of housing for frail older people will probably have to be organized and managed at the local level by essentially nonprofessional persons who have, first and foremost, a genuine desire to provide such housing and also the practical knowledge to carry out their commitment to serving older people.

A vital society adapts to new needs and priorities as they emerge. In the future, there will not be an automatic government response to these needs, and therefore there will be a necessity to adapt to the decreased public resources. We must devise new ways to give meaning to the longer life span that technology and medical science have given us. Most of our social system has been based on the historical ideals of rugged individualism and self-sufficiency, but this orientation does not direct attention to the problems of a large number of frail elderly.

In the past, many people in the social sciences have turned to "political" means for doing good. They have believed that passing laws to insure that needs are met and justice is accomplished is the most effective way to handle social problems. However, we are nearing a limit to the public means to pay for all the good causes that various groups recognize and for which they raise a demand. There is no longer willingness to use public funds to solve all of our human service problems.

Yet there will be continued demand from interest groups and their paid lobbyists for their "share" of the available public monies. Priorities will emerge out of the give and take of the political process, with both selfish and benevolent interests involved. These priorities will shape the way public resources are used. Given the need of housing for a growing number of frail older people, and the increased recognition of their political power, one can hope that their need will be recognized by policy makers who control the public purse.

ZONING AS AN IMPEDIMENT TO SHARED HOUSING

One of the central policy issues that inhibits the spread of shared housing results from the difficulties with zoning, ordinances, regulations, and the granting of variances by local government agencies. Simply stated, the practical problem is that a suitable structure is often in an area zoned for single-family dwelling units. Since shared housing often involves five or more unrelated adults living together, frequently a variance must be obtained. Traditionally, the regulation of land use has resided in local government units. This reflects law and practice which has deep roots in American and British society. In recent decades, however, the proliferation of laws, programs, and regulations at the state and federal level has challenged the practice of local autonomy in matters of zoning. For example, the federal government may specify that unless a policy (like deinstitutionalization) is carried out according to federal rules and specifications, funds will be withheld. This has resulted in some fierce battles on the local level, as group homes for the developmentally handicapped have been placed in residential areas. In the future, there may be restraints placed on local zoning bodies if charges of discrimination against certain citizens are raised, or if they fail to provide for the outcomes of modernization—that is, a large older population, particularly the frail elderly. The common good—care of *all* frail elderly regardless of where they happen to have been born (in or out of state) or to whom in the household they are related—may have to take precedence over local land-use law and customs.

The placement of group housing of any sort is opposed by the residents of many local neighborhoods. One of the major criticisms raised is that group homes will reduce property values in the neighborhood. The number of shared housing units for elderly is relatively small, and to our knowledge no systematic studies have been carried out on their impact on property values. However, there are eight studies that examine in detail the impact of homes for persons with developmental disabilities. All eight report uniformly that group homes have *no effect on the property values* or the rate of property turnover (Lauber 1982). One study, which is methodologically and statistically sound, illustrates that property values in communities with group homes had the same change in market prices as in matched control areas (Wolpert 1978). This study was carried out in forty-two neighborhoods within ten municipalities in New York. Matched neighborhoods were selected on key variables so there were equivalent control sites for neighborhoods in which group homes were located. Thus, the fears of neighborhood groups concerning property values appear to be unjustified. None of the eight studies involved group homes for the elderly; in fact, it would be our contention that such homes would have only a minor impact upon the "normal" neighborhoods, and therefore they would meet less resistance than other types of group homes. Some neighborhood associations, however, fear any precedent that might effect a change in their locality. We would suggest these associations still hold to the sentiments of an earlier era and have not adjusted to the housing needs of a modern society.

The matter of zoning is an area marked by confusion and vagueness, competing and conflicting ordinances, and antiquated or obscure regulations, which can be brought out to block a project if neighborhood groups wish to do so. Many of these issues were highlighted in a hearing before the Subcommittee on Housing and Consumer Interests of the Select Committee on Aging of the House of Representatives on November 17, 1981.

One of the issues brought forth in the hearing was the negative attitude of the general public toward boarding homes and the anxiety that their own neighborhood may be "tainted" by them. Insofar as shared living is defined as a boarding home, many people will be negative in their attitudes toward it and will consider that it might reduce the value of their property. Drayton Bryant, an urban planner in Philadelphia, in a prepared statement to the hearing, stated that the category "group dwellings" carries a negative connotation in the minds of many people, for

they are sponsors of a range of social services, halfway houses for drug and alcohol abuse, youthful offenders, battered women, pregnant girls or those removed from destructive home situations, retarded or disturbed patients with resident staff, or nonprofit boarding homes for the frail elderly or permanently 'convalescent.' All of these have many unfortunate, low-status, or Four-D connotations: Disadvantaged, Depressed, Deprived, and Depraved. (Bryant 1981:42)

He added that sharing of housing is vaguely associated with skid row, high transiency, irresponsibility toward property, and "cults" rather than denominations. Unfortunately, this typifies the kind of stereotypes held by many of the general public, which become obstacles to sponsors of shared housing.

Bryant stressed that zoning ordinances are a major obstacle to shared housing, for most ordinances say a "family" can take in only one or two unrelated adults. He said that he knows of many instances of shared housing where people are responding to the "economics of the day" and "moving in," without licenses, zoning, or building permits. Often these are younger people who simply go ahead with their scheme and ignore the regulations. We would add that the religious organizations, which are often the groups sponsoring shared living for the elderly, adhere to the law. Bryant stressed that it is imperative to enact modern zoning regulations that do not respond to *past* conditions. He asserted that zoning is ten to thirty years behind reality.

We reported in chapter 6 the difficulties that the Jewish Council on the Aging encountered in Skokie, Illinois, to get a zoning variance to build Robineau House—the only purpose-built house we have located. Two of the court cases concerning group housing were presented in chapter 9. Another example of zoning problems that came to our attention was a case in which neighborhood residents blocked use of a home for six elderly people because they claimed that, while they personally did not object to the elderly, "this variance will pave the way to let in a bunch of drug addicts."

Congresswoman Pat Schroeder, who was present at the hearing, stated that there is a real need for housing, but "there is absolutely no money for it. Shared housing becomes a real solution to a critical problem." She urged that model codes be developed and presented to city council members. She added, however, that neighborhood associations have many basic fears and have made their views known. "Because of the stereotypes involved, the problem is that the city councils are afraid the neighborhood groups will absolutely eat them alive" (Schroeder 1981: 45).

The role of the federal government in promoting shared housing was also discussed at the hearing. Philip Abrams, general deputy assistant secretary for housing, Department of Housing and Urban Development, stated:

For shared housing to be most effective and responsive to the communities' and the shared-housing residents' needs, we believe the projects should be locally conceived, developed, and managed. Through this mechanism, the program can grow rapidly and effectively without being constrained by the Federal bureaucracy and Federal regulations. (Abrams 1981:5)

Other persons at the hearing, however, took issue with this recommendation, pointing out that this seems like an avoidance of responsibility. Reverend Day-Lower said there should be a federal commitment to offering technical assistance to local groups in order to avoid the two- or three-year time period of establishing a household. Bryant also urged that the federal government could play an important role in "seeding the field," sending out information to state agencies to initiate demonstration programs or assisting with partial funding.

He stated:

Shared housing, its concepts, creation, financing and responsible operations are a voluntary area of initiative and leadership for constructive action. Governments at various levels should not stand in the way by zoning exclusions and excessive restrictions, but can facilitate this normal and useful part of the social structure and strengthen the faltering economics of housing in this difficult time, to better preserve and maintain the existing housing stock, and to build confidence in the feasibility of a valued part of the housing spectrum.

All people want to make choices within their means, whether young or elderly, single or in continued relations. The poor, ill, elderly handicapped, frail or impaired have even less choice. Shared housing choices should be reasonably available to the present wide range of those who might benefit. Improvement of clarity and recognition in zoning is a critical early step for useful shared housing. (Bryant 1981:42–43)

THE ENERGY ISSUE AND SHARED HOUSING

The continuing concern about energy resources and their costs requires persistent, imaginative planning and implementation for all persons in the world, and especially for the elderly in developed nations like the United States and the United Kingdom. Energy and the needs of the frail elderly have policy implications because as these persons age, they have fewer resources—economic, physical, social, and psychological— and therefore they have fewer means for meeting their problems in comparison to other segments of the population. Furthermore, impairment of the thermo-regulatory system is one of the characteristics of aging in some people. Various factors are involved, such as diminished metabolic rate, lack of exercise, or the effect of drugs. In addition, it is believed that aging itself has effects on the cerebrovascular system and on the body's thermostat. This combination of factors results in the generalization that older persons often feel the cold more intensely and need a warmer temperature in their homes than other age groups (Rango 1980).

Shared housing is a more economical way for older people to live, for they can reduce energy costs. Obviously, it costs less to supply heat and light for six to eight people sharing a home than if they lived in separate residences. This is the basic premise underlying such designs as the Solar Group Home of the Tennessee Valley Authority, Share-A-Home, and others.

The shared living models and TVA's Solar Group Home discussed in previous chapters serve to point out two very important aspects of modern society's attempts to deal with the energy cost problems of its elderly citizens: these models represent a recognition that there exists a problem, and, more importantly, they provide a set of tools with which to address that problem. In some projects established for social benefits, savings in energy and food costs are of secondary concern. In other projects, such as the TVA model, energy economy is part of the primary design characteristics. In both types, cost savings are part of the tangible benefit that recommends the establishment of shared living facilities.

The awareness of the elderly of high energy costs is illustrated by the results of a recent research study on bringing nutritious frozen meals to home-bound people. The program was deemed unsuccessful, for the recipients felt that the cost of heating the frozen meals was too high in comparison to the benefit of the meal.

Professor Jack Meltzer (1980) of the University of Chicago's School of Social Services Administration has made the important distinction between energy needed for survival and energy needed to enhance the quality of life. In considering shared housing and its energy implications, one must keep this in mind. A great deal of energy consumed by people in developed countries is done to enhance the quality of life. The policy that emphasizes keeping the elderly in their homes as long as possible is cost-inefficient in the use of energy for individuals and for the community. The question is whether public policies should be set forth that encourage the frail elderly to consider some kind of group living arrangements like those described in this book in order to enjoy a greater amount of personal comfort and effect a more efficient use of energy. The loss of privacy and problems of adaptation have to be weighed against the lower energy costs and a more comfortable environment.

LONG LIFE, ADAPTABILITY, AND SHARED HOUSING

Social policy makers and administrators at state and national levels have established a policy of keeping people in their own homes as long as possible, and bringing to them an array of services. This may not be a sound policy if one weighs a combination of social, economic, and psychological factors. Moreover, the policy and the publicity supporting it are predicated on stability and nonmovement, when perhaps the message should instead stress change and adaptation.

Gerontologists have generally embraced the idea that it is highly undesirable to move the elderly. When surveys ask older people what they prefer, they usually say they want life to remain as it has been. The elderly do not generally look forward to changes. However, recent reviews of a large body of research on relocation of the elderly in nursing homes show that the negative consequences have been overstated (Borup 1981; Borup, Gallego, and Heffernan 1979; Borup and Gallego 1981; Coffman 1981).

The financial considerations are also important. According to Bane:

Most notably, the transfer system purchases the ability to live independently and maintain separate households for many elderly people and many single mothers. The privacy and autonomy that most elderly, disabled and single people seem to prefer is probably the most expensive new service purchased by the social welfare system. (1983:97)

Perhaps gerontologists should stress that people may have to move—that mobility in old age is part of American life. When people cannot drive, cannot shop, and their family is far away geographically, they may have to make new arrangements. The model of life in a small village with caring neighbors is not valid for many older Americans. This is not to suggest that we value mobility for the sake of mobility. It is part of the changing nature of American society, for neighborhoods change, economic conditions change, and the social and mental health conditions of persons over 75 change.

Yet the prospect of moving to a shared living environment is met with resistance by many persons—old and young—because such a move is perceived as a sudden change away from the familiar and the known environment to one that is unfamiliar and unpredictable. Shared living is not compatible with some of our cherished American ideals of independence and individuality. Yet sometimes, at the end of life, over-emphasis on independence may be counterproductive.

Rosow (1974) has pointed out that socialization to old age is difficult because the norms and situations are ambiguous. A change in living arrangements might constitute a stressful move to an ambiguous situation. Yet in terms of policy decisions for our older citizens, attention and emphasis should be given to the necessity of change and adaptation and not to continuing the old patterns of life. Some of the aging population may have to realize that living to an old age means that a person cannot necessarily remain in the same lifetime groove, but must accept the possibility of change and relocation, perhaps to a shared living facility with its advantages and its disadvantages. With a restricted economic condition predicted for the future of our country, and with resources that are limited, not expanding, we need to consider new adaptations.

Modernization has enabled many older persons to live longer. Because the survivors are often more adaptable people, the move to a new living arrangement like shared housing need not necessarily be traumatic. It can be part of the adaptability of the older person to a new environment, which may be life enhancing, enriching, and personally satisfying.

We predict that shared housing will be among those programs that receive increased interest from the general public and greater awareness from policy makers, resulting in appropriation of public resources for their initiation and support. These factors, combined with grass-roots participation by volunteers in local communities, will shape the future of shared households to meet the changing needs of America's elderly.

MODERNIZATION AND SHARED HOUSING: A SUMMING UP

The broad theme presented in chapter 1 is that one of the major consequences of modernization in developed societies is an aging population—larger numbers of persons who reach old age and an increasing proportion of the elderly. The accompanying health and medical technologies have been the antecedent for the graying of the population. In the foreseeable future, this gerontological "revolution" will include about

15 to 20 percent of the noninstitutionalized elderly, who are called the frail elderly.

The care of the frail elderly has traditionally been the responsibility of women relatives, principally daughters. With the increasing number of women in the labor force, the number of family members who can assume care-taking roles has declined, and will continue to do so. For those who do become caretakers, the responsibilities often become burdensome and debilitating.

Social problems resulting from modernization are conventionally considered to be solved by modern methods, namely, development of large-scale bureaucratic programs and technologies that can be standardized and delivered to meet the shelter and service needs of a frail older population. But the "quick fix" of technological, bureaucratic, and computerized cost efficiencies are often ineffective in dealing with many of the nonstandardized tasks that must be performed for these older people.

Some of the variable, idiosyncratic human needs may not be easily met by standardized computerized solutions. It is a paradox that the approaches we have described in this book are essentially "old-fashioned" solutions to modern problems. Our society has developed sophisticated technology to deal with health and medical problems and extend peoples' lives. However, the needs of the elderly are complex and should have inputs from a number of systems other than the health care system to make the extended lives livable.

Government agencies have been reluctant to move into this area because government policy makers and administrators, of necessity, usually must provide alternatives that are standardized and may be applied on a broad scale in many states and localities. In the United States, these programs are usually prescribed and structured by lawyers who approach most public issues and social programs in a legalistic way. Lawyers often shape the thinking of legislative bodies and administrative agencies. However, the elderly and their needs for shelter are difficult to encompass in conventional legal concepts and language (see the discussion of "family" and zoning earlier in the book). One cannot write a regulation which says "do what needs to be done," because it would immediately be challenged as a vague law which could not be enforced.

A few years ago, the conventional thinking of many economists was challenged by E. F. Schumacher's (1973) book, *Small Is Beautiful: Eco-*

nomics as if People Mattered. In our approach to this modern problem of a large number of frail elderly who need a supportive environment, we also assert that people really do matter. Small may not be beautiful, but it is *appropriate.* Beauty is an esthetic characteristic and rests in the eyes of the beholder, but appropriateness is a more rational, testable matter and is not judged by esthetic standards. Small size can result in personalized attention and permit freedom of choice, which is not possible in large social organizations. Many observers have pointed out that modern societies tend to be fragmented, uncoordinated, and lacking in social solidarity. It seems possible that small group homes like those we have described, which are rooted in the community and depend on the concern and good will of neighbors and strangers, can bring about a new solidarity that helps to involve community residents. These pockets of social concern may enhance generational cohesion.

A continuing concern of sociologists through the last hundred years has been the divisiveness of societies as they became modern. Writers of various political persuasions have expressed the fear that the emphasis on growth, technology, and raising the standard of living would cause the sense of community to be lost. In Maurice Stein's (1960) phrase, there would be an "eclipse of community." In this book, we have presented a description and analysis of a number of small-scale social experiments that draw upon the basic motives of good will, charity, and neighborliness. We cannot forecast whether the number and scale of these experiments to deal with older people and their needs will be expanded further. This rests not with the older generation but with the decisions and values of younger people. Such intergenerational cooperation provides the possibility for citizens of modern societies to contribute to the solution of this ongoing problem and perhaps create the kind of society they will find waiting for them when they, too, become elderly.

Methods of Research

Since shared living arrangements are amalgam groups, we combined research methods to deal with both primary groups and formal organizations. This was necessary both in the design of the study and in the techniques of research. We have used participant observation, informal observation, formal interviews, mail surveys, and available information such as staff reports, brochures, directories, and magazine and newspaper articles.

In studying an organization, a first research priority is to obtain entry to the organization so one can observe and interview the persons involved. We were fortunate in receiving a high degree of cooperation from the organizers, administrators, and staff of all of the projects and houses we visited. This ease of access for the researchers occurs because the persons involved in organizing shared housing are proud of what they are trying to provide and want others to know about their activities. They hope that others who know of their experience might become involved in similar kinds of work. Open institutions thus constitute very positive research sites.

We combined the methods of field work, participant observation and interviewing, with the methods of survey research in two countries, giving our study a cross-national comparative perspective.

These are the main components of the research process, which was conducted over a five-year period:

1. Informal observation of Share-A-Home "families" throughout the United States, interviews with the founder, and attendance at meetings of boards of directors.

2. Participant observation in the homes: one of the authors lived in the Florida households for six months.

3. Formal interviews with Share-A-Home residents and staff.

4. Comparative research: visits to and observation of other shared facilities throughout the United States. Informal interviews with residents, staff, board members.

5. Diffusion research: mail survey of readers of *Modern Maturity* who wrote for information about shared living.

6. Mail survey of organizers or managers of other shared facilities in the United States.

7. Assessment of the "market" for shared housing: mail survey of the interest in this kind of facility of residents in two Florida retirement communities.

8. Cross-national research: visit to Abbeyfield Society headquarters in Great Britain, visits to Abbeyfield houses, collection of reports and secondary analysis of Abbeyfield survey data. Interviews with paid staff, volunteers. Attendance at meetings of boards and committees.

9. Preparation of a manual for community groups on how to start and operate a Share-A-Home.

10. Conducting workshops and seminars for interested groups.

This research started as a sociological study in which we focused our attention on small group living arrangements and their family-like characteristics. It was secondarily a study of older individuals and their adaptations and attitudes. As our knowledge of these small groups increased, we became aware that they involved organizational components that required us to conceive of the groups as amalgams. The awareness of the formal organizational side of small group arrangements required us to investigate the sponsorship and financial aspects of the projects, because careful control of economics is necessary for survival.

As our focus shifted from group structure and process to organizational survival, we saw the importance of investigating how these projects were involved with other groups and organizations. Hence it was necessary to devote attention to the organizational linkages to social service agencies, sponsoring religious organizations, and government funding sources. It was essential to examine the way shared living groups were connected to the economy, the polity, and other institutional structures.

The independent variable in this investigation was the small group environment. The dependent variable was the quality of life provided by this kind of living arrangement for the elderly—how adequate it is in terms of providing basic shelter, food, and security, along with some degree of companionship and sociability. We recognized that the environments were more complex than we had orginally thought and therefore our research attention was directed to unfolding the complexities of these settings as the independent variable.

The typical ideal research design is to determine the effect of the major variable on the phenomena to be explained. The investigator makes the assumption that other major factors or influences are equal or somehow held constant. In this investigation, we described those other factors that are considered as constants or sometimes as intervening variables: the way other organizations or institutions influenced the structure and function of the living arrangements and their sponsors. For example, we studied how a unit of government, a court or an administrative agency, aided or impeded the operation of a particular project.

To increase our understanding of these linkages between living unit, project, and institutional context, we compiled an inventory of 80 shared houses in the United States and visited 40 of them. We also visited 15 of the 900 houses in Great Britain in order to have a comparative data base that would provide descriptive generalizations of the living arrangements located in a different society. We were interested in determining the interorganizational linkages between these living arrangements, their sponsoring organizations, and the governmental structure of Great Britain.

Although the major focus of this study was on groups and organizations, we also obtained data based on individuals as the observation unit. This focus on the human actor was accomplished through observation, participant observation, interviewing, and questionnaire survey research. In addition to providing information on how individuals felt and behaved in these new "family" environments, this work enabled us to refine our understanding of group dynamics.

To enhance the validity of this research and to provide a realistic and contextual picture, we obtained the views of both insiders and outsiders. The insiders in this instance were the residents of these living units, whom we interviewed. In the case of Abbeyfield, we had access to the survey research conducted by a professional research organization, and we were able to conduct a secondary analysis of these materials. The outsiders included, of course, the researchers themselves, the organizers, and other persons who were not residents of these units but acted as informants about them. This blending of observations of the phenomenon from the inside in terms of the standpoint of the actors provided a qualitative dimension, while the outsiders' views provided a more detached set of observations. Our task was to attempt to generalize about these variant living units and, at the same time, present specific insights into the meaning of shared living for older people.

Instruments

Resident Interview Guide

STUDY OF ALTERNATIVE LIVING ARRANGEMENTS

Subject ID#_____

University of Florida
Department of Sociology
Center for Gerontological Studies
September 1978

DATE_____

This is a confidential study which will be used for research purposes only. Participants will not be identified by name. Participation is voluntary.

Consent obtained_____
(Signature)   (Date)

Other persons present during much of interview?
_____Yes   _____No
Specify whom_____

Informant:
_____None
_____For less than 5 questions
_____For substantial part of interview
_____For all of interview

Informant:
_____None
_____Lives with subject
_____Does not live with subject

Adapted from instruments developed at the Philadelphia Geriatric Center, Philadelphia, Pennsylvania.

A. BACKGROUND

(After consent form has been signed, record type of housing, sex, and race below:)

1. Type of Housing:
   _____Housing especially for the elderly
   _____Single-family detached house
   _____Multiple dwelling house: row, duplex, semi-detached
   _____Apartment in house with one or more apartments (apartment *has* kitchen)
   _____Boarding house, rented room(s) in house (room has no private kitchen)
   _____Apartment building (approximate number of units—by
inspection # _____)
   _____Other_____
              (specify)
2. Sex: _____Male _____Female

3. Race: _____White _____Black _____Other

---

4. What do you like most about Share-A-Home?

5. What do you like least about Share-A-Home?

6. Why did you move to Share-A-Home?

7. If you did not live in Share-A-Home, where could you live?

8. What is today's date:

	CORRECT		
	YES	NO	NA
Month_____	_____	_____	_____
Date_____	_____	_____	_____
Year_____	_____	_____	_____

(Probe): What (month/date/year) is it now?

9. How long have you lived at this address? _____years

10. About how far away was the home you lived in before this? Was it:_____
_____in this neighborhood (within 8 blocks or a half mile), in this city (town) but in a different neighborhood, or
_____in another city (town)?

11. Did you live alone? _____Yes   _____No

12. Who lived with you?

13. How was the person(s) related to you?

14. How old was the person(s)?

    12. Name   13. Relationship   14. Age

_____   _____   _____

_____   _____   _____

_____   _____   _____

Number of *other* persons then living in household: _____

These are some questions about you.

	CORRECT NO,		
	YES	DK	NA

15. How old are you? _____ ____ ____

16. When were you born?
    Month_____   ____ ____
    Date_____   ____ ____ ____
    Year_____   ____ ____ ____

17. Were you born in the United States or in another coun-try? ____U.S.____Other country

18. Have you ever been married:
    ____Yes____No

19. Are you presently:
    ____Married
    ____Widowed
    ____Separated
    ____Divorced

20. What religion are you?
    ____Protestant   ____Jewish   ____Other
    ____Catholic   ____None

21. What kind of work did *you* do most of your working life?
    _____ ____Never employed
    (occupational title or duties)

22. What kind of business or company was that?
    _____
    (industry or type of business)

23. Do you work now?
    ____Yes   ____No

24. Do you work:
    ____Full time   ____Just once in a while
    ____Part time

25. What kind of work did your spouse do most of his (her) working life?
    _____
    (occupational title or duties)

26. What kind of business or company was that?
    _____
    Industry or type of business)

27. What was the highest grade of school you completed?
    ____years

28. Did you ever attend any business school or trade school?
    ____Yes   ____No

29. How many years did you attend (business school/trade school)?
    ____years

30. What is your exact address?

CORRECT
NO,
YES   DK   NA

_____   ____ ____ ____

31. Where is it located?
    (city, section)

    _____

    _____   ____ ____

B. PHYSICAL HEALTH

32. How would you rate your overall health at the present time?—
    ____Excellent   ____Good   ____Fair   ____Poor   ____NA, DK

33. Is your health *now* better, about the same, or not as good as it was three
    years ago?
    ____Better   ____Same   ____Not as good   ____NA, DK

34. Do your health problems stand in the way of your doing the things you
    want to do—not at all, a little, or a great deal?
    ____Not at all   ____A little   ____A great deal

35. Would you say that your health is better, about the same, or not as good as most people your age?

_____ Better _____ Same _____ Not as good _____ NA, DK

36. How good is your eyesight (with glasses if used)? Is it good (adequate) or poor, or are you blind?

_____ Good or adequate _____ Poor or partially blind
_____ Totally blind _____ NA, DK

37. How good is your hearing (with hearing aid if used)? Is it good (adequate) or poor, or are you deaf?

_____ Good or adequate _____ Poor or partially deaf
_____ Totally deaf _____ NA, DK

38. About how many times did you see *any type* of doctor during the past twelve months? (Do not include doctors seen while a patient in a hospital)

_____ Number of times

39. About how many days have you spent in a hospital during the past twelve months?

_____ Number of days

40. About how many days during the past twelve months have you been sick in bed at home all or most of the day?

_____ Number of days

41. In the past year, have you had:

	Yes	No	DK
a. diabetes or sugar sickness?	_____	_____	_____
b. high blood pressure or hypertension?	_____	_____	_____
c. heart trouble?	_____	_____	_____
d. circulation problems, hardening of the arteries?	_____	_____	_____
e. been paralyzed in any way?	_____	_____	_____
f. any other effects of stroke?	_____	_____	_____
g. arthritis, rheumatism?	_____	_____	_____
h. a stomach ulcer?	_____	_____	_____
i. emphysema or asthma?	_____	_____	_____
j. glaucoma, pressure behind the eye?	_____	_____	_____
k. cataracts?	_____	_____	_____
l. a tumor or growth, cancer?	_____	_____	_____
m. liver trouble or jaundice?	_____	_____	_____
n. gall bladder trouble?	_____	_____	_____
o. kidney trouble?	_____	_____	_____
p. bladder trouble?	_____	_____	_____
q. a broken hip?	_____	_____	_____
r. other broken bones?	_____	_____	_____

s. anemia? ___ ___ ___
t. Parkinson's disease? ___ ___ ___
u. trouble sleeping, insomnia? ___ ___ ___
v. nervousness, tenseness? ___ ___ ___

42. Anything else? Yes No DK
a. other (specify) ___ ___ ___
b. other (specify) ___ ___ ___
c. other (specify) ___ ___ ___

43. Do you use any of the following aids: Yes No
a. cane? ___ ___
b. walker? ___ ___
c. wheelchair? ___ ___
d. leg brace? ___ ___
e. back brace? ___ ___
f. hearing aid? ___ ___
g. pacemaker? ___ ___
h. colostomy equipment? ___ ___
i. catheter? ___ ___
j. geriatric chair? ___ ___
k. glasses? ___ ___
l. artificial limb? ___ ___
m. other device (specify) ___ ___

44. (Check by observation)   Number of arms missing___
Number of legs missing___

45. On the average, about how often do you go out of this (house/building) in good weather?
___Never   ___Once a week
___Less than once a month   ___2–4 days a week
___Once a month   ___5 days a week or more
___2–3 days a month

46. About how often do you leave the neighborhood?
(In completely rural areas, ask:) About how often do you go into town?
___Never   ___Once a week
___Less than once a month   ___2–4 days a week
___Once a month   ___5 days a week or more
___2–3 days a month

C. INSTRUMENTAL ACTIVITIES OF DAILY LIVING (IADL)

47. Did you use the telephone where you lived before Share-A-Home?
    ____ without help (including looking up numbers & dialing)
    ____ with some help (answer phone, dial operator in an emergency, but have a special phone or help in getting a number or dialing), or
    ____ don't you use the telephone at all?

48. Why is it that you (had some help/didn't use the telephone)?

49. Can you use the telephone now?
    ____ without help
    ____ with some help, or
    ____ are you completely unable to use the telephone?

50. Did you get to places out of walking distance where you lived before SAH?
    ____ without help (travel alone on buses, taxis, or drive your own car)
    ____ with some help (have someone to help or accompany), or
    ____ don't you go at all (unless arrangements are made for a specialized vehicle like an ambulance)?

51. Why is it that you (had some help/didn't go at all)?

52. Can you get to places out of walking distance now?
    ____ without help
    ____ with some help, or
    ____ are you completely unable to travel unless special arrangements are made?

53. Do you (or your husband/wife) own *and* drive a car now?
    ____ Yes   ____ No

54. Did you go shopping for groceries where you lived before SAH?
    ____ without help (take care of all shopping needs yourself)
    ____ with some help (have someone to go with you on all shopping trips). or
    ____ don't you shop for groceries at all?

55. Why is it that you (had some help/didn't shop at all)?

56. Could you go shopping for groceries now?
    ____ without help
    ____ with some help, or
    ____ are you completely unable to do any shopping?

57. Did you prepare your own meals where you lived before SAH?
    _____ without help (plan and cook full meals)
    _____ with some help (prepare some things but don't cook), or
    _____ don't fix any meals at all?

58. Why is it that you (had some help/didn't fix any meals at all)?

59. Could you prepare your own meals now?
    _____ without help
    _____ with some help, or
    _____ are you completely unable to prepare any meals?

60. Did you do your own housework where you lived before SAH?
    _____ without help (do heavy housework, scrub floors, etc.)
    _____ with some help (do light housework but have help with heavy work), or
    _____ don't you do housework at all?

61. Why is it that you (had some help/didn't do housework at all)?

62. Could you do your housework now?
    _____ without help
    _____ with some help, or
    _____ are you completely unable to do any housework?

63. Do you make your own bed?
    _____ without help
    _____ with some help, or
    _____ are you completely unable to make your bed?

64. Did you do your own handyman work where you lived before SAH?
    _____ without help
    _____ with some help (do some things, not others), or
    _____ don't you do handyman work at all?

65. why is it that you (had some help/didn't do handyman work at all)?

66. Could you do your own handyman work now?
    _____ without help
    _____ with some help, or
    _____ are you completely unable to do any handyman work?

67. Did you do your own laundry where you lived before SAH?
    _____ without help (take care of all laundry or all except sheets and towels)
    _____ with some help (do small items only), or
    _____ don't you do any laundry at all?

68. Why is it that you (had some help/didn't do laundry at all)?

69. Could you do your own laundry now?
    ——Yes ——No

70. Do you take any medicines or use any medications?

71. Do you administer your own medicine?
    ——Yes ——No

72. If you had to take medicine, could you do it?
    ——without help (in the right doses at the right time)
    ——with some help (take medicine if someone prepares it for you and/or reminds you to take it), or
    ——(are you/would you be) completely unable to take your own medicines?

73. Why is it that you (have some help/need medicine given)?

74. Do you need (more) help with taking your medicines?
    ——Yes ——No ——DK

75. Did you manage your own money where you lived before SAH?
    ——without help (write checks, pay bills, etc.)
    ——with some help (manage day-to-day buying but have help with managing your checkbook and paying your bills), or
    ——don't you handle money at all (no day-to-day buying)?

76. Why is it that you (have some help/don't handle money)?

77. Do you handle your own money now?
    ——without help
    ——with some help, or
    ——are you completely unable to handle money?

78. Do you need (more) help with handling your money?
    ——Yes ——No ——DK

D. STAFF

79. What qualities, skill, or training do you think the manager of a Share-A-Home should have?

80. What do you believe is the most important duty the manager has?

E. PERSONAL SELF-MAINTENANCE ACTIVITIES (PSMA)

81. Do you eat?
    ____ without help
    ____ with some help (cutting food, identifying for blind, etc.)
    ____ or does someone feed you?

82. Do you need (more) help with eating?
    ____ Yes ____ No ____ DK

83. Do you dress and undress yourself?
    ____ without any help (pick out clothes, dress and undress self)
    ____ with some help (dressing *or* undressing)
    ____ or does someone dress *and* undress you?

84. Do you need (more) help with dressing and undressing?
    ____ Yes ____ No ____ DK

85. Do you take care of your own appearance, things like combing your hair and (for men) shaving?
    ____ without help
    ____ with some help
    ____ or does someone do all this type of thing for you?

86. Do you need (more) help with care of your appearance?
    ____ Yes ____ No ____ DK

87. Do you get around your (house/apartment/room)?
    ____ without help of any kind (except for a cane)
    ____ with some help (from a person or using walker, crutches, chair)
    ____ or don't you get around your home at all unless someone moves you?

88. Do you need (more) help with getting around your (house/apartment/room)?
    ____ Yes ____ No ____ DK

89. Do you get in and out of bed?
    ____ without any help or aid,
    ____ only with some help (from a person or device)
    ____ or don't you get in and out of bed unless someone lifts you?

90. Do you need (more) help with getting in and out of bed?
    ____ Yes ____ No ____ DK

91. Do you bathe—that is, take a bath, shower, or sponge bath?
    ____ without help
    ____ with some help (from a person or device)
    ____ or only when someone bathes you (lifted in and out or bathed)?

92. Do you need (more) help with bathing?

      ____Yes   ____No   ____DK

F. ACTIVITIES

93. Of all the things you do, either as a pastime or as part of your daily routine *or* work, what one thing do you like to do the most?

(For each item, ask):

1 Never	5 2–3 × month
2 3 × yr or less	6 1 × week
3 4–10 × yr	7 2–4 × week
4 1 × month	8 5 × week/more

94. In the past year, how often have you: FREQUENCY

   a. Gone to a senior center, or attended a senior citizen's group: ____

   b. Attended a church or synagogue service?   ____

   c. Gone to meetings of a church group or other groups or clubs?   ____

   d. Gone to the movies, theater, concert or lecture?   ____

   e. Gone to a sporting event?   ____

   f. Participated in a sport like swimming, fishing, hunting, bicycling, golf?   ____

   g. Played cards, bingo, pool, or some other game?   ____

   h. Taken care of house plants or done any outdoor gardening?   ____

   i. Worked on a hobby or handwork like sewing, knitting, or woodworking?   ____

   j. Painted pictures or played a musical instrument?   ____

   k. Eaten out at a restaurant for a special occasion with friends or relatives?   ____

   l. Babysat for grandchildren or other children?   ____

   m. Visited a friend or relative out of town for overnight or longer?   ____

   n. Gone out of town for (a/another) vacation?   ____

   o. Had a visit from a friend or relative out of town for overnight or longer?   ____

   p. Done volunteer work?   ____

95. How often have you: FREQUENCY

   a. Played bingo at Share-A-Home?   ____

   b. Attended a prayer meeting at Share-A-Home?   ____

   c. Attended films or musical performances at Share-A-Home?   ____

96. Do you usually vote in elections for the President?
    ____Yes   ____No

97. Who is the President of the United States?   *CORRECT*
                                                       ____*Yes* ____*No*
98. Who was the President before him?   ____*Yes* ____*No*

G. SOCIAL RELATIONS

99. Is there anyone in particular in whom you confide or talk to about your problems?
    ____Yes ____No

100. Who is that? (check only one)
     ____Friend inside SAH   ____Other relative
     ____Spouse   ____Child
     ____Other relatives   ____Friend or neighbor outside SAH

101. Do you ever do favors for or help out any of the residents here at Share-A-Home?
     ____Yes ____No

102. If yes, what do you do?

103. Do any of the residents ever do favors for you or help you out?
     ____Yes ____No

104. If yes, what do they do?

105. Do you ever help out the staff?
     ____Yes ____No

106. If yes, what do you do?

107. If you had a problem with your roommate (or next door neighbor) what would you do?

108. How satisfied do you think most people are in this Share-A-Home?
     ____Very satisfied   ____Fairly satisfied
     ____Not very satisfied

109. Compared to the last place you lived, has it been harder or easier to make friends at Share-A-Home?
     ____Harder ____Easier ____No difference

110. If you received some good news, is there anyone you would tell at Share-A-Home?

_____Yes   _____No

111. If yes, whom?

112. If you received some bad news, is there anyone you would tell at Share-A-Home?

_____Yes   _____No

113. If yes, whom?_____

Now some questions about your family

	Yes	No
114. Do you have any living children?	____	____
115. Do you have any living brothers or sisters?	____	____
116. Are there any other relatives to whom you feel very close?	____	____

(If no relatives, skip to question 123)

117. Now please think of your relatives that you feel close to: your (children/brothers or sisters/other relatives).
What are their first names?
(Ask 118 through 122 for each relative)

1 Never	2 3×yr. or less	3 4–10×yr.
4 1×month	5 2–3×month	6 1 week
7 2–4 week	8 5×week or more	

118. How is (name) related to you?

119. Where does (name relative) live?

120. About how often do you talk with (name) on the phone?

121. About how often do you visit (name) in (his/her) home?

122. About how often does (name) visit you in your home?

Q 117 First Name	Q 118 Relationship	Q 119 Where Lives (specify) What: neighborhood, intersection, or address Other: town & state	Q 120 Phone	Q 121 S Visit Others	Q 122 Others Visit S

123. In the last year, how often have you:
     (Ask items a through d below)

                                                                Frequency
     a. Dropped in or visited friends who live in this neighbor-
        hood or elsewhere in the (city/area)?   _____
     b. Had friends who live in (this neighborhood or elsewhere
        in the city/area) drop in or visit you?   _____
     c. Talked on the phone to friends, or written letters to them?   _____
     d. Arranged to meet with a friend away from your (Share-
        A-Home) home or his?   _____

                          FREQUENCY:
              1 Never   5 2–3 × month
              2 3 × yr or less   6 1 × week
              3 4–10 × year   7 2–4 × week
              4 1 × month   8 5 × week or more

                          H. MORALE

We would like to know how you feel about a number of things. You can
just answer "yes" or "no."

124. Do things keep getting worse as you get older?
     ____Yes ____No ____NA, DK

125. Do you have as much pep as you did last year?
     ____Yes ____No ____NA, DK

126. How much do you feel lonely? (READ RESPONSES TO SUBJECT)
     ____Not much ____A lot ____NA, DK

127. Do little things bother you more this year?
     ____Yes ____No ____NA, DK

128. Do you see enough of your friends and relatives?
     ____Yes ____No ____NA, DK

129. Do you feel that as you get older you are less useful?
     ____Yes ____No ____NA, DK

130. Do you have a lot to be sad about?
     ____Yes ____No ____NA, DK

131. Do you take things hard?
     ____Yes ____No ____NA, DK

132. Do you get upset easily?
  ____Yes   ____No   ____NA, DK

I. ENVIRONMENT

133. How satisfied are you with Share-A-Home as a place to live? Are you:
  ____Not very satisfied?
  ____Fairly satisfied
  ____Very satisfied

134. Would you like to move to another place?
  ____Yes   ____Not certain, DK   ____No

135. Do you feel that this house is:
  ____Very well built
  ____Fairly well built, or
  ____Not very well built

136. Overall, how attractive do you consider the inside of this house? Is it:
  ____Very attractive
  ____Fairly attractive, or
  ____Not very attractive?

137. How satisfied are you with the state of repairs or maintenance of this house? Are you:
  ____Very satisfied
  ____Fairly satisfied, or
  ____Not very satisfied?

138. How comfortable is the temperature in this house during the winter? Is it:
  ____Always comfortable
  ____Fairly comfortable, or
  ____Often too cold?

139. How about during the summer? Is it:
  ____Always comfortable
  ____Fairly comfortable
  ____Often too hot?

140. How much does any noise from the outside bother you?
  ____A lot
  ____A little, or
  ____Not much?

141. Would you say you have all the space you need in this house, that it is a little small, or that it is much too small?

_____ All you need

_____ A little small, or

_____ Much too small?

142. How satisfied are you with the amount of privacy you have here: that is, being able to do what you wish without other people seeing you or hearing you? Would you say that you are:

_____ Very satisfied

_____ Fairly satisfied, or

_____ Not very satisfied?

143. Do you ever wish you had more people to talk with and visit with here?

_____ Often

_____ Sometimes

_____ Never

(Check by observation)

144. Condition of building and dwelling unit is generally sound (not dilapidated)

_____ Yes   _____ No

145. Furnishings are generally sound (not dilapidated)

_____ Yes_____ No

146. Dwelling unit has:

a. flush toilet, tub or shower, piped hot water, central heat (all four)

b. telephone

c. refrigerator and stove

d. television

e. radio

147. Number of steps:

a. From street to dwelling unit

_____ No steps   _____ 1–3 steps   _____ 4 or more

b. From first floor of unit to bedroom or bathroom

_____ no steps   _____ 1–3 steps   _____ 4 or more

148. Would you say that you like this neighborhood:

_____ Very much   _____ Somewhat

_____ Not much, or   _____ Not at all?

149. How satisfied are you with the peace and quietness of the neighborhood?
    ____Not very satisfied
    ____Fairly satisfied, or
    ____Very satisfied?

150. How convenient is this neighborhood for shopping and getting the things you need?
    ____Very convenient
    ____Fairly convenient, or
    ____Not very convenient?

151. Is this house within four blocks (or a ten-minute slow walk) of a store?
    ____Yes   ____No

152. How convenient is this place for visiting with friends? Is it:
    ____Very convenient
    ____Fairly convenient, or
    ____Not very convenient?

153. How convenient is this place for getting medical care? Is it:
    ____Very convenient   ____Fairly convenient, or
    ____Not very convenient?

154. How satisfied do you feel with this town as a place to live? Would you say that you are:
    ____Very satisfied
    ____Fairly satisfied, or
    ____Not very satisfied?

155. How satisfied are you with the public transportation around here? Are you:
    ____Very satisfied
    ____Fairly satisfied, or
    ____Not very satisfied?

156. Is this house within four blocks (or a ten-minute slow walk) of public transportation?
    ____Yes   ____No

157. What about the conditions of the houses in this neighborhood? Would you say that they are?
    ____Very well kept up
    ____Fairly well kept up, or
    ____Not very well kept up?

158. What about the people who live around here? As neighbors, would you say that they are:

_____Very good neighbors

_____Fairly good neighbors, or

_____Not very good neighbors

	Yes	No
159. Do you feel safe in your house at night?	____	____
160. Do you feel safe in your *neighborhood* during the *day?*	____	____
161. Do you feel safe in your *neighborhood* at night?	____	____
162. Have you been robbed or attacked or the victim of any other crime?	____	____

(If YES): When? (year)_____

Please describe what happened:

J. SERVICES

163. Are you now: (Read a–h). (If YES): From whom?

	Are you now?		
	Yes	No	From Whom?
a. receiving help with finding another place to live?	____	____	_____
b. receiving help with getting into a nursing home?	____	____	_____
c. receiving help with finding more or better medical or nursing care?	____	____	_____
d. seeing someone about personal or family problems?	____	____	_____
e. getting legal services?	____	____	_____
f. receiving help with anything else?	____	____	_____

164. Do you feel that you need (more) help with:

a. finding another place to live?	____Yes	____No
b. getting into a nursing home?	____Yes	____No
c. finding more or better medical or nursing care?	____Yes	____No
d. personal or family problems?	____Yes	____No
e. getting legal services?	____Yes	____No
f. anything else: (Specify)		

165. Do you feel that you have:
    a. enough interesting things to do?   ____Yes ____No
    b. a chance to be with people enough?   ____Yes ____No
    c. someone to check on you enough to make sure ____Yes ____No
    you are all right?

K. EXPERIENCES

In the past year, have you:

	Yes	No	DK NA
166. been severely depressed?	___	___	___
167. had major fears or anxieties, i.e., you worried a very great deal about something?	___	___	___
168. heard voices when nobody was there?	___	___	___
169. had suicidal thoughts or wishes?	___	___	___
170. felt that you couldn't stand having anybody around you?	___	___	___
171. had a problem with alcohol?	___	___	___
172. had major problems with your memory?	___	___	___
173. sometimes not known the time of day, day of week, or season?	___	___	___
174. sometimes not known where you are?	___	___	___
175. sometimes become confused in conversation?	___	___	___
176. Have you ever had a nervous breakdown? (If YES ask:) About how many years ago?____	___	___	___
177. Have you felt like you were *going to have* a nervous breakdown *within the past year*?	___	___	___

L. INCOME

178. Thinking about your money situation, would you say you:
    ____can't make ends meet

    ____have just enough to get along on, or

    ____are you comfortable?

M. SELF-PERCEIVED CHANGE

179. Would you say you have changed in any of the following ways since moving here in the past six months?

   a. Do you feel:
      ( ) More safe   ( ) Less safe   ( ) Same
   b. Are you:
      ( ) Better off financially   ( ) Less well off financially   ( ) Same
   c. Do you worry about money:
      ( ) Less   ( ) More   ( ) Same
   d. Do you have:
      ( ) More energy   ( ) Less energy   ( ) Same
   e. Is your health:
      ( ) Better   ( ) Worse   ( ) Same
   f. Are you:
      ( ) More active   ( ) Less active   ( ) Same
   g. Do you have:
      ( ) More friends   ( ) Fewer friends   ( ) Same
   h. Do you eat:
      ( ) Better   ( ) Worse   ( ) Same
   i. Do you see your family:
      ( ) More often   ( ) Less often   ( ) Same
   j. Do you see your friends:
      ( ) More often   ( ) Less often   ( ) Same
   k. Do you sleep:
      ( ) Better   ( ) Worse   ( ) Same
   l. Do you get out:
      ( ) More often   ( ) Less often   ( ) Same
   m. Are you:
      ( ) Happier   ( ) Less happy   ( ) Same
   m. Do you follow the news:
      ( ) More closely   ( ) Less closely   ( ) Same
   o. Do you dress up:
      ( ) More often   ( ) Less often   ( ) Same
   p. Do you watch T.V.:
      ( ) More often   ( ) Less often   ( ) Same

Staff Interview Guide

Name_____

Position_____

Date_____

Location_____

1. Current job situation
   a. Length of current employment
   b. How learned of position
   c. Description of typical work day (specific assigned duties, primary and secondary; any informal duties)
   d. Importance of this job in successful functioning of SAH
   e. Types of skills, qualifications, personality characteristics, training need for this job (formal training/education? on the job training? Age, sex, religion, etc?)
   f. Perception of other staff positions (qualifications, skill, etc. required for other staff positions)
   g. What advice would you give to someone considering working in this type of setting?
   h. If you were helping to start a new SAH how would you go about staffing the home? Would you add or eliminate any positions?
   i. Could SAH improve anything regarding staffing arrangements?
   j. How would you describe the contact between the staff here?
   k. Do you feel that the residents' expectations regarding the staff are being met?

2. Background
   a. Summary of education and training
   b. Summary of previous employment
   c. Future job goals
   d. Age____
   e. Marital status_____
   f. Religion_____

Architectural Plans for TVA's Solar Group Home

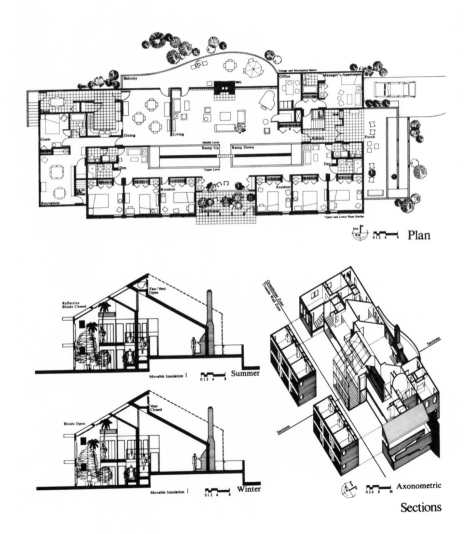

Plan

Summer

Winter

Axonometric

Sections

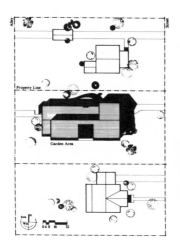

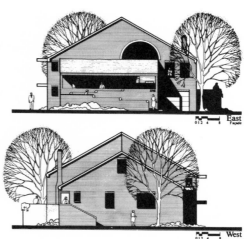

East
Façade

West

Typical Site Plan
Elevations

South

North

Elevations

Shared Housing Projects in the United States

ARIZONA

Senior Village
Dept. of Health Services for Long-Term Care, Maricopa County
3521 Dogel
Phoenix, AZ 85021

ARKANSAS

Sunset Lodge, Mt. Ida, Arkansas
c/o West Central Arkansas Area Agency on Aging
624 Malvern Ave.
Hot Springs, AK 71901

CALIFORNIA

Action for Better Living for Elders (ABLE)
1095 Market St., Rm. 212
San Francisco, CA 94103

Alternative Living for the Aged
7563½ Beverly Blvd.
Los Angeles, CA 90048

It should be noted that this list was compiled in 1982–83 and some of the homes may no longer be in operation. The list was compiled from the following sources: the University of Florida list was compiled during research funded by a grant from AOA 04-AM-000003/01 (3); *The National Directory of Shared Housing Programs, September 1982,* Shared Housing Resource Center, Inc., 6344 Greene Street, Philadelphia, PA 19144; *Shared Housing Arrangements for Older Persons,* Cooperative Living for older Persons, Alternatives for the Aging Program, American Baptist Board of National Ministries, ABC/USA, Valley Forge, PA 19481.

California Jewish Home
7150 Tampa Ave.
Reseda, CA 91335

Chula Vista Senior Service Center
360 Third Ave.
Chula Vista, CA 92010

City of Santa Ana Shared Housing
424 W. Third
Santa Ana, CA 92701

City of Visalia
Leisure Services RSVP
415 N. Locust
Visalia, CA 93291

E. Co. Council on Aging
Shared Housing Program
220 Avocado Ave.
El Cajon, CA 92020

ECHO Housing Assistance Center
3774 Peralta Blvd.
Fremont, CA 94536

ECHO Housing Assistance Center
3311 Pacific Ave.
Livermore, CA 94550

Golden Timers Shared Housing
114 E. 19th St.
Costa Mesa, CA 92627

Gray Panthers of Sonoma County
P.O. Box 296
Santa Rosa, CA 95402

H. Louis Lake Senior Citizen Center
11300 Stanford
Garden Grove, CA 92640

Home-Again Plan, Inc.
Family Services Association
P.O. Box 35
Chico, CA 95926

Home Sharing Program–RSVP
Humboldt State University
Arcata, CA 95521

The Housing Connection
Community Council of Stockton & San Joaquin County
1525 Pacific Ave., Rm. 101
Stockton, CA 95204

Housing Desk-Reseda Senior Citizen Multi-Purpose Center
7222 Reseda Blvd.
Reseda, CA 91335

McGarr Senior Center
Catholic Social Services
46 Mariposa Ave.
San Anselmo, CA 94960

Project Scout
1126 Soquel Ave.
Santa Cruz, CA 95062

RSVP Housing Project
24300 Narbonne Ave.
Lomita, CA 90717

SHARE Program
1450 Venice Blvd.
Los Angeles, CA 90006

Shared Homes for Seniors
Human Investment Projects, Inc., of San Mateo County
Fidelity Savings & Loan
11 E. Third Ave.
San Mateo, CA 94401

Shared Housing
1 Civic Center Circle
Brea, CA 92621

Shared Housing
201 E. Colorado
Glendale, CA 91205

Shared Housing
Echo Housing Assistance Center

770 A St., #309
Hayward, CA 94541

Shared Housing
124 N. Sullivan
Huntington Beach, CA 92703

Shared Housing
P.O. Box 19575–9575
Irvine, CA 92713

Shared Housing
Box 1343
Laguna Beach, CA 92654

Shared Housing
170 South Olive
Orange, CA 92666

Shared Housing
P.O. Box 82
San Clemente, CA 92672

Shared Housing
Park & Recreation Program
32506 Poseo Adelanto
San Juan Capistrano, CA 92675

Shared Housing
300 Centennial Way
Tustin, CA 92680

Shared Housing
205 Modoc Pl.
Woodland, CA 95695

Shared Housing Program
Co. Housing Alliance of Contra
Costa County, Inc.
2480 Pacheco St.
Concord, CA 94520

Shared Housing for Seniors
% People's Federal Savings & Loan
23688 El Toro Rd.
El Toro, CA 92630

Shared Housing Project for Singles
2175 The Alameda, #101
San Jose, CA 95112

Shared Housing for Seniors
2600 Middlefield Rd.
Redwood City, CA 94063

Shared Senior Housing
Jewish Family & Children Service
1600 Scott St.
San Francisco, CA 94115 *or*
1100 Gough St., #10A & #11A
San Francisco, CA 94118

Van Nuys Multi-Purpose Center
6514 Sylmar Ave.
Van Nuys, CA 91401

Ventura Senior Homesharing
461 Main St., Suite C
Ventura, CA 93001

Wilkinson Multi-Purpose Senior Center
8956 Vanalden Ave.
Northridge, CA 91324

COLORADO

1390 Housing Project
P.O. Box 10848
Edgemont Branch
Golden, CO 80401

DELAWARE

Brandywine House
Wilmington Senior Center, Inc.
9 W. 18th St.
Wilmington, DE 19802

Laurel Group Home
Route #3, Box 370
Laurel, DE 19965

St. Patrick's Home, Inc.
St. Patrick's Roman Catholic Church
115 E. 14th St.
Wilmington, DE 19801

DISTRICT OF COLUMBIA

Christian Communities Group Homes
1419 V St., N.W.
Washington, DC 20009

Harvest House & Senior Center
150 Rhode Island Ave., N.E.
Washington, DC 20002

Richmond Fellowship Creative Housing for Older Persons
Richmond Fellowship of Metro. Washington
1829 Kalorama, N.W.
Washington, DC 20009

St. Francis de Sales
2017 Fulton Pl., N.E.
Washington, DC 20018

FLORIDA

Share-A-Home of America, Inc.
701 Driver Ave.
Winter Park, FL 32789

Share-A-Home of the Golden Triangle
27 S. Dewey St.
Eustis, FL 32726

Share-A-Home/Riverside
107 Riverside
Cocoa, FL 32922

Share-A-Home/St. Charles
P.O. Box 507
San Antonio, FL 33576

Share-A-Home of Upper Pinellas
1930 Union St.
Clearwater, FL 33515

Suncoast Shared Living
10051 5th St. N.
St. Petersburg, FL 33702

Wilbon Family
720 N. Lakemont Ave.
Winter Park, FL 32789

GEORGIA

Louis Kahn Group Home
Jewish Family & Children's Bureau
1753 Peachtree Rd., N.E.
Atlanta, GA 30809

Share-A-Home of Gainesville
313 Boulevard, N.E.
Gainesville, GA 30501

HAWAII

Small Group Homes-Hawaii Co.
Office of Aging
34 Rainbow Dr.
Hilo, HI 96720

Small Group Homes for Older Adults/Paired Housing
Catholic Social Services
250 S. Vineyard St.
Honolulu, HI 96813

ILLINOIS

Lieberman Geriatric Health Center
Council for Jewish Elderly
9700 Gross Point Rd.
Skokie, IL 60076

Weinfeld Group Living Residence
Council for Jewish Elderly
1015 Howard St.
Evanston, IL 60202

INDIANA

Simeon House
1801 Poplar St.
Terre Haute, IN 47803

KENTUCKY

Share-A-Home of Louisville
2901 Lexington Rd.
Louisville, KY 40205

MARYLAND

Group Home Program
Jewish Council for the Aging of Greater Washington
6111 Montrose Rd.
Rockville, MD 20852

Home Care Research, Inc.
30 E. Patrick St.
Frederick, MD 21701

Hurwitz House
133 Slade Ave.
Baltimore, MD 21208

Levindale Hebrew Geriatric Center
2434 W. Belvedere Ave.
Baltimore, MD 21215

Small Group Homes
Jewish Family & Children's Service Bureau
5750 Park Heights Ave.
Baltimore, MD 21215

MASSACHUSETTS

Amherst Council on Aging
70 Bottwood Walk
Amherst, MA 01002

Amherst Housing Authority
33 Kellogg Ave.
Amherst, MA 01002

Belknap House
207 Main St.
Concord, MA 01742

Bradford-Russell Home of Fairhaven, Inc.
62 Centre St.
Fairhaven, MA 02719

Captain Clarence Eldridge House
Barnstable Housing Authority
30 Pine St.
Hyannis, MA, 02601

CLOE (Cambridge Living Options for Elders)
99 Bishop Richard Allen Dr.
Cambridge, MA 02139

Cooperative Living of Newton, Inc.
Coop Metro. Ministries
53 Crescent Ave.
Newton, MA 02159

ECHO, Inc. (Elder Cooperative Housing Options)
186 Hampshire St.
Cambridge, MA 02139

Elderly Center & Congregate Housing Facility
Cambridge Housing Authority
116 Norfolk St.
Cambridge, MA 02139

Jewish Family & Children's Service
31 New Chardon St.
Boston, MA 02146

Roxbury Action Program
Linwood St.
Boston, MA 02174

MICHIGAN

Dorothy Robb
2501 Brockman Blvd.
Ann Arbor, MI 48104

OREGON

Homesharing Program
Housing Authority & Community Service Agency of Lane County
172 E. 8th St.
Eugene, OR 97401

PENNSYLVANIA

Group Living Homes
Presbyterian Association on Aging, Inc.
1215 Hulton Rd.
Oakmont, PA 15139

Lutheran Service of Lehigh Valley
330 Ferry St.
Easton, PA 18042

Share-A-Home of Bryn Mawr
Saints Memorial Baptist Church
47 Warner Ave.
Bryn Mawr, PA, 19010

Share-A-Home of the Lehigh Valley
321 Wyandotte St.
Bethlehem, PA 18015

Wellsboro Shared Homes, Inc.
27 Bacon St.
Wellsboro, PA 16901

RHODE ISLAND

Cooperative Living Project
126 Pierce St.
East Greenwich, RI 02818

Unitarian Church
112 Everett Ave.
Providence, RI 02906

TEXAS

Dallas Home & Hospital of Jewish Aged
2525 Centerville Rd.
Dallas, TX 75228

VERMONT

Northern Cooperative Resources
18 Langdon St.
Montpelier, VT 05602

VIRGINIA

Madonna Home
814 West 37th St.
Norfolk, VA 23517

WISCONSIN

Colonial House
Colonial Club
124 Dewey
Mailing Address: Box 134
Sun Prairie, WI 53590

Other Source Materials on Shared Housing

The Center for Gerontological Studies, University of Florida has published *An Experiment in Shared Living for Older People: A Description and Guide for Action*, by Gordon F. Streib and Mary Anne Hilker. This manual may be ordered from:

Center for Gerontological Studies
University of Florida
3357 GPA
Gainesville, FL 32611

The price is $7.50.

The Shared Housing Resource Center of Philadelphia promotes intergenerational housing alternatives for older people. This organization has the following goals and activities:

The national office will *develop and distribute new educational information* through religious, community, and human service networks on the desirability and how-to of shared living.

S.H.R.C. will directly *advise, resource, and facilitate local groups* desiring to establish shared households.

S.H.R.C. will *advocate through testimony and legislative proposals for the removal of barriers that inhibit the development of shared housing* at federal, state, and local levels.

S.H.R.C. will work to *create linkages between individuals, groups, churches, and human service agencies who are planning and/or living in shared households*, developing a support network where experience and information may be shared.

The center has a number of publications for sale. For more information:

Shared Housing Resource Center, Inc.
6344 Greene St.
Philadelphia, PA 19144
(215) 848-1220

Two community agencies in Boston have published *Planning and Developing a Shared Living Project: A Guide for Community Groups* (120 pages). For a copy of the manual and other information:

Action for Boston Community Development, Inc.
178 Tremont St.
Boston, MA 02111
(617) 357-6000

Concerned Boston Citizens for Elder Affairs
178 Tremont St.
Boston, MA 02111
(617) 357-6000

The Abbeyfield Society of Great Britain has the following publications for sale with the price and postage list in pounds sterling:

Code	Item	Cost	Postage
AFD 1	What Is Abbeyfield	3p ea.	26p
AFD 2	Abbeyfield Booklet	24p ea.	68p
AFD 4	Start an Abbeyfield	2p ea.	26p
AFD 6	Some of your Questions Answered	3p ea.	26p
AFD 7	Forming a Local Abbeyfield	2p ea.	26p
AFD 17	Members Handbook	40p ea.	82p
AFD 20	Why Volunteer?	3p ea.	26p
AFD 21	Understanding Extra Care	60p ea.	68p
	A Housekeeper Brief	3p ea.	26p
	Building Extra Care	£2.00 ea.	£2.50
	Abbeyfield Extra Care Manual	£20.00 ea.	£6.14
	The Lights are Green	£3.00 ea.	£5.16
	Survey in Abbeyfield House	£3.00 ea.	£5.44
	Abbeyfield House of the Future	£1.50 ea.	£1.80
	Abbeyfield Bulletin (current issue)	30p ea.	96p

For further information write:
The Abbeyfield Society,
186-192 Darkes Lane,
Potters Bar,
Herts. EN6 1AB
ENGLAND

References

Abbeyfield Extra Care. n.d. Potters Bar, Herts., England: The Abbeyfield Society.

Abbeyfield Society Bulletin, No. 1. n.d. Potters Bar, Herts., England.

Abbeyfield Society Commission on Growth. 1979. *The Lights Are Green.* Potters Bar, Herts., England: The Abbeyfield Society.

Abbeyfield Society Manual of Information. 1976. Potters Bar, Herts., England.

Abbeyfield Society Members *Handbook.* n.d. Potters Bar, Herts., England: The Abbeyfield Society.

Abrams, Mark. 1978. *Beyond Three-Score and Ten: A First Report on a Survey of the Elderly.* Mitcham, Surrey: Age Concern.

Abrams, Philip. 1981. Testimony before the Hearing of the Subcommittee on Housing and Consumer Interests of the Select Committee on Aging, House of Representatives, November 17, 1981. "Shared Housing," Comm. Pub. No. 97-321. Washington, D.C.: GPO.

Achenbaum, Andrew. 1978. *Old Age in a New Land: The American Experience since 1790.* Baltimore: Johns Hopkins University Press.

Albrecht, R. 1969. "Retirement Hotels in Florida." In C. C. Osterbind, ed., *Feasible Planning for Social Change in the Field of Aging,* pp. 11–82. Gainesville: University Presses of Florida.

Ball, Donald W. 1972. "The Family as Sociological Problem: Conceptualization of the Taken for Granted Prologue to Social Problem Analysis." *Social Problems* 19:295–307.

Bane, Mary Jo. 1983. "Is the Welfare State Replacing the Family?" *The Public Interest* 70:91–101.

Barr, Donald F. 1977. Residents' Evaluation of Hawthorne at Leesburg. Unpublished survey prepared for Marketing Research Department. Philadelphia: Colonial Penn Insurance. Mimeograph.

Baum, Martha and Rainer C. Baum. 1980. *Growing Old: A Societal Perspective.* Englewood Cliffs, N.J.: Prentice-Hall.

Bengtson, Vern, James Dowd, David Smith, and Alex Inkeles. 1975. "Modernization, Modernity and Perception of Aging: A Cross-Cultural Study." *Journal of Gerontology* 30:688–695.

Berghorn, Forrest J., Donna E. Schafer, Geoffrey H. Steere, and Robert F. Wiseman. 1978. *The Urban Elderly: A Study of Life Satisfaction.* Montclair, N.J.: Allanheld, Osmeen.

Black, C. E. 1966. *The Dynamics of Modernization*. New York: Harper & Row.

Blau, Peter M. 1956. *Bureaucracy in Modern Society*. New York: Random House.

Borup, Jerry H. 1981. "Relocation: Attitudes, Information Network and Problems Encountered." *The Gerontologist* 21:501–511.

Borup, Jerry H. and Daniel Gallego. 1981. "Mortality as Affected by Institutional Relocation: Update and Assessment." *The Gerontologist* 21:8–16.

Borup, Jerry H., Daniel Gallego, and Pamela Heffernan. 1979. "Relocation and Its Effects on Mortality." *The Gerontologist* 19:135–140.

Branch, Laurence G. 1980. *Vulnerable Elders*. Gerontological Monographs No. 6. Washington, D.C.: Gerontological Society of America.

Brody, Elaine. 1978. "Community Housing for the Elderly. The Program, the People, the Decision-Making Process and the Research." *The Gerontologist* 18:121–128.

Brody, Elaine and Bernard Liebowitz. 1981. "Some Recent Innovations in Community Living Arrangements for Older People." In Powell Lawton and Sally Hoover, eds., *Community Housing Choices for Older Americans*, pp. 245–258. New York: Springer.

Bryant, Drayton. 1981. Testimony Before the Hearing of the Subcommittee on Housing and Consumer Interests of the Select Committee on Aging, House of Representatives, November 17, 1981. "Shared Housing," Comm. Pub. No. 97-321. Washington, D.C.: GPO.

Bultena, G. L. and V. Wood. 1969. "The American Retirement Community: Bane or Blessing?" *The Journal of Gerontology* 24:209–217.

Butler, Alan, Christine Oldman, and Richard Wright. 1979. *Sheltered Housing for the Elderly: A Critical Review*. Department of Social Policy and Administration Research Monograph. Leeds: University of Leeds.

Butler, Robert. 1975. *Why Survive? Being Old in America*. New York: Harper & Row.

Butterfield, Fox. 1982. *China, Alive in the Bitter Sea*. New York: Times Books.

Buxton, Christopher. 1977. Abbeyfield Society Bulletin. Potters Bar, Herts., England.

Campbell, George. 1981. Letter to the authors.

Carp, Frances. 1966. *A Future for the Aged*. Austin: University of Texas Press.

Carp, Frances. 1975. "Long-Range Satisfaction with Housing." *The Gerontologist* 15:68–72.

Carp, Frances. 1976. "Housing and Living Environments of Older People." In Robert H. Binstock and Ethel Shanas, eds., *Handbook of Aging and the Social Sciences*, pp. 244–271. New York: Van Nostrand, Reinhold.

Castles, Francis G. 1978. *The Social Democratic Image of Society*. London: Routledge & Kegan Paul.

Chadwick, Terry B. 1976. Review of *The Honorable Elders* by Erdman Palmore. *The Gerontologist* 16:560–561.

Charles, D. A. L. 1982. Personal communication to authors.

Cherry, Ralph and Scott Magnuson-Martinson. 1981. "Modernization and the Status of the Aged in China: Decline or Equalization?" *Sociological Quarterly* 22:253–261.

Coffman, Thomas. 1981. "Relocation and Survival of Institutionalized Aged: A Reexamination of the Evidence." *The Gerontologist* 21:483–500.

Collins, Randall. 1975. *Conflict Sociology: Toward an Explanatory Science*. New York: Academic Press.

Comptroller General of the United States. 1979. Report to the Chairman, Subcommittee on Human Services, House Select Committee on Aging (HRD-80-7). Washington, D.C.: GPO.

Conard, Richard. 1982. "A Medical/Social Model for Development and Management of Sheltered Living for the Elderly." Lecture given at Programming and Economics: Housing Design for the Elderly, University of Florida College of Architecture, October 28.

Cottrell, Fred. 1960. "The Technological and Societal Basis of Aging." In Clark Tibbitts, ed., *Handbook of Social Gerontology*, pp. 92–119. Chicago: University of Chicago Press.

Cowgill, Donald O. 1974. "Aging and Modernization: A Revision of the Theory." In J. F. Gubrium, ed., *Late Life: Communities and Environmental Policy*, pp. 123–146. Springfield, Ill.: Charles Thomas.

Cowgill, Donald O. and Lowell D. Holmes. 1972. *Aging and Modernization.* New York: Appleton-Century-Crofts.

Day-Lower, Dennis. 1981. Testimony Before the Hearing of the Subcommittee on Housing and Consumer Interests of the Select Committee on Aging, House of Representatives, November 17, 1981. "Shared Housing," Comm. Pub. No. 97-321. Washington, D.C.: GPO.

Ehrlich, Phyllis and Ira Ehrlich. 1982. "SRO Elderly: A Distinct Population in a Viable Housing Alternative." In Gari Lesnoff-Caravaglia, ed., *Aging and the Human Condition*, pp. 71–82. New York: Human Sciences Press.

Ellul, Jacques. 1978 *The Technological Society.* New York: Knopf.

Erickson, R. and K. Eckert. 1977 "The Elderly Poor in Downtown San Diego Hotels." *The Gerontologist* 17:440–446.

Estes, Carroll. 1979. *The Aging Enterprise.* San Francisco: Jossey-Bass. Federal Council on Aging. 1978. *Public Policy and the Frail Elderly.* Washington, D.C.: United States Department of Health, Education, and Welfare. DHEW Publication No. (OHDS) 79-20959.

Ferkiss, Victor. 1969. *Technological Man: The Myth and the Reality.* New York: New American Library.

Fischer, David H. 1978. *Growing Old in America.* New York: Oxford University Press.

Florida, Department of Health and Rehabilitative Services. 1983. "Guidelines for Zoning and Special Community Housing." Tallahassee: Health and Rehabilitative Services (1317 Winewood Blvd., 32301).

Florman, Samuel C. 1981. *Blaming Technology: The Irrational Search for Scapegoats.* New York: St. Martin's Press.

Frankel, Charles. 1959. *The Case for Modern Man.* Reprint. Boston: Beacon Press (New York: Harper, 1955).

Freeman, Howard E. 1977. "The Present Status of Evaluation Research." In Marcia Guttentag, ed., *Evaluation Studies*, pp. 17–51. Beverly Hills, Calif.: Sage.

Galper, Jeffrey H. 1981. "The Political Function of the Social Services." In George T. Martin, Jr. and Mayer N. Zald, eds., *Social Welfare in Society*, pp. 167–193. New York: Columbia University Press.

Getze, Linda H. 1980. "New Idea: Share-A-Home." *Modern Maturity* (March) 23:19–20. .

Glasscote, Raymond et al. 1976. *Old Folks at Home*. Washington, D.C.: Joint Information Service.

Gouldner, Alvin. 1970. *The Coming Crisis of Western Sociology*. New York: Basic Books.

Gubrium, J. F. 1973 *The Myth of the Golden Years*. Springfield, Ill.: Charles Thomas.

Gubrium, J. F. 1975. *Living and Dying at Murray Manor*. New York: St. Martin's Press.

Guion, Edward. 1981. Letter to authors.

Haas, William. 1980. "The Social Ties Between a Retirement Village and the Surrounding Community." Ph.D. dissertation, University of Florida.

Habenstein, R. W., C. Kiefer, and Y. Wang. 1976. *Boarding Homes for the Elderly: Overview and Outlook."* Columbia: Center for Aging Studies, University of Missouri.

Hare, Patrick H. 1982. "Why Granny Flats Are a Good Idea." *Planning* (February), pp. 15–16.

Heclo, Hugh. 1974. *Modern Social Politics in Britain and Sweden*. New Haven: Yale University Press.

Heintz, Katherine M. 1976. *Retirement Communities: For Adults Only*. New Brunswick: Center for Urban Policy Research, Rutgers, State University of New Jersey.

Heumann, Leonard and Duncan Boldy. 1982. *Housing for the Elderly: Planning and Policy Formulation in Western Europe and North America*. New York: St. Martin's Press; London: Croom Helm.

Hilker, Mary Anne. 1983. "Shared Living in Florida: Alternative Living Arrangements for Older People. Ph.D. dissertation, University of Florida.

Hirsch, Carol Schreter. 1977. "Integrating the Nursing Home Resident Into a Senior Citizens Center." *The Gerontologist* 17:227–234.

Hochschild, Arlie. 1973 *The Unexpected Community*. Englewood Cliffs, N.J.: Prentice-Hall.

Hollander, P. J. 1973. *Soviet and American Society: A Comparison*. New York: Oxford University Press.

Hoyt, G. C. 1954. "The Life of the Retired in a Trailer Park." *American Journal of Sociology* 59(4):361–370.

Jacksonville Community Council. 1980. "But Not in My Neighborhood." Jacksonville, Florida.

Jacobs, J. 1974. *Fun City: An Ethnographic Study of a Retirement Community*. New York: Holt.

James, Marlise. 1972. "A Commune for Old Folks." *Life Magazine*, (May 12), 72:53–57.

Johnson, J. L. and Cantor, M. N. 1979. "Situational Aspects of Frailty." *The Gerontologist* vol. 19, no. 5, part II, p. 96.

Johnson, S. K. 1971. *Idle Haven: Community Building Among the Working Class Retired*. Berkeley: University of California Press.

Kahn, Robert L. and Toni Antonucci. 1981. "Convoys Over the Life Course: Attachment, Roles, and Social Support." In P. B. Baltes and O. Brim, eds., *Life Span Development and Behavior*, 3:383–405. New York: Academic Press.

Katz, Elihu and Brenda Danet. 1973. "Introduction: Bureaucracy as a Problem for Sociology and Society." In Elihu Katz and Brenda Danet, eds., *Bureaucracy and the Public*, pp. 3–27. New York: Basic Books.

Khurana, Barbara. 1980. Personal communication.

Kiefer, Christie. 1976. Review of *The Honorable Elders* by Erdman Palmore. *Contemporary Sociology* 5:576–575.

Kosberg, Jordon I. and S. S. Tobin. 1972. "Variability Among Nursing Homes." *The Gerontologist* 12:214–219.

Kutza, Elizabeth Ann. 1981. *The Benefits of Old Age*. Chicago: University of Chicago Press.

Lally, M., E. Black, M. Thornock, and J. D. Hawkins. 1979. "Older Women in Single Room Occupant (SRO) Hotels: A Seattle Profile." *The Gerontologist* 19:67–74.

Landes, David S. 1969. *The Unbound Prometheus: Technological Change and Industrial Development in Western Europe from 1750 to the Present*. London: Cambridge University Press.

Lasch, Christopher. 1977. *Haven in a Heartless World: The Family Besieged*. New York: Basic Books.

Laslett, Peter. 1976. "Societal Development and Aging." In Robert H. Binstock and Ethel Shanas, eds., *Handbook of Aging and the Social Sciences*, pp. 87–116. New York: Van Nostrand, Reinhold.

Laslett, Peter. 1979. "The Traditional English Family and the Aged in our Society." In David D. Van Tassel, ed., *Aging, Death, and the Completion of Being*, pp. 97–113. Philadelphia: University of Pennsylvania Press.

Lauber, Daniel. 1982. "Impacts of Group Homes on the Surrounding Neighborhood: An Evaluation of Research Findings." Illinois: Planning/Communications. Mimeographed.

Lawton, M. Powell. 1980. *Environment and Aging*. Monterey, Calif.: Brooks/Cole.

Lawton, M. Powell. 1981. "Alternative Housing." *Journal of Gerontological Social Work* 3:61–80.

Lawton, M. Powell and Elaine M. Brody. 1969. "Assessment of Older People: Self-Maintaining and Instrumental Activities of Daily Living." *The Gerontologist* 9:179–186.

Lerner, Daniel. 1958. *The Passing of Traditional Society: Modernizing the Middle East*. Glencoe, Ill.: Free Press.

Leslie, Gerald. 1979. *The Family in Social Context* (4th ed.). New York: Oxford University Press.

Litwak, Eugene. 1965. "Extended Kin Relations in an Industrial Society." In Ethel Shanas and Gordon Streib, eds., *Social Structure and the Family*, pp. 290–323. Englewood Cliffs, N.J.: Prentice-Hall.

Litwak, Eugene and J. Figueira. 1968. "Technological Innovations and Theoretical Functions of Primary Groups and Bureaucratic Structures." *American Journal of Sociology* 73:466–481.

Litwak, Eugene and Henry Meyer. 1974. *School, Family, and Neighborhood: The Theory and Practice of School-Community Relations*. New York: Columbia University Press.

Lowenthal, Marjorie Fiske. 1964. *Lives in Distress: The Paths of the Elderly to the Psychiatric Ward*. New York: Basic Books.

Lowenthal, Marjorie Fiske and Clayton Haven. 1968. "Interaction and Adaptation: Intimacy As a Critical Variable." *American Sociological Review* 33:20–30.

McConnell, S. R. and C. F. Usher. 1979. *Intergenerational House-Sharing.* Los Angeles: University of Southern California, Andrus Gerontology Center.

Maddox, G. L. and D. C. Dellinger. 1978. Assessment of Functional Status in a Program of Evaluation and Resource Allocation Model." *Annals of the American Academy of Political and Social Science* 438:59–70.

Manatee County Planning and Development Department. 1979. Report to the Manatee County Planning Commission: Zoning Ordinance Amendment Z-115, Residential Care Facilities. Bradenton, Florida.

Mangum, Wiley. 1979. "Retirement Villages: Past, Present, and Future." In Patricia Wagner and John McRae, eds., *Back to Basics: Food and Shelter for the Elderly,* pp. 88–97. Center for Gerontological Studies and Programs, University of Florida. Gainesville: University Presses of Florida.

Mangum, Wiley. 1983. "Not in My Neighborhood: Preliminary Results of a Study of Community Resistance to Housing for the Elderly." In *A Report of the Housing Task Force in the International Exchange Center on Gerontology at the University of South Florida,* pp. 9–29. Xerox.

Meltzer, Jack. 1980. Statement at Hearing Before the Special Committee on Aging, United States Senate, November 26, 1979. "Energy and the Aged: A Challenge to the Quality of Life in a Time of Declining Energy Availability." Washington, D.C.: GPO.

Mendelson, M. A. 1974. *Tender Loving Greed.* New York: Random House.

Merton, Robert K. 1957. "Bureaucratic Structure and Personality." In Robert K. Merton, *Theory and Social Structure,* pp. 195–206. Rev. ed. Glencoe, Ill.: Free Press (original publication, 1940).

Merton, Robert K. 1976. "The Ambivalence of Organizational Leaders." In Robert K. Merton, *Sociological Ambivalence and Other Essays,* pp. 73–89. New York: Free Press.

Modell, John and Tamara K. Hareven. 1973. "Urbanization and the Malleable Household: An Examination of Boarding and Lodging in American Families." *Journal of Marriage and the Family* 35:467–479.

Modern Maturity. 1982. "Hope for the Elderly in Housing Concept" (October–November), 25:7.

Morton-Williams, Jean. 1979. *Survey in Abbeyfield Houses.* Potters Bar, Herts., England: Abbeyfield Society.

Nagi, Saad. 1975. *An Epidemiology of Adult Disability in the United States.* Columbus: Mershon Center, Ohio State University.

Newman, Evelyn and Susan Sherman. 1979. "Foster-Family Care for the Elderly: Surrogate Family or Mini-Institution?" *International Journal of Aging and Human Development* 10:165–176.

Newman, S. J. 1976. "Housing Adjustment of the Disabled Elderly." *The Gerontologist* 16:312–317.

Norbeck, Edward. 1978. *Country to City: The Urbanization of a Japanese Village.* Salt Lake City: University of Utah Press.

NRTA-AARP. 1981. Conference Report: Granny Flats Forum. Washington, D.C.: National Retired Teachers Association, American Association of Retired Persons.

Nydegger, Corinne. 1983. "Family Ties in Cross-Cultural Perspective." *The Gerontologist* 23:26–32.

Olson, Laura. 1982. *The Political Economy of Aging.* New York: Columbia University Press.

Oltman, Ruth. 1980. "The Small Group Home." *Perspective on Aging* (January/February), 9:14–15.

Osgood, Nancy J. 1982. *Senior Settlers: Social Integration in Retirement Communities.* New York: Praeger.

Palmore, Erdman. 1975. *The Honorable Elders: A Cross-Cultural Analysis of Aging in Japan.* Durham, N.C.: Duke University Press.

Peace, Sheila. 1981. "Small Group Living in Institutional Settings." *Ageing International* (Spring), 8(1):13–16.

Pfeiffer, Eric. 1976. *Multidimensional Functional Assessment: The OARS Methodology.* Durham, N.C.: Center for the Study of Aging and Human Development, Duke University.

Pierson, Ann. 1982. Senior Village Status Reports. Mimeographed quarterly reports. Phoenix, Arizona: Maricopa County Health Department.

Pierson, Ann. 1983. Personal communication to authors.

Plath, David W. 1972. "Japan: The After Years." In D. O. Cowgill and L. D. Holmes, eds., *Aging and Modernization,* pp. 133–150. New York: Appleton-Century-Crofts.

Quadagno, Jill. 1982. *Aging in Early Industrial Society.* New York: Academic Press.

Rango, Nicholas. 1980. "Energy and the Aged: A Challenge to the Quality of Life in a Time of Declining Energy Availability." Hearing Before the Special Committee on Aging, United States Senate, November 26, 1979. Washington, D.C.: GPO.

Rogers, Everett M. 1962. *Diffusion of Innovations.* New York: Free Press.

Rose, Arnold M. 1962. "The Sub-culture of the Aging: A Topic for Sociological Research." *The Gerontologist* 2:123–127.

Rosenmayr, Leopold and Eva Köckeis. 1963. "Propositions for a Sociological Theory of Aging and the Family." *International Social Science Journal* 15:410–426.

Rosow, Irving. 1967. *Social Integration of the Aged.* New York: Free Press.

Rosow, Irving. 1974. *Socialization to Old Age.* Berkeley and Los Angeles: University of California Press.

Rosow, Irving. 1976. "Status and Role Change Through the Life Span." In Robert H. Binstock and Ethel Shanas, eds., *Handbook of Aging and the Social Sciences,* pp. 457–482. New York: Van Nostrand, Reinhold.

Sauer, Elizabeth T. 1983. Personal communication to authors.

Scholen, Ken and Yung-Ping Chen. 1980. *Unlocking Home Equity for the Elderly.* Cambridge, Mass.: Ballinger.

Schreter, Carol A. 1982. "House Sharing by Non-frail Older Persons." In *Housing Options for the Community Resident Elderly: Policy Report of the Housing Choices of Older Americans Study,* ch. 5. Bryn Mawr, Pa.: Graduate School of Social Work and Social Research, Bryn Mawr College.

Schreter, Carol A. 1983. "Room for Rent: Shared Housing with Nonrelated Older Americans." Ph.D. dissertation, Bryn Mawr College.

Schroeder, Pat. 1981. Testimony before the Hearing of the Subcommittee on Housing and Consumer Interests of the Select Committee on Aging, House of Representatives, November 17, 1981. "Shared Housing," Comm. Pub. No. 97-321. Washington, D.C.: GPO.

Schulz, James. 1980. *The Economics of Aging.* Belmont, Calif.: Wadsworth.

Schulz, James, G. Carrin, H. Krupp, M. Peschke, E. Sclar, and J. Van Steenberge. 1974. *Providing Adequate Retirement Income: Pension Reform in the United States and Abroad.* Hanover, N.H.: University Press of New England.

Schumacher, E. F. 1973. *Small Is Beautiful: Economics as if People Mattered.* New York: Harper & Row; London: Blond & Briggs.

Select Committee on Aging, House of Representatives. 1982. *Every Ninth American.* Comm. Pub. No. 97-332. Washington, D.C.: GPO.

Shambaugh, B. M. H. 1932. *Amana That Was and Amana That Is.* Iowa City: State Historical Society of Iowa.

Sherwood, Sylvia, David S. Green, John N. Morris, Vincent Mor, and Associates. 1981. *An Alternative to Institutionalization: The Highland Heights Experiment.* Cambridge, Mass: Ballinger.

Simons, Lee. 1982. "The Elderly Plow New Ground Together." *Lerner News,* April 5.

Smith, K. F. and V. L. Bengtson. 1979. "Positive Consequences of Institutionalization: Solidarity Between Elderly Patients and Their Middle-aged Children." *The Gerontologist* 19:438–444.

Smith, Robert J. 1978. *Kurusu: The Price of Progress in a Japanese Village, 1951–1975.* Stanford, Calif.: Stanford University Press.

Stein, Maurice. 1960. *The Eclipse of Community.* New York: Harper & Row.

Stephens, J. 1976. *Loners, Losers, and Lovers: Elderly Tenants in a Slum Hotel.* Seattle: University of Washington Press.

Stockard, Susan. 1981. Testimony Before the Hearing of the Subcommittee on Housing and Consumer Interests of the Select Committee on Aging, House of Representatives, November 17, 1981. "Shared Housing," Comm. Pub. No. 97-321. Washington, D.C.: GPO.

Stoddard, Sandol. 1978. *The Hospice Movement.* New York: Vintage Books. Random House.

Streib, Gordon F. 1972. "Older Families and Their Troubles: Familial and Social Responses." *The Family Coordinator* 21:5–19.

Streib, Gordon F. 1978. "An Alternative Family Form for Older Persons: Need and Social Context." *The Family Coordinator* 27:413–420.

Streib, Gordon F. 1980. Field notes, Evanston, Illinois.

Streib, Gordon F. and William H. Haas, III. 1983. "Plans for the Future: Attitudes of Retirement Community Residents." Paper presented at annual meeting, Southern Sociological Society, Atlanta, Georgia, April 1983.

Streib, G., A. LaGreca, and W. E. Folts. "Retirement Communities: People, Planning, Prospects." In Robert J. Newcomer, Powell Lawton, and Thomas Byerts, eds., *Housing an Aging Society.* Stroudsburg, Pa.: Hutchinson and Ross. (In press.)

Streib, Gordon F. and Ruth B. Streib. 1975. "Communes and the Aging: Utopian Dream and Gerontological Reality." *American Behavioral Scientist* 19:176–189.

Struyk, Raymond. 1977. "The Housing Situation of Elderly Americans." *The Gerontologist* 17(2):130–139.

Struyk, Raymond and Beth Soldo. 1980. *Improving the Elderly's Housing.* Cambridge, Mass.: Ballinger.

Stub, Holger R. 1982. *Social Consequences of Long Life*. Springfield, Ill.: Charles Thomas.

Sussman, Marvin B. 1976. "The Family Life of Old People." In Robert Binstock and Ethel Shanas, eds., *Handbook of Aging and the Social Sciences*, pp. 218–243. New York: Van Nostrand, Reinhold.

Tinker, Anthea. 1976. "Housing the Elderly: How Successful Are Granny Annexes?" Social Research Division, Occasional Paper 1/76, Department of the Environment, Housing Development Directorate, London.

Tobin, S. S. and R. A. Lieberman. 1976. *Last Home for the Aged*. San Francisco: Jossey-Bass.

Townsend, Claire. 1971. *Old Age: The Last Segregation*. New York: Bantam Books.

U.S. Department of Health, Education, and Welfare. 1978. *Health: United States*. DHEW Publication No. (PHS) 78-1232. Washington, D.C.: GPO.

Usher, Carolyn and Stephen McConnell. 1980. "House-Sharing: A Way to Intimacy?" *Alternative Lifestyles* (May), 3:149–166.

Village Green, Inc. 1983. "Village Green: For Retired People, Maybe It's the Answer." Greensboro, N.C. Brochure.

Wax, Judith. 1976. "It's Like Your Own Home Here." *New York Times Magazine*, November 21.

Webber, I. 1954. "The Organized Social Life of the Retired: Two Florida Communities." *American Journal of Sociology* 54:340–348.

Weber, Max. 1947. *The Theory of Social and Economic Organization*. New York: Oxford University Press.

Wilensky, Harold. 1975. *The Welfare State and Equality*. Berkeley: University of California Press.

Williamson, John B., Linda Evans, and Lawrence Powell. 1982. *The Politics of Aging: Power and Policy*. Springfield, Ill.: Charles C. Thomas.

Wolpert, Julian. 1978. "Group Homes for the Mentally Retarded: An Investigation of Neighborhood Property Impacts." Report for New York State Office of Mental Retardation and Developmental Disabilities, Albany, N.Y.

Yankelovich, Daniel. 1982. *New Rules: Searching for Self Fulfillment in a World Turned Upside Down*. New York: Bantam Books.

Name Index

Abrams, Mark, 177
Abrams, Philip, 242
Achenbaum, Andrew, 19, 22
Albrecht, R., 28
Antonucci, Toni, 217

Baldwin, Leo, 152
Ball, Donald W., 211
Bane, Mary Jo, 245
Barr, Donald F., 27, 33
Baum, Martha, 17
Baum, Rainer C., 17
Bengtson, Vern, 22
Benning, Walter, 154
Berghorn, Forrest J., 25n, 32
Black, C. E., 21
Blau, Peter M., 14
Boldy, Duncan, 156n, 235
Borup, Jerry H., 245
Branch, Laurence G., 13
Brody, Elaine, 50, 121
Bryant, Drayton, 241, 243
Bultena, G. L., 27, 33
Butler, Robert, 31, 156
Butterfield, Fox, 18
Buxton, Christopher, 158–59

Campbell, George, 104
Cantor, M. N., 13
Carp, Frances, 23, 33–34
Carr-Gomm, Richard, 157–58
Carrin, G., 17
Castles, Francis G., 3n
Chadwick, Terry B., 21
Charles, D.A.L., 161
Chen, Yung-Ping, 26
Cherry, Ralph, 22

Coffman, Thomas, 245
Collins, Randall, 3n, 218
Conard, Richard, M.D., 131–32
Cooper, Barry, 153
Cottrell, Fred, 21
Cowgill, Donald O., 8–10, 22

Danet, Brenda, 14
Day-Lower, Dennis, 238, 243
Dellinger, D. C., 13
Dowd, James, 22
Dys, Peter, 152

Eckert, K., 29
Ehrlich, Ira, 29, 34
Ehrlich, Phyllis, 29, 34
Erickson, R., 29
Estes, Carroll, 228–30
Evans, Linda, 19

Figueira, J., 15
Fischer, David H., 19, 22
Folts, W. E., 27
Frankel, Charles, 7
Freeman, Howard, 175

Gallego, Daniel, 245
Galper, Jeffrey H., 229
Getze, Linda H., 82
Gillies, James, 37–38, 78
Glasscote, Raymond, 31
Gouldner, Alvin, 4n
Green, David S., 36
Gubrium, J. F., 31, 33
Guion, Edward, 153

Haas, William, 28, 220
Habenstein, R. W., 29
Hare, Patrick H., 152
Hareven, Tamara K., 147
Haven, Clayton, 65
Heclo, Hugh, 3n
Heffernan, Pamela, 245
Heintz, Katherine M., 28
Heumann, Leonard, 156n, 235
Hilker, Mary Anne, 42
Hochschild, Arlie, 32, 69
Hollander, P. J., 18
Holmes, Lowell D., 8, 22
Hoyt, G. C., 27

Inkeles, Alex, 22

Jacobs, J., 27, 32–33
James, Marlise, 81
Johnson, J. L., 13
Johnson, S. K., 27, 33

Kahn, Robert L., 217
Katz, Elihu, 14
Khurana, Barbara, 114
Kiefer, Christie, 21, 29
Köckeis, Eva, 16
Kodaira, Yutaka, 130
Krupp, H., 17
Kuhn, Maggie, 32
Kutza, Elizabeth Ann, 17

La Greca, A. J., 27
Lally, M., 29
Landes, David, 21
Lasch, Christopher, 215
Laslett, Peter, 19
Lauber, Daniel, 240
Lawton, M. Powell, 25n, 33, 50, 121, 148–49
Leibowitz, Bernard, 121
Lerner, Daniel, 21
Leslie, Gerald, 210
Lieberman, R. A., 31
Litwak, Eugene, 15, 16
Lowenthal, Marjorie, 50, 65

McConnell, S. R., 147–48
Maddox, G. L., 13
Magnuson-Martinson, Scott, 22

Mangum, Wiley, 25, 25n, 206
Meltzer, Jack, 244
Mendelson, M. A., 31
Merton, Robert K., 14, 209
Meyer, Henry, 15–16
Modell, John, 147
Mor, Vincent, 36
Morris, John N., 36
Morton-Williams, Jean, 165, 177–78

Nagi, Saad, 13
Newman, Evelyn, 149–50
Newman, S. J., 23
Norbeck, Edward, 21–22
Nydegger, Corinne, 19

Olson, Laura, 17, 228–30
Oltman, Ruth, 128
Osgood, Nancy J., 33

Palmore, Erdman, 21
Peace, Sheila, 132
Peschke, M., 17
Pfeiffer, Eric, 13
Pierson, Ann, 106n, 107
Plath, David, 21
Powell, Lawrence, 19

Quadagno, Jill, 22

Rango, Nicholas, 243
Rose, Arnold M., 32
Rosenmayr, Leopold, 16
Rosow, Irving, 32, 216, 246
Roybal, Edward R., 126

Sauer, Elizabeth T., 183n
Scholen, Ken, 26
Schreter, Carol A., 148
Schroeder, Pat, 242
Schulz, James, 3n, 17
Schumacher, E. F., 247
Sclar, E., 17
Shambaugh, B.M.H., 154
Sherman, Susan, 149–50
Sherwood, Sylvia, 36
Simons, Lee, 120
Smith, David, 22
Smith, Robert J., 21

Soldo, Beth, 25n, 26, 34, 229
Stein, Maurice, 248
Stephens, J., 28–29
Stockard, Susan, 238
Stoddard, Sandol, 76–77
Streib, Gordon F., 15, 27, 119, 154, 218, 220
Streib, Ruth B., 154
Struyk, Raymond, 25n, 26, 34, 229
Stub, Holger R., 9
Sussman, Marvin B., 15

Tinker, Anthea, 151–52
Tobin, S. S., 31
Townsend, Claire, 31

Usher, C. F., 147–48

Van Steenberge, J., 17

Wang, Y., 29
Wax, Judith, 118–19
Webber, I., 27
Weber, Max, 14, 218
Weismehl, Ronald, 119
Wilensky, Harold, 3n
Williamson, John B., 19
Wolpert, Julian, 240
Wood, V., 27, 33
Wright, H. Beric, 174–75

Yankelovich, Daniel, 225

Zwerger, Mark, 139–40

Subject Index

AARP (American Association of Retired Persons), 82, 152

AARP/NRTA (American Association of Retired Persons and the National Retired Teachers Association), 82

"Abandonment of the elderly," 20

Abbeyfield, 2, 140–41, 143, 156–85, 219, 235, 251; advantages, 178; anticipated needs, 184; applicants, 163; basic principles, 163; criticisms, 178; description of houses, 166; description of purpose-built houses, 171; drugs, prescription, 164; extra care houses, 173–75; first residents, 158; funding, 159–61; Friends of Abbeyfield, 163; future, 183–85; happiness of residents, 178; health of residents, 177; house committee, 163–65; housekeeper, 164–65, 178; housekeeper duties, 164; houses, 165–66; houses, examples of, 166–71; inner cities problems, 161; lifestyle, 164; location of houses, 165–66; magazine, 161; Manual of Information, 164; National Executive Committee, 160; national organization, 160–62; number of residents, 166; paid employees, 165; policy disagreement, 158–59; purpose, 163; purpose-built houses, 171–73; resident, sponsor of, 163; residents, 163–64; residents' chores, 164; restricted to elderly, 158–59; social activities, 163; strength, 161; success, 160–61; temporary residence, 164

Abbeyfield Commission on Growth, 165

Abbeyfield growth: limiting factors, 184

Abbeyfield house: description, 156–57; Belfast, Northern Ireland, 169–70; Central Edinburgh, 168–69; Colwyn Bay, Wales, 166–68; Suburban Edinburgh, 170–71

Abbeyfield residents: dependency, 173; illness, 173

Abbeyfield self-evaluation: areas of study, 176; report on organization's future, 176, 183; survey of residents, 176

Abbeyfield self-evaluation survey: activities, 178–79; character of respondents, 176–77; coming to Abbeyfield, 179; happiness of residents, 177–78; health of residents, 177; hearing about Abbeyfield, 179–80

Abbeyfield Society, 2, 77, 143, 156, 229; attitude toward integration, 182–83; collaboration, 160; communication, 160; cross-national comparison, 180–83; decision to self-evaluate, 175–76; description, 157; description and organization, 162–63; development committee, 162; and Extra Care Houses, 173–75; goals for Extra Care Houses, 175; history and organization, 157–60; house committee, 162; an international society, 162; local committee, 162; local societies, 162; prestige, 181–82; and purpose-built houses, 173; representation, 160; self-evaluation, 175–80; summary evaluation, 184–85; volunteers, 162

Abbeyfield Society Commission on Growth, 176

Abuse, safeguards against: shared living, 232–34

Abuse of elderly: nursing homes, 232–33; family, 233; shared living, 234

Acquisition and renovation costs, 192

Adaptation, 246

Adapted structures, 133–34

Administration on Aging, Department of Health, Education and Welfare, 4; grant, 104

Administrative costs, 190

Adult group home, 96

Affectional ties, 17

Age: density, 32; integration, 32; segregation, 32

Age-concentrated environments vs. age-integrated environments, 32–33

Age Concern (British organization), 177

Age-dense environments, 32–33
Aging, and loss of institutional roles, 216
Allocative process, 220
Alternative housing, 9; awareness of elderly's need for, 6; existing households, 146–55
Alternative living arrangements, 15, 238–39; apartments, 26; available range of, 25; Board and Care Homes, 29–31; Board and Care Homes in Missouri, 30; condominiums, 26; conventional housing, 25–26; high-rise apartments, 28; legal basis for, 15; life care facilities, 30; manufactured (mobile) home parks, 27; need for, 12; nursing homes, 25, 29, 31–32; retirement communities, 27–28; retirement hotels, 28; shared living homes, 29; slum hotels, 29
Amalgam: family and bureaucracy, 218–20; a mixed social structure, 16
Amalgam group, 2, 15; bureaucratic component, 219–20; definition, 218; primary group aspects, 218–20; uniform and nonuniform tasks, 15
Amalgam groups, 220, 250
American Association of Retired Persons (AARP), 82, 152
American Association of Retired Persons and the National Retired Teachers Association (AARP/NRTA), 82
American Baptist Churches: CLOP (Cooperative Living for Older Persons), 107
Area Agency on Aging, 105
Arnold Ross and Associates, 4

Back Bay Aging Concerns Committee (BBACC), 124–25, 144
Boarding and lodging, 147
Boarding home: as housing category, 96
Boarding homes: attitudes toward, 241
Boarding house, 78
Boston Shared Living Project: age-integrated, 127; federal classification, 126–27; intergenerational housing, 126–27; intergenerational living, question regarding, 126; organizational difficulty, 126; rent supplements, 126; rent supplement elligibility, 126; residents, 127; Section 8 assistance, 126–27; success, 127
Bureaucracies and families: differences, 16; distinction between, 15

Bureaucracy: elderly and the increase of, 230–36; increase in modern society, 230; modernization and shared housing, 14–16; needs of elderly, 230; reports and records, 234–35; resistance to change, 230
Bureaucratic procedures, disadvantages for frail elderly, 231
Bureaucratic regulations, 232
Bureaucratization, characteristics, 14

Change, in old age, 246
Changing society: needs, 239; priorities, 239
Chronically impaired, 36n
Cleveland study (by General Accounting Office), 13
Coastal Colony Corporation, 152–53
Commune, 81
Communication networks, see Mass media
Community housing for the elderly in Philadelphia, 120–21, 142
Comparative studies, 2
Comptroller General of the United States, 13
Congregate care facility, 96
Contingency fund, 190
Converted houses, disadvantages of, 171
Convoy, concept of, 217–18
Cooperative Living for Older Persons (CLOP), 107
Costs, 99, 188–93, 197; estimates of, 189–92
Council of International Urban Liaison, 153
Council for Jewish Elderly, 114, 119; activities, 115; funding, 115; organization, 115
Court decisions, 78
Cross-national perspective, 249
Cultural divergences: American and British, 180–82
Cultural similarities: American and British, 180–81

Department of Health, Education and Welfare, 124
Dependency levels, and distribution of population, 14
Differences, shared living and nursing homes, 233–34; in profit making, 233; in residents' health, 234; in sponsorship, 234; in "visibility," 234
Diffusion, of Share-A-Home model, 76–77, 83, 87–88

Diffusion, shared living: avenues of, 224–27; citizen involvement and commitment, 224–26; profit making, 224, 226; public resources, 225–27

Displacement of old, 9

Domain assumptions, 4n

Duke University Older Americans Resources and Services (OARS), 13

Duke University study, 13

ECHO Housing (Elder Cottage Housing Opportunities), 152–53; evaluation, 154; zoning laws and, 152

Economic supplements, 35

Economic technology, as inanimate power, 9

Economic viability, 187

Education, 10

Elder Cottages, as village community, 153

Elderly: autonomy, 10; and change, 245; demography, 11–14; dependency, 8; economic security, 8; economic situation, improved, 17; energy costs, 243; in historic past, 19; household management, 8; independent living, 10; living arrangements, 8; loneliness, 8; lowered status, 8; mythic past, 19; in other societies, 19; perception of shared housing, 220–23; problem meeting, 243; relations with children, 16; resources, 243; respect for, 19; romantic portraits, 18; thermo-regulatory system of the, 243; withdrawn, 132

Elderly housing alternatives: remodeling of old hospital, 133; remodeling of old hotels and motels, 133–34

Emotional ties, 17

Energy: planning for elderly, 243; quality of life, 244; survival, 244

Energy cost efficiency, and group living, 244

Energy costs: addressing problem, 244; elderly, 244; recognition of problem, 244; shared housing, 244

Enriched Housing, New York, 107–10, 123, 141; applicants' interpersonal skills, 108; black staff, 109; description, 107; difficulty attracting residents, 108; establishment, 107; funding, 107; house rules, 107; housekeeper, 107; housing choice, 109; integration by sex and race, 109; licensing, 109; monthly cost, 108; outside activities, 108; positive features, 109; recreation, 108; registered nurse, 107; re-

sources (public and private), 109; SICM, 109; SSI payments, 108; success, 109; transportation, 107

Establishment problems, 186

Evaluation research, 175

Extra Care Houses: funding, 175; locations, 174–75; medical services, 175; residents, 174

Family, 218; abuse of elderly, 233; concept of, 210–11, 211n; support for elderly, 221–22

"Family," 78–80, 201; as unrelated adults, 2

Family group living, 132

Family groups, traditional, 15

Family relations: autonomy, 16–18; changing, 16–18; independence, 16–18

Family Service Society of Nassau County, New York, 147

Federal Council on Aging, 12

Federal Housing Administration, "236" Rehabilitation Program, 121

Federal Housing Law, 34; Boston Shared Living Project and, 126; rent supplements, 126; Section 8, 126–27

Females, death rates, 11

Field sociologist: justification of research, 5; methods, 5

Financial exploitation: frail elderly, 234; in Share-A-Home, 234

Florida retirement communities, 220–21; description of residents, 220–21; survey of residents, 220–21

Focus of study, 251

Food costs, 189

Food stamps, 193

Formal organizations, 249; in shared living arrangements, 218

Foster care: caretakers, 149; family integration, 150; family participation, 150; former residents, 150; given by families, 149; relationships under, 149; residents, 150; social distance, 150; social interaction, 150

Foster family care, 149–150; definition, 149; variant of house sharing, 149

Foster homes, 146; evaluation, 154

Frail elderly, 13, 107, 133; care, 247; characteristics, 13; financial exploitation, 234; future care, 240; housing needs—physical structure approach, 34, social approach, 35, supplement approach, 35; housing orientations, 33–

Frail elderly *(Continued)*
 36; income, 13; long-term care, 13; in Massachusetts, 13; need for housing, 210; needs, 106, 230–31; in New York City, 13; private care, 231; public care, 231; over 75 (old-old), 8; role behavior, 216; "small" approach, 248; social environment, 35
Frailty, increasing, 199

Gemeinschaft, 218
"Gerontological miracle," 9
Gerontological "revolution," 246–47
Gesellschaft, 218
Goals of this research, 3–4
Grandmothers, and child care, 18
Granny Annexes: Amana Colonies in Iowa, 154; description, 151; ECHO Housing, an American version, 152–53; problems, 151; purpose, 151
Granny Flats, 146, 150–54; in Australia, 151, 153–54; evaluation, 154; in Great Britain, 151; origin and purpose, 151
Granny Flats Forum, 153–54
Gray Panthers, 144; of Greater Boston, 124
Great Britain: housing options for elders, 156; sheltered housing for elderly, 235; supplements, Abbeyfield, 237; *see also* Abbeyfield
Group dwellings, connotation of, 241
Group Home Program, Washington, D.C., 121–24; high-rise apartment buildings, 121; Jewish Council for the Aging of Greater Washington, Inc. (JCA), 122
Group Homes, Washington, D.C., 142
Group housing: compatibility of residents, 108; court cases, 242; neighborhood fears, 240; neighborhood opposition, 240; property turnover, 240; property values, 240
Group process, 250
Group structure, 250

Haven in a Heartless World: The Family Besieged, 215
Health and medical problems, 198–200
Health and Rehabilitative Services of Florida, Department of (HRS): "Guidelines for Zoning and Special Community Housing," 204
Health technology, 9
Homecall, home services for older people, 129
Home Care Research, 128–29

Home Close, Great Britain, 102, 132–33, 142; description, 132; model for others, 133; positive results, 133; residents, 133; success, 133
Home ownership, 12
Home Sharing for Seniors, Seattle, Washington, 147
Honorable Elders, The, 21
Hospice, Inc., 76
Hotels: residents of, 29; retirement, 29; slum, 29
Hotels and motels, former: costs, 137; disadvantages, 137; public areas' advantage, 138; rooms, short-term design, 138; value of land, 137
Household, 211
House sharing, 146–49; boarding and lodging, 146; definition, 146; difficulties, 155; evaluation, 154; intergenerational, 147–48; intragenerational, 147; older homeowners' view, 147; payments, 148; services, 148; SSI and, 148
House staff, 195
Housing: crises, 78–80; for elderly, 156, 239; inadequacies, 12; needs of elderly, 101; needs of frail elderly, 34–35; policy and existing programs, 229; programs, costs of, 238
Housing Act, 1959, 34
Housing Act, 1974, 34, 159–60
Housing alternatives for elderly: children's homes, 24; home care services, 24; nursing homes, 23; relatives' homes, 23
Housing and Community Development Act of 1974, 35n
Housing Assistance Payments Program, 35n
Housing Law, 119
Housing and Urban Development, Department of (HUD), 119, 152, 237; Section 8, 122, 193; shared housing recommendations, 242
Housing stock, 130–40; adapted structures, 133–34; purpose-built homes, 130; single-family homes, 130; units within larger institution, 130–31
HRS, 204
HRS Reorganization Act, 204
HUD, *see* Housing and Urban Development, Department of

Income of elderly, adequacy, 17
Incremental change, elderly's attitude toward, 230

Independence of elderly, 17; economic, 17
Industrialized society and the family, 215
Innovation, 2, 77; diffusion of, 2; social and technological, 2
Integration, American requirements, 183
Intergenerational households: Russia, 18; China, 18
Intergenerational living, 17, 124
Intergenerational solidarity, 17
International Federation on Ageing, 153
Interpersonal transactions: affect, 217; affirmation, 217; aid, 217
Institutionalization: alternatives to, 36n; effects of, 31
Isolation, 12
Ithacare, Ithaca, New York, 138–40, 143; activities, 140; board of directors, 138n; church services, 140; college and university affiliation, 138; day care, 139–40; director, 139; fees, 139–40; frail elderly, 138–39; hospital, former, 138; HUD financing, 138; Ithaca College, relationship with, 140; Ithacare scholarships, 13; kitchen and dining arrangements, 139; licensing, 139; location, 138; New York State Department of Social Services, 139; opening, 139; renovation of building, 139; residents, 139

Japan: changes from modernization, 22; status of elderly, 22
Jewish Council for the Aging of Greater Washington, Inc. (JCA): fees, 122; financial assistance to Group Home Residents, 123; Group Home Program, 122–24; group living, 122; housing projects, 122; information and referral, 122; resident subsidies, 122; total cost of housing, 122; transportation, 122
Jewish Federation of Metropolitan Chicago, 114, 142; activities, 115; subsidies to Weinfeld residents, 116

"Kangaroo Houses," 151

Labels, significance, 211n
Law, and needs of elderly, 247
Legal issues, 200–1
Legal relationships, 201

Leisure Living Center, Bradenton, Florida, 131–32; description, 131; family-like unit included, 131; nursing home, 131; residents, 131–32; Retirement Corporation of America, 131
Licensing, 90, 95–96, 206–8
Licensure, 95–96, 186
Life Magazine, 81
Lifestyle of generations, 17
Lights Are Green, The, 184
Living arrangements, 11; continuum of, 25–32; intergenerational cooperative, 124; older people, 23–36; social context, 7; unrelated adults in family-like, 7
Local control, 91–92
Loneliness, 12
Low income: mortgage funds, 77; residents, 197; supplements in shared housing, 237

Manufactured Housing Institute, 154
Marital status, 11
Mass media, and images of the old, 18–20
Matching services, housemate, 147
Mechanical solidarity, 218
Medical Advisory Committee (Abbeyfield), 174
Medical Services, 96–97
"Minimum intrusion," principle of, 128
Minorities: Britain, 182; United States, 182
"Missionary work at home," 110
Mobility, elderly, 245–46
Modernization, 7–22; advantages/disadvantages, 20; aging population, 246; antecedent factors, 9; approaches for study, 22; change, 7; community and society, 248; comparative history, 21; consequences, 11, 20; Cowgill's theory of, 10, 14; cross-national, 21; defined, 7, 21; demographic trends, 1; framework, 8; industrial, 9; institutional structures, 8; intergenerational solidarity, 17; Japan, 21; longer life, 246; nursing homes, 20; orientation, 8; positive and negative features, 8; ramifications of, 8; salient aspects, 9; shared housing, 246–48; social problems and their solution, 247; social processes, 8; systems and efficiencies, 9; theory, 8
Modern Maturity, 82, 152, 222
Monthly costs, 98
Motels and hotels: group living, 134; semipermanent housing, 134; SRO, 134

Mt. Vernon Lodge, Ocala, Florida, 136–38, 143; description, 136–37; fees, 137; former motel, 136; profit operation, 136; services, 137

National Assistance Act of 1948 (Great Britain), 164
National Cancer Society, 224
National Retired Teachers Association, American Association of Retired Persons and the (NRTA, AARP/), 82, 153, 222
National Society for Muscular Dystrophy, 224
National Survey of Housing Choices of Older Americans, 148
Natural family: "bad times" or crisis, 214–15; "good times," 214; history, 214; nurturance, 215
NBC, "American Family," 81
Neighborhoods, 32–33
Networks, 15
New Jersey (State of New Jersey vs. Dennis Baker), 203–4, 203n
New York Department of Social Services, 141
Nonprofit corporation, 79, 90, 201
Nonprofit organization, 99
Normalization principle, 204–5
NRTA, AARP/ (National Retired Teachers Association, American Association of Retired Persons and the), 82, 153, 222
NRTA-AARP Andrus Foundation, 4, 82
Nursing homes, 132; abuse of elderly, 232–33; Arizona residents, 104; physical setting, 31; research on, 245; social structure, 31; see also Differences, shared living and nursing homes

OAA Title III, 147
Office on Aging, 152
Old-age homes, British, 133; adaptation to small group living, 133
Older Americans Resources and Services, Duke University (OARS), 13
Older houses: financing, 238; renovating, 238
Older persons: health, 12; income, 12; need for supportive environments, 12
Older women, housing arrangements, 12
Orange County vs. Share-A-Home Association of Winter Park, Florida et al., 43, 202n, 202–3
Organic solidarity, 218
Organizational survival, 250
"Overhoused," 12

Pensioner population, 16
Philadelphia Geriatric Center, 120–21; activities, 121; description of row homes, 121; intermediate housing, 120; remodeled row housing, 120; residents' contact with staff, 121; social services, 121
Phoenix project, 105–7; see also Senior Village, Phoenix, Arizona
Physical structures, services, 34
Physician, role in decision to move elderly, 30
Policy, 247; adaptation, 245; change, 245; funding, 240; implications of energy and needs of elderly, 243; staying in own home, 245
Population: dependency levels and distribution, 14; older, United States, 11; total, United States, 11
Practical information, 4
Preterminal deterioration, 9
Primary groups, 249; in shared living arrangements, 218
Private housing market, 228
Project Match, San Jose, California, 147
Project Share, Hempstead, New York, 147
Project staff, 195
Property: acquisition, 187; location, 187
Proprietary sponsorship, 129–30
Public funding: housing of elderly, 231–32; shared housing, 231–32
Public housing, 34; for elderly in Great Britain, 156; project, 33–34
Public issues, 247
Public sponsorship, 102–10
Purpose-built homes: Abbeyfield Society, 130; Robineau House, 130; TVA plans, 130; University of Florida College of Architecture, 130

Quality of life, in small groups, 250

Recruitment: residents, 91, 97, 193–94
Regional Housekeeping Registrars, 165
Regulation, 186
Regulatory agencies, 91
Religious sponsorship, 110–24
Renovation, 94; costs, 191; retrofitting, 187–88
Rental/purchase of property, 91
Rents, 188–89
Rent subsidy programs, 35
Requirements for admission, 96–97

Research: components of, 249–50; data, 251; design, 251; goals, 3–4; inside views, 251–52; methods of, 249–52; outside views, 251–52; priority, 249; sociological study, 250; study of older individuals, 250

Residence of elderly: location in United States, 23

Residential concentration, 32

Residential density, 32

Residents: location, 193; recruitment, 91, 97, 193

Respondents to surveys, comparison, 223

Retirement communities, 32–33; "geriatric playpens," 32

Retirement Corporation of America, 131

Retirement environment: desirable, 33; optimum, 33; realistic alternatives, 33

Ridgeview, Largo, Florida, an integrated Share-A-Home, 183n

Risk, in care of elderly, 234

Robineau Group Living Residence (Robineau House), 114, 142, 242; authorization, 119; community reaction and questions, 119–20; funding, 119; Jewish Council, 119; opening, 120; public hearings, 119; purpose-built structure, 119–20; residents, 120; residents' reaction, 120; site, 119; Skokie, Illinois, 119; zoning, 119–20

Role change, through life span, 216

Roles, informal, frail elderly, 218

Rollins College, 80

Scarcity of homes, 80

Schenectady Inner City Ministry (SICM), 107; see also Enriched Housing, New York

Secular-Charitable Sponsorship, 124–29; Abbeyfield Society houses, 124; Boston Shared Living Project, 124; Share-A-Homes, 124

Seed money, 191

Select Committee on Aging of the House of Representatives, 11, 237

Self-care, 34

Senility, circumstantial, 132

Senior Village, Phoenix, Arizona, 102, 107, 141, 200; activities, 105; Activity Club, 105; fees, 105; houses, 104; manager, 104; nursing home alternative, 104; project, 104; quarterly reports, 106; residents, 104–5; revenue-sharing funds, 104; staff, 105

Separate living arrangements, 17

Services, 99

Sex ratios, 11

Share-A-Home, 76–87, 90–91, 93–94, 102, 141, 143, 211n, 219, 224, 244; analysis of information requests, 222; attitudes toward, 221; caring environment, 214; diffusion of idea, 100; diffusion of model, 76–100; dissemination, 81; establishment, 87–88; financial exploitation, 234; founder, 2, 37–38, 78; governmental intervention, 212–13; philosophy, 235; requests for information, 222; residents, 150; sponsorship, 87; see also Survey, Share-A-Home correspondents; Share-A-Home of America, Inc.; Share-A-Home in Florida; Share-A-Home model

Share-A-Home of America, Inc., 38, 79

Share-A-Home in Florida, 37–75; administration, 38, 73; admission to, 47, 60; board of directors, 38; changes in self-care capacity, 71; community acceptance, 53–54; community involvement, 53–54, 56; confidants, 65, 73; "family" model, 37, 42–48, 55–56, 58–59, 61, 73, 75; field study, 42, 48, 65; goal of, 42; helping roles, 63, 65, 67–71, 73–74; history, 37–42; household staff, 51–53; Instrumental Activities of Daily Living scale, 50; interpersonal conflict, 65–66, 74; interpersonal relationships, 65–69; intimacy, 73; licensing issues, 43; mental impairment, 71, 75; Physical Self-Maintenance scale, 49–50; physical structures, 38; policies and procedures, 46–48; record-keeping, 46–47; relatives of residents, 44; resident compatibility, 60–61; resident satisfaction, 70; resident socialization, 58–63; resident-staff relationships, 71–73; resident turnover, 70, 74; residents' alternatives to, 58–59; residents' characteristics, 47–51; residents' costs, 45, 60; residents' daily routines, 55–57; residents' families, 63–64; residents' friends in the community, 63–64; services provided, 44–45; "sibling collusion," 69; staff characteristics, 51–52, 72; staff duties, 62–63, 68, 72; staff qualifications, 46; staff responsibilities, 55, 73–74; staff training, 43–44; staff turnover, 52–53, 74; termination of residency, 47, 74–75; thirty-day trial period, 62; zoning issues, 43, 54

Share-A-Home model, diffusion of, 76–100

Shared functions, theory of, 15

Shared Home, Wellsboro, Pennsylvania, *see* Wellsboro Shared Homes, Pennsylvania

Shared housing: and adaptability, 245–46; agency-assisted, 148; agency-sponsored, 148; and energy, 243–46; financing and policy, 236–39; funds, 242; incremental change, 228–30; and long life, 245–46; model of, 148; need for, 222, 242; neighborhood attitudes, 242; policy consideration, 236; policy implications, 228–48; private funding, 236; relationship to social welfare, 229; role of federal government, 242; self-initiated, 148; suitable structure, 240; supportive services, 228; zoning and spread of, 240; zoning ordinances, 241–42

Shared housing "movement," 76

Shared housing organiations, procedural advantages for frail elderly, 231

Shared housing policy: experimental programs, 238; financial devices and considerations, 236–37; financial problems, 237

Shared housing recommendations: Dennis Day-Lower, 243; Drayton Bryant, 243; HUD, 242

Shared living, 91, 186; Abbeyfield, 212; admissions requirements, 96–97; American-British contrast, 223–24; authority structure, 213; in "bad times" or crisis, 214–15; burnout (organizers), 198; choice, 212; compared with natural family, 211; cross-national comparisons, 180–83; daily life, 98; decision making, 87; differences with natural family, 211–15; diffusion of, 76, 223–24 (*see also* Diffusion, shared living); economic arrangements, 212; external factors, 200–9; financial sponsorship, 197; in "good times," 214–15; governmental intervention, 212–13; high-rise, Bradenton, Florida, 142; individual foibles, 213; internal factors, 187–200; medical services, lack of, 198–200; nurturance, 214–15; older people, 1; physical setting, 213; primary group nature of, 220; racial integration, 214; residents' obligations, 212; retarding factors in America, 223–24; social integration, 213–14; social roles and, 215–18; sponsorship, structure, and cost-case studies, 101–45

Shared living arrangements, 5; amalgam group, 216, 249; aspect of contemporary American culture, 3; expected role behavior, 216–17; formal structures, 216; option for elderly, 4;

primary group resemblance, 16; real families, 211–15; significance of categories, 211n; suitability of former hotels and motels, 137

Shared living environment, 97

Shared living facilities, 94–100; autonomy, 198; high-rise buildings, 121–24; organizational dilemmas, 209; problems in establishing, 186; services based on ability to pay, 108

Shared living groups: common characteristics, 143–45; costs, 144; as families, 210–11; financing, 144; goals and aims, 141; as "households," 210–11; locations, 144; philosophy, 144; physical structures, 144–45; as primary groups, 210; social structures, 144–45; sponsors, 144

Shared living homes, 36; characteristics, 101; classification, 101, 103; housing stock, 130–40; noninstitutional living arrangements, 101; public sponsorship, 102; religious sponsorship, 110; residents, 102; *see also* Differences, shared living and nursing homes

Shared living project, motivation for, 2

Shared Living Project, Boston, 124–28, 142; American Baptist Extension Corporation, 125; BBACC, 125–26; change to nonprofit organization, 126; fees, 125; funding sources, 125; gentrification, 124; "house facilitator," 125; intergenerational living, 124; original model, 125; rent subsidies, 10; residents, 124–25; routine, 125; seed money, 125; services not provided, 125; target population, 125; urban renewal, 124

SICM, *see* Schenectady Inner City Ministry

Single-family homes, and Cases 1 through 9, 102–29

Single-room occupancy (SRO), 134

Small group environment, 250–51

Small Group Homes, Frederick, Maryland, 128–29, 142

Small Group Homes in Hawaii, 102, 113–14, 141; applications, 114; Area Agency on Aging, 114; beginning, 114; Catholic Social Service, 113; community leaders, 114; leases, 114; noteworthy features, 114; number of houses, 113; operation, 113; organization, 114; referrals, 114; rent, 113–14; residents, 113; seed money, 114

Small group living arrangements, involvement with other organizations, 250

Small groups: formal organization, 250

Small Is Beautiful: Economics as if People Mattered, 247–48
Social and Community Planning Research, 176
Social change, 78
Social context: new living arrangements, 8
Social innovation, 76
Social programs, 247
Social support networks, 217–18
Social supports: defined, 217
Socialization: to old age, 246
Societal restructuring: and services to elderly, 229–30
Sociological goals: "aesthetic" or "dramatic" approach, 3n; applied, 3; explanatory, 3; ideological, 3
Sociology of organizations, 2
Solar Group Home, 93–94, 244
SRO (Single-room occupancy), 134
SSI (Supplementary Security Income), 139, 148, 193
SSI payments, in shared housing, 237
Staff, 195–96; costs, 189–90; recruitment, 195
Staffing, 99
State of New Jersey vs. Dennis Baker, 203–4, 203n
State regulation, 208
Structure, types, 83, 94–95
Subcommittee on Housing and Consumer Interests, 237
Subsidies, 98, 197; low-income residents, 77
Sunset Lodge, Hot Springs, Arkansas, 135–36, 143; activities, 136; Area Agency on Aging, 136; Attendant Care Facilities, 135; budget, 136; description, 135–36; fees, 136; food costs, 136; managers, 136; organization, 135–36; purpose, 135
Supplemental Security Income (SSI), 139, 148, 193
Supplements: government programs, 35; rent, 35
Supportive environment, need for, 12
Survey, Share-A-Home correspondents, 220–23; evaluations of curent housing, 222; reactions to shared living, 222–23
Swedish approach, compared with American, 3

Target population, 194
Tasks: for expert, 16; for nonexpert, 16; *see also* Amalgam group

Tax exempt status, 201
Tennessee Valley Authority (TVA), 92–94, 244; Community Resource Development Branch, 92; Older Americans Initiative, 92
Transportation costs, 190

United Fund, 107
Units within larger institution, discussion of, 130–31
University of Florida Foundation, 4
Urbanization, 10
Utility costs, 190

Viability, 196–98
Village Green, Greensboro, North Carolina, 134–35, 143; activities director, 135; description, 135; fees, 135; Greensboro Housing Authority, 134; nurse, 135; services, 134–35; support services, 135
"Vulnerable elders": *see* Frail elderly, 13

"Warehousing" of elderly, 232
Weinfeld and Robineau Residences, Illinois, 114–20; evaluation, 120; sponsorship, 115; success, 114–15
Weinfeld Group Living Residence, 114, 142; applications, 116; arrangement of units, 115–16; Council for Jewish Elderly, 116; daily life, 118–19; financial arrangements, 117; housekeeping, 118; meals, 117–18; monthly charge, 116; operation, 119; origin, 115; project description, 116; residents, 116–17; staff, 118; success, 119; support, 116; *see also* Jewish Federation of Metropolitan Chicago
Welfare state: basis for, 9
Wellsboro, Pennsylvania, 141
Wellsboro Shared Homes, Pennsylvania, 110–13; admission, 112–13; applicants, 110; Baptist Church, 110, 112; beginning, 110; description of house, 113; donor, 110; fees, 110; location, 110; manager, 112; operation, 112; pastor, 112; physician, 112; project, 113; residents, 110, 112; temporary residence, 113; volunteers, 112
Widows/Widowers, 11–12
Women: death rates, 11; living arrangements, 11–12
World Health Organization (WHO), 166

Youth and job opportunities, 10
Youth Opportunity Program, Great Britain, 161

Zoning, 78–79, 90, 186, 201–2, 205; as block to project, 241; future, 240; impediment to shared housing, 239–43; local autonomy, 240; *Orange County vs. Share-A-Home Association of Winter Park, Florida et al.,* 202; ordinances, shared housing, 241–42; problems, 242; *State of New Jersey vs. Dennis Baker,* 203–4